Practitioner Series

Springer
London
Berlin
Heidelberg
New York
Barcelona
Hong Kong
Milan
Paris
Singapore
Tokyo

Other titles in this series:

Richard Veryard

The Component-Based Business:

Plug and Play

 Springer

Richard Veryard
Veryard Projects, London

Practitioner series ISSN 1439-9245

ISBN 1-85233-361-8 Springer-Verlag London Berlin Heidelberg

British Library Cataloguing in Publication Data
Veryard, R. (Richard)
    Component-based business. – (Practitioner series).
    1. New business enterprises 2. Consolidation and merger of
    corporations 3. Industrial organization 4. Organizational
    change
    I. Title
    658.1'6
    ISBN 1852333618

Library of Congress Cataloging-in-Publication Data
Veryard, R. (Richard)
    Component-based business / Richard Veryard.
        p. cm. – (Practitioner series, ISSN 1439-9245)
    Includes bibliographical references.
    ISBN 1-85233-361-8 (alk. paper)
        1. New business enterprises. 2. Consolidation and merger of corporations. 3. Industrial
    organization. I. Title. II. Practitioner series (Springer-Verlag)

    HD62.5 .V456 2000
    658.1'6—dc21

                                                    00-061903

Typesetting: camera ready by author
Printed and bound by the Athenæum Press Ltd., Gateshead, Tyne & Wear
34/3830-543210 Printed on acid-free paper SPIN 10777455

Series Editor's Foreword

Component Based Software Architectures are in fashion at the time of writing, and I am not alone in researching this area, albeit I have the privilege of having a major government funded grant to help users, developers and software tool suppliers in trying to understand how to make this work.

But this is not what this book is about. Software enables. The new technologies give business's opportunities to use components, and their relationships, to produce new assembled businesses. This requires planning and imagination, a manageable approach to change, and a strategy(ies). This book demonstrates techniques to handle these business opportunities. It explains how Component Based Software Engineering is far from sufficient in taking these opportunities if the organisational aspects are neglected. The risks associated with the latter are carefully explained.

Component Based Business is about adapting the business for survival in the new age of eCommerce and of instant information that the Internet provides. The building blocks necessary to provide this adaptability are described, and how then systems may be built from these blocks. The different principles for designing and using the blocks are elucidated. The quality of the block interfaces and the question of trust are shown to be essential ingredients for success. An evolutionary approach are both recommended and explained.

Clearly this book is essential reading for practitioners so that the technical approaches adopted avoid organisational failure. It should also be required reading for undergraduate and postgraduate students of any aspect of IT, since it provides a well-considered explanation of why technical solutions, logic and rationality (whose?) are not sufficient for success.

Ray Paul

Contents

Introduction

We are in the Middle Ages. Knights chase around the forest after mythical beasts, encumbered by heavy armour and ancient weapons. Wizards camp in the clearings, selling silver bullets and magic potions. Kings build castles to assert their unshakeable power. And lovers attach themselves to unattainable dreams.

We are in the Middle Ages. System engineers try to capture The Business Requirements, to which they can develop an ageless Solution. Vendors and users quibble about the magical powers of one or other Device. Businessmen and investors try to build a permanent position of Competitive Advantage or Profit, from which they can be safe from the dragons of Uncertainty and Risk. And customers dream of Frustrations finally Alleviated, Demands Satisfied at last.

Everyone acknowledges that the landscape for business and IT has changed. Many people admit that the rules of the game have changed. But most practitioners continue to set themselves the same old tasks, attempt to erect the same old defences against the same old monsters.

The traditional goals are increasingly meaningless. What good are Efficiency or Control or Integration, if you've sacrificed Flexibility? How important is Certainty or even Identity, in a fluid world where "stationary" apparently means "stagnant"? What Trust can be invested in business relationships and software artefacts? We still need people who are successful at delivering projects and developing solutions, but more than ever we need people who are aware of the new forces, and who can play a new fast-moving game

This book doesn't equip you with an alternative suit of armour, magic weapons, a new way of constructing castles in the air. It tries to help you improve how you think through the practical difficulties and opportunities of what's really going on in the forest.

And remember: we're still in the Middle Ages. The forest is still full of knights lumbering about with lances. At some point you may decide to discard your own lance altogether – but you might need it for a little while longer. Don't suddenly stop doing things in the old ways – the old ways are often convenient, sometimes even necessary – but you may start loosening your attachment to them. And if your competitors are still firmly attached to the old ways, it should be easy to get the better of them, by paying attention to some of the things they are overlooking.

What is Component-Based Business?

This book describes an increasingly popular and prevalent approach to business: Component-Based Business. In this introduction, I'm going to provide a sketch of Component-Based Business: what it is, where it came from, who is doing it, what are its potential business benefits and risks.

There is currently an explosion of new businesses – not just small start-ups but substantial launches. Many well-known brand-names are being cut-and-pasted onto new products and services. And not just e-versions of existing businesses either, although that's certainly part of the story. A grocery store opens a bank or an insurance company. An insurance company opens a hospital or car breakdown service. Suddenly, and without warning, there's a new player in the marketplace.

Is this new? No, of course not. But what is new is the way it's done, and the speed. Thanks to the plug-and-play approach, a new business can be rapidly assembled as a loosely coupled set of partnerships and services, with a complex business process spanning many organizations. These business structures (and the software and services that support them) evolve in complex ways, beyond the control of any single player. Even a substantial company can now be viewed as a component of a much larger system, rather than as a self-contained business operation, and this has huge implications for planning and managing at all levels.

Component-based business means creating a business operation or process by connecting "components" together from different sources.

In this book, we're going to explore these new business opportunities in terms of components, relationships between components, and the assembled systems. We're going to demonstrate techniques for planning and managing evolutionary change, and identify strategies for business survival and success.

From vertical integration to deintegration.

For most of the twentieth century, management aimed to control and integrate as much of the business process as possible, from end to end. This strategy is known as **vertical integration**. Many industries were dominated by a small number of vertically integrated firms – and some still are today.

But by the end of the twentieth century, it became apparent that the strategy of vertical integration was vulnerable to a radically different strategy: value chain specialization. IBM's dominant position in the computer industry was challenged, and then overtaken, by such firms as Microsoft and Intel, which focused on specific steps in the computing value chain. In his book on **Profit Patterns**, Adrian Slywotzky cites this as an example of what he calls the "Deintegration" pattern, and estimates the value released at $600 billion.

In the past, thin slices of the value chain were often overlooked by the big players, and were left as niches for small companies to occupy. Today's business dynamics can catapult a niche player into the major league almost overnight. This is particularly evident in telecommunications, where a combination of deregulation and technological change has created many opportunities for high value specialization.

Management trends.

Component-based business represents a convergence of management trends and technology trends.

In some respects, component-based business is merely the logical extension of outsourcing. In traditional outsourcing, a firm contracts out some well-defined support processes (such as IT, property services or logistics), allowing it to focus on the primary value-adding or customer-facing processes. The benefits and dangers of outsourcing have been well rehearsed in the management literature, and I'm not going to repeat them here. Component-based business goes a step further than outsourcing, since it typically involves partitioning the primary value-adding process between two or more independent partners. This raises critical issues about ownership of (and access to) a series of intangible assets such as customers, brands, data and knowledge. Component-based business often also takes on some elements of franchising, where the partners are jointly exploiting some brand or other assets.

If a complex business is unbundled into separate components, or if a new enterprise is configured from separate components, each component can be easier to manage. Unbundling also provides greater transparency to outsiders, including investors and regulators. When large conglomerates are demerged, the separate parts can turn out to be worth more (in market capitalization) than the whole, reflecting a perceived net benefit either to the firms themselves or to their investors.

Technology trends.

In addition to these business trends, some of the impetus for component-based business has come from Information Technology. There are several strands to this, which we can bring together under three headings: Internet, CSCW and software componentry.

First and foremost, there is the Internet, which provides new methods of interconnecting separate firms with each other and with their customers. Such jargon as e-this or e-that, B2C, B2B, or even B2B2B have been scattered across the media. To the extent that these technologies drive down the transaction costs for connecting business processes across organizational boundaries, they make the traditional hierarchical organization much less attractive from an economic point of view.

Alongside the growth of the Internet, there has been a parallel, although less hyped, growth in Computer-Supported Cooperative Work (CSCW). There has been an explosion of tools and methods aimed at supporting cooperation between workers separated by geography, culture or organizational allegiance. CSCW allows a complex task or process or workflow to be carried out by a virtual organization or team, and is an important technological prerequisite for some aspects of component-based business. Sometimes workflow tools are seen as liberating, apparently providing support for self-governing teams; but sometimes the same tools are used to exert greater management control over a complex business process.

Thirdly, we should mention Component-Based Software Engineering (CBSE). (People who restrict their thinking to software, or who cannot imagine developing anything other than software, refer to this as Component-Based Development.) This is a method for the construction of large flexible software systems from kits of standard, reusable software components. These components are often distributed across multiple platforms, and may be owned and operated by separate commercial entities. As the software components themselves increasingly become standard commodities, we can see software suppliers moving up the service supply chain, in many cases offering a full range of business services rather than simply selling lumps of software, and becoming active participants in a range of business ventures. The traditional split between business and IT isn't going to go away altogether, but it's getting much more complicated.

Assessing the overall significance of these trends is difficult. Is the Internet going to trigger a revolutionary transformation in society; is it a revolutionary technology equivalent to or greater than the mechanical clock, crop rotation, railways or electricity? Will workflow tools turn out to be a force for liberation or constraint? Will Component-Based Software Engineering gradually or suddenly replace other forms of software engineering? We can leave these questions to future historians. For our purposes, it is enough to note the existence of these trends, and their impact on component-based business.

Plug-and-play.

In many domains, we expect components from different manufacturers to work properly together. For example, a consumer with no electronics expertise can easily plug a Panasonic VCR into a Sony television, or even an HP printer into a Compaq computer. And I can send faxes anywhere in the world from my ancient Canon fax machine, without my needing to know anything about the fax machine at the other end. The notion of plug-and-play implies instant connection and instant operation – ideally, you shouldn't need to restart your computer, or go through an elaborate installation routine. It also implies that you can unplug and you're back to where you started – ideally your computer shouldn't remain littered with memories of devices you have no intention of using again.

What is involved in plugging businesses together? You might need to negotiate a business relationship between two or more legal entities, involving service levels, ownership of customers and intellectual property, as well as specifying the distribution of costs, benefits and risks. This could take anything from months (if the legal department gets involved) to micro-seconds (if the relationship can be based on standard protocols implemented by an electronic broker).

Plugging business components together usually involves, among other things, plugging together the computer systems on both sides. If the computer systems were already built to accommodate such relationships, this would be practically instantaneous, once the legal departments on both sides had done their stuff. In practice this is rarely the case, and the IT departments often delay things even more than the legal departments.

Notwithstanding the impatience of the typical businessman, the IT and legal departments are both essential to the success of component-based business. The role of the lawyers is to anticipate the ways in which the relationship might need to be unplugged. Putting the worst case into the contract might sometimes be a way to make sure it doesn't happen, or it may sometimes be a way of ensuring that there is a clean and efficient way of terminating something that isn't working.

In most cases nowadays, plugging the computer systems together is an obvious precondition for a successful joint operation. But if this task is difficult, it will often divert attention and resources from "softer" preconditions, such as getting the people and the human systems to work effectively together.

 People in some walks of life are accustomed to working rapidly and effectively with strangers. A hundred professional musicians can be assembled into a brand-new orchestra in the morning, and perform a concert on the same evening. How long would it take the people in your organization to work effectively with people from another organization?

Who is doing component-based business?

Example: bank and supermarket.

In many countries recently, joint ventures of various kinds have been established between banks and supermarkets, to deliver banking services to the supermarket's customers.

If we look at this from the perspective of the supermarket, we can think of it as plugging a "bank-in-a-box" into the supermarket's operations. If all goes well, the supermarket can achieve a kind of virtual diversification at high speed, low cost and low risk.

The bank may be providing a similar set of services to firms in other industries as well, and this can become one of the bank's standard offerings. As the banking services to the end-customers may become a standard commodity, the relationship to the joint venture partners becomes a well-understood and easily repeatable service. This may reduce still further the time and expenditure needed to establish another new joint venture.

From the perspective of the bank, the supermarket provides access to a further set of customers and some new distribution channels, under a different brand name. Indeed, some financial institutions will wish to concentrate business strategy on developing third party distribution channels, and may even pull out altogether from direct relationships with end-customers. For example, an insurance company may become a "manufacturer", concentrating on product development and underwriting, and leaving "distribution", including sales and marketing, to other organizations.

But these joint ventures can bring further benefits. One leading UK bank, the Royal Bank of Scotland, is currently involved in three separate joint ventures: with Tesco (supermarket), Virgin (multiple sectors), and Scottish Power (utility). Each of these four organizations has a different corporate culture, and a different view on customers and their needs. This diversity has proved to be a valuable source of innovation and market trial; the Royal Bank of Scotland has more than once developed extra capabilities initially for its joint venture partners, which it has subsequently rolled out to its own customers.

From application service providers to business service providers.

The traditional software industry involves the sale of software artefacts by specialist software producers to other business organizations (known as user organizations), which then use these artefacts to operate or support some business processes. The user organization either funds the development of the software, or purchases a licence to use the software.

As we saw earlier, some software suppliers are now starting to sell business services rather than software artefacts. This may simply involve operating software applications or other technical services for customers, perhaps charging on a different basis (e.g. pay-per-use). Companies offering these services are known as Application Service Providers (ASPs).

Some software suppliers are moving still further up the supply ladder, to provide a complete business service. A company specializing in software for insurance companies can plug in some additional capabilities, including underwriting, and then offer a full insurance back-office service to retailers. We'll explore this trend further in Chapter 3.

What are the potential benefits and risks?

A large UK insurance company wanted to set up a new line of business in medical insurance. It plugged in a quick solution from the USA as a way of getting off the ground quickly. Given the costs and risks of developing a solution slowly inhouse, this enabled a rapid entry into a new market. The bought-in solution represented an entire customer proposition, not just a software package.

But there was a sting in the tail. The company was left with an organizational legacy (in the form of head office structures and procedures), as well as a computer legacy. The bought-in systems and procedures embedded a fixed notion of market demand, and it was difficult to move to respond to a dynamic market. Organizational learning took place – but it was ad hoc and haphazard. Energy was diverted to dealing with minor infelicities in the systems, and to correcting operational mistakes – in one instance, policies were sent to the wrong customers.

At first sight, component-based business seems to offer great benefits to all and sundry. Some firms can exploit their assets (tangible and intangible) by packaging them into black boxes, for sale to other firms. These other firms can then achieve the benefits of diversification, with virtually no lead time, and at a greatly reduced cost and risk. Existing firms can grow into new markets, while well-focused start-up firms can convert a small niche into a world-beating product or service. Managers can increase the flexibility of business processes and operations while reducing their complexity. Everyone shares the benefits from reduced transaction costs. Investors can "cherry pick" the components that represent the most attractive business opportunities. Competition becomes fairer and more open. Business excellence abounds.

But there are hidden costs, and hidden risks, to all players. Many of the potential benefits of component-based business are not realised, for various reasons. Many ventures are poorly negotiated, poorly structured and poorly managed. The primary transaction costs may be reduced, but unplanned secondary costs may spring up. And some ventures are ill-conceived from the start, with no consideration of the profound ability of large complex systems to defeat any human efforts to control them. (Instead of reducing overall complexity, you may merely succeed in suppressing complexity in one place, only to see greater complexity spring up somewhere else.)

The components can be problematic. There may be a lack of quality, the component may demand too much attention or may require special effort to achieve a non-standard connection. And the usage of components can be problematic: there may be a lack of availability or choice, or there may be an effective monoculture or monopoly.

The apparent ability to enter a new market, or to make short-term gains, may discourage longer term planning and investment. A firm may rush to deliver a box of services, but the internal design may be a mess, and this may compromise many of the potential benefits of the component-based approach. A firm may rapidly plug in some new capability, and find that it's not so easy to unplug. A firm may gain commitments and risks, which it finds itself unable to control.

Benefits to some stakeholders may be at the expense of other stakeholders.   For example, if investors can cherry pick, this may make it more difficult to raise funds for the less glamorous, but nonetheless essential components of the whole system.   And ultimately the investors themselves may suffer, if their cherry-picking tactics damage the financial viability of the whole.

What is the potential scope for component-based business?

There are several points where component-based business appears relevant to business strategy, including diversification, mergers and demergers, as well as simple improvements in business structures, processes and operations.   We'll just mention them briefly here in the Introduction.

Articulation.

A properly articulated business, structured from loosely coupled components, can often be more flexible and manageable than a monolithic structure.

If the structure is well chosen, it can enhance the adaptability to changing business demands, as well as allowing the contribution and competitiveness of separate units to be more clearly visible.   But that's an important IF.   As we shall see, it's not easy to get the structure right.

Diversification.

As we have seen, a company can use a component-based approach as a route into a new business.   This may take several forms:

➢ plugging in capability from another source
➢ packaging capability for distribution through new channels and intermediaries, perhaps under alternative brand names
➢ franchising.

Mass customization.

The component-based approach strongly supports the ability to reconfigure a set of standard services for each customer.   Most of the popularly quoted examples of mass customization are fairly trivial, but e-commerce enables some more complex (and interesting) examples.

Merger.

When two companies merge, there is often an expectation that the back-office processes and systems supporting the two businesses will merge onto a single platform. Indeed, this is typically the basis for much of the promised synergies and cost-savings.

This can be regarded as a form of component-based business. Instead of a single platform supporting a single business, the merged company operates a single platform that provides services to multiple businesses.

If the prior operating configurations of the merging companies were favourable, we might imagine that the post-merger integration could be effected extremely quickly and easily, simply by plugging them together as components of an enlarged structure. At present, this remains an unrealized dream for most large industries currently undergoing consolidation. However, component-based thinking is still valuable in managing the post-merger integration programme, and in preparing organizations and systems for potentially easier mergers in future.

Demerger.

Demergers are typically done for one of two apparently contradictory motives: either to increase shareholder value or to increase competition and customer value. In either case, separating a large operation into its constituent parts is much easier if there are already well-managed interfaces between these parts.

A financial services company recently announced an intention to convert an existing branch network into a franchise network. In any franchise situation, but particularly in this one, we can expect to see a complicated set of services provided by the franchiser to the franchisee, and an equally complicated set of information flows in both directions.

Demergers are often fiercely resisted, especially when they are imposed by regulators or by hostile takeovers. In fact, any move towards decoupling the business is often interpreted as a step towards demerger, and is sometimes resisted for this reason. Such resistance can be conscious as well as unconscious, and can include the design of the organization's structure.

 What mechanisms can be used by an organization to delay or remove the threat of demerger? Whose interests does this serve?

Pitfalls, risks & nightmare scenarios.

➤ Two large companies with incompatible strategies or cultures, inextricably entangled in multiple joint products, services or processes. Adhoc wiring.

➤ Partner component failure or loss of service, with no immediate or short-term replacement.

➤ Excellent component, servicing whole market including you. Effective monopoly or monoculture means effective entrapment, with no possible replacement or contingency.

➤ Adhoc componentry. Components are hacked, cloned or bodged, inefficient and unreliable. Capability is not robust or scaleable.

➤ Baroque componentry. Excess functionality, excess complexity, excess cost.

➤ Relationship demands too much management attention.

➤ Duplicated capability. Checks and balances, redundant effort, in order to guarantee business critical or safety critical service.

➤ Autodisintermediation. You can't keep up with the rest of the consortium. You're the one that gets sidelined, bypassed, squashed out.

Tips & best practices.

➤ Let go the old goals: efficiency, control, certainty, integration.

➤ Balance short-term problem-solving with longer-term adventure. Operate at two strategic levels: core components and overall configuration.

• Identify what components (or component strategies) are likely to be successful, and position yourself to share in the success. Core components must be world-beating. Focus on areas where you have, or can achieve leadership and excellence. Develop new areas of excellence. Acquire and maintain "rising stars" as well as maximizing "cash cows".

➤ Promote excellence in partners. Be prepared to switch partners regularly. Exercise the switch. Don't let partners take you for granted. Don't take your partners for granted. Develop commitment and trust in balance with partners.

➤ Follow standard frameworks for articulating your business. This makes it easier for you to learn from others, to acquire patterns and best practices as well as standard business components. It also increases the range and value of potential partnerships.

➤ Develop deal-making as the primary strategic ability at all levels of management. (Many firms limit this ability to top management.) This includes: consortium management, risk management, supply chain management and procurement, and above all relationship management.

➤ Strategic advantage: pay attention to aspects that your competitors are overlooking.

About the book – and other resources.

The remainder of the book is a more detailed exploration of various aspects of component-based business.

Chapter 1	**Building Blocks**

A large range of manufactured products can be built from pre-existing (and potentially interchangeable) components. Complex systems and artefacts can be explained by decomposing them into components. Increasingly, IT solutions are constructed from software components. The next step is to construct a whole business from building blocks. There are some notable pitfalls of componentry. However, components are not a choice: they represent a new game.

Chapter 2	**Systems constructed from Building Blocks**

Assuming we have some basis for understanding the success of large complex systems, we can identify two desirable system properties: Intelligence and Character. Some systems lack intelligence, character or both.

Increasing the componentry of a system increases a property called **Articulation**. Articulation can alter both intelligence and character.

Chapter 3	**Principles Governing the Design and Use of Building Blocks**

We identify four contexts for making judgements about components.

  ° Solution-oriented judgements

  ° Technically-oriented judgements

  ° Components respecting ecological principles

  ° Components possessing character

Chapter 4	**Intelligent and Trustworthy Interfaces**

If the building blocks are well designed and well chosen, the focus of management attention shifts to where it should have been all along: the business relationships between the building blocks.

Interfaces connect and separate components or subsystems. The quality of the interfaces affects the quality of the larger system. Some of the significant system properties can be seen as located in the interfaces. Significant changes to systems usually involve boundary changes. Business relationships are dynamic and require trust and character.

Chapter 5	**Evolutionary Change**

One of the motives for component-based business is that it increases adaptability. So we need to look closely at the process of adaptation, and see how componentry may affect it.

Traditional modes of business planning and IT planning have proved themselves incapable of delivering flexible organizations and systems. So an alternative approach is required.

A few examples of component-based business are included in this book, for the purposes of illustration. However, as this is rapidly developing field, more up-to-date and more detailed examples, as well as further background material, can be found on the website associated with the book: http://www.component-based-business.com.

The book contains a series of suggested questions to take your thinking further. The http://www.component-based-business.com website contains open forums, in which these and other questions can be discussed.

Thanks.

To my clients for keeping me busy while writing the book. (John Cage once wrote that being interrupted by the telephone "opens us to the world outside".)

To various friends and associates who have kindly read and commented on earlier drafts, including: Adrian Apthorp, Hans Fugers, Pat Green, Brian Henderson-Sellars, Michael Jackson, Nic Holt, Kathy Maitland, June Melody, David Sprott and Ken Veryard. Aidan Ward read the entire manuscript through twice, and his support and encouragement has been invaluable.

To various additional friends and associates who have stimulated or educated my thinking, or provided ideas and material. These include: Ian Alexander, Paul Allen, Philip Boxer, Bernie Cohen, John Dobson, Ian Graham, Jeremy Hadden, Clive Mabey, Mike Martin, Mike Mills, Bashar Nuseibeh, Chris Russell, Lawrence Wilkes, and Alan Cameron Wills.

To the organizers and audiences of various seminars and workshops at which I've presented some of this material, for stimulation and feedback.

To the CBDi Forum team and members, for support and encouragement.

To the Springer-Verlag team, for all the hard work they've still got to do after I've written this.

And above all to my family: June, Anthony and Dominic, for keeping me sane.

1. Building Blocks

It's child's play. If you know what you want, you can assemble it from building blocks. Business services, application services, application software – whatever you might need is being packaged in the form of components. Furthermore, we are invited to see the world – whatever world we happen to inhabit – as a single large, extremely complex system, composed of interacting agents and artefacts. Whatever we assemble, from components or otherwise, is still only a tiny part of a much larger system.

So componentry is both a way of understanding the world, and a way of taking effective action within the world. There are both commercial and intellectual reasons for the dominance of the component paradigm. There is increasing pressure to think components – in a broad range of domains. There is increasing pressure for an enterprise to configure itself in the form of components.

And yet we need to be careful. It is tempting to regard components as black boxes, whose contents can be disregarded, and whose proper functioning can be taken for granted (after a one-time exercise of due diligence and acceptance testing). Indeed, it is often both convenient and necessary to ignore the contents of these black boxes, and to assume that they provide a satisfactory service, in order to be able to grapple with complexities elsewhere. But if we regard a component simply as a static device, we shall fail to anticipate some of the hidden forces and dangers of a component-based world. Components are provisional, encapsulation and control are always provisional. There are no certainties.

Thus component thinking is both a necessary convenience, and a potential danger. A given decomposition of a whole into parts should always be provisional. A component is a dynamic relationship, not a fixed device. If an organization or market has configured itself around a set of business services or components, then this can be both a source of strength and a source of weakness. There is no perfect and timeless architecture that is invulnerable to change.

In this chapter, we shall review the use of building blocks in a wide range of fields – both for understanding things and for making things – before zooming in on two strongly related fields: Business and Information Technology (IT). This prelude aims to help readers coming from either a business background or an IT background to see the building block approach from a new angle, and thereby to appreciate both some of its opportunities and some of its limitations.

A large range of manufactured products can be built from pre-existing (and potentially interchangeable) components.

When I was a child, I played with Lego. My sons now play with Lego. It is a simple toy, with infinite possibilities, and well deserves its lasting popularity.   Given the assumption that everyone (at least in the Western world) has some experience of Lego, it is tempting to use Lego (or some other construction toy) as a metaphor for describing and explaining the building block approach.

> What are the essential characteristics of the Lego experience? How does this differ from the use of building blocks in other domains?

Examples: Bicycles, Guns.

The bicycle is a consumer product that is assembled from prefabricated components, and provides a good illustration of the component-based approach within manufacturing.   There are also some interesting lessons about components from the manufacture of guns.

Let's start by looking at the early history of the bicycle in England.   Bicycles were manufactured in Coventry, using components from several other industrial towns and cities. See Figure 1.1.

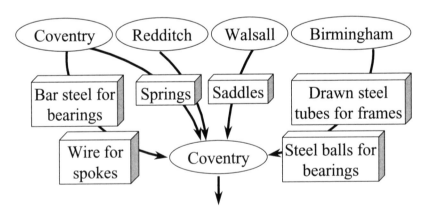

Figure 1.1: Bicycle components in the 1870s.
[Source: Bijker]

> "Since the beginning of the cycle industry, local blacksmiths and mechanics have participated in constructing small numbers of bicycles to order. … Standardization … had two opposite effects on industry: it further enhanced mass production, and it strengthened the position of those small workshops. A considerable number of local bicycle makers could offer a "home-made" product to the residents of their small village at a price somewhat lower than that of factory-produced bicycles because of their lower overhead costs. Some large companies had specialized in the manufacture of standardized components, delivering them to both bicycle factories and local workshops. Thus three classes of machine could be distinguished. First, there were the mass-produced bicycles made by bicycle factories. Only the largest of these factories manufactured all components themselves; most of them had contracted out the manufacture of saddles, tires, and the like. Second, there were bicycles made by local workshops, constructed from proprietary components made by specialized firms. And the third class of bicycles, made by special departments of factories as well as by small workshops, was known as "de luxe" machines, produced without much regard for costs."

Case 1.1: Early Bicycle Industry.
[Source: Bijker]

Thus the building block approach offers the end user a choice of products (standard, modified, hand-built) with different cost–quality equations. Similar trends can be identified in business services, as well as application software.

Q When do you think that hand-built solutions are worth the extra cost?

Another interesting feature of this historical example is the evolution and reuse of an industrial legacy. A network of mechanics and workshops, which established itself in the 1870s for the bicycle industry, subsequently provided the capability to manufacture and service motor cars. Thus the early motor car industry reused the factories and workshops, inter-firm relationships, engineering and commercial skills, and even some of the specific components and tools, that had been developed for the bicycle industry some decades before. And for that matter, the bicycle industry had reused a large legacy network of blacksmiths, who provided services to bicyclists alongside their original function of shoeing horses and repairing carts.

It is standard practice for consultants nowadays to develop a highly abstract business description, or encourage their clients to do so. A modern strategy consultant might see the transformation of the role of the blacksmith, from the horse and cart via the bicycle to the car, as a confirmation of this approach. If we had a time machine, and could send this consultant back into the Victorian era, we could imagine him saying to the blacksmith: "But Sir, you shouldn't see yourself as in the Horse-Shoeing Business but in the Personal Transport Facilitation Business." (Perhaps this could be the basis for an amusing but informative exercise for a business studies student.)

Q To do this exercise properly, what techniques would you use? What data would you need? What resistance would you expect from the blacksmith?

Another good example of component-based manufacture is provided by the gun. Two hundred years ago, Eli Whitney amazed his contemporaries by assembling guns rapidly from prepared parts, without the need for careful filing and fitting. At that time, the assembly of guns had been a slow craft, requiring skills and special equipment. Whitney's components were interchangeable for two reasons. Firstly, he had designed a standard connection, so that the parts fitted together in a standard way. Secondly, he had designed some tolerance into the connection, so that the parts didn't have to be accurate to the smallest fraction of a millimetre. Whitney certainly wasn't the first person to make that type of gun. He wasn't even the first person to make guns out of separate bits. What was important was the way he made the bits, and the way he assembled these bits into guns.

 How can we apply Witney's innovation to business or system relationships? How much tolerance is designed into standard business contracts or software interfaces?

Potential benefits: economies of scale, ease of repair and upgrade.

Economies of scale.

One of the most obvious advantages of the building block approach to manufacture is that it sometimes enables economies of scale. In manufacturing of physical products, economies of scale are obtained by two main factors.

1. Firstly, long production runs tend to be more economic than short production runs. If you have to keep stopping the machine to change the settings, then this interferes with productivity. Although modern computer-based machine tools allow for considerable variability within a single production run, the general principle still holds valid.

2. Secondly, the more of a given product you make, the better you get at making it – economists call this **learning by doing**.

Kevin Kelly quotes the example of Fairchild Semiconductor, whose newly developed transistor would replace a valve used in a range of military equipment. Only problem: the valves cost $1.05 each. Based on initial production runs, the transistor was going to cost $100 each.

 As an exercise in persuasion: what tactics would you use to persuade a hard-nosed general to pay a large premium price for a new (and unknown) technology?

Even when economists predict that production will get cheaper over time, it takes courage (or desperation) for businessmen to do what Fairchild Semiconductor did. They sold the transistor for $1.05, taking a huge financial loss.

 As another exercise in persuasion: what tactics would you use to persuade a hard-nosed banker (or venture capitalist) to extend your overdraft, based on this cost equation?

History is written by the victors. The transistor triumphed, and so did Fairchild Semiconductor. Within two years, they had a 90% market share, and were selling the transistor for 50¢. And making a profit.

So if the building block approach means that you are using larger volumes of a small number of interchangeable parts, then this can yield significant economies of scale. But it doesn't always mean that. Sometimes each end-product requires a completely different set of building blocks, so there is little or no reuse from one end-product to the next.

 In physical manufacturing, is there a benefit from the building block approach even if there is no reuse from one end-product to another? And what about business services or software?

Repair and upgrade.

Separately from the production economies, the building block approach ought to simplify repair and upgrade. If a component is faulty, it can be replaced. If a better component becomes available, it can be substituted.

 If componentry is to lead to simplified repair and upgrade, what other conditions need to be satisfied? (Draw from the following examples, and from your own experience.)

We're now going to look at two examples of practical problems with repair and upgrade: the rear light assembly on a German car, and the power switch on a home computer. These examples show that componentry is not sufficient, and that there are other conditions that need to be satisfied.

My friend David, who is an expert on software components, recently complained about the maintenance on his expensive German automobile. He wanted the garage to fix a faulty rear light. It turned out that the light was part of a larger component and he needed to have the entire rear light cluster replaced, costing several hundred pounds.

He asked who made the decision to set the unit of replacement at the level of the rear light cluster. Was it a production engineering decision? Surely the marketing role would not have misrepresented customer requirements so badly?

Sadly for us consumers, the key question for many marketing departments is not (i) *which component architecture would be most convenient for most of our customers?* but (ii) *does this component architecture make any difference to the likely volume of sales?*

In other words, does the car maker care whether it costs you more to fix your rear light? How much money do they make from selling spare parts?

We'll come back to this story later, because it illustrates some useful points in relation to component architecture, and the different interests that may be served by different design principles.

Meanwhile, here's a related story. My father recently had a problem with his home computer. He phoned the technical support line, and told them that the grey knob on the front had broken. Which grey knob? The one he used for switching the computer on and off.

To my father's logical mind this description seemed both simple and sufficient, but it puzzled the technical support staff. It took them some time to work out that my father was referring to the component officially known as The Power Switch.

When one buys a complex item of equipment, one doesn't necessarily know the official names of all the components. This doesn't matter when everything is working, but it can cause huge problems when things start to fail. How do I reinstall or replace a faulty component, and how do I even know whether a given component is still in use, when the suppliers' names for the components are obscure and undocumented?

 If you have access to a Windows computer, look how many DLL files are installed. Do you know the purpose of any of them? Do you know where they are used? Do you imagine that anyone within Microsoft has a complete understanding of all the DLL files?

Once my father had overcome the barrier of terminology, he thought it would be a simple matter to persuade technical support to supply him with a new "Power Switch".

Not simple at all. It turns out that the makers of this brand of computer have used a variety of different Power Switches, without properly keeping track. Although the technical support division was supposedly in possession of a complete specification of my father's computer, this specification failed to tell them which of several different (and incompatible) Power Switches had been used in this particular assembly.

It was therefore necessary to replace the entire front panel. Sounds familiar?

Q How many different companies share responsibility for the componentry in a typical home computer? How likely do you think it is that they all use the same names for the components?

Q What are the mechanisms used within the software industry to control such situations? In your experience, do they work effectively?

Design is often dominated by the components that exist.

Designer chooses component as quickest and cheapest route to solution.

Given the complexity of a typical design task, it may be impossible for a designer to rethink every part from scratch. The only way to manage this complexity is to use standard components.

For example, the designer of a new electric gadget may save time (and money) by using a standard on-off switch, or a standard power cable, taken out of a supplier's catalogue, rather than designing each component from first principles.

However, this is in many cases a conscious design decision. The designer reserves the option to design his own switch, if he cannot find one that fits.

Q What criteria would you expect the designer to use, to decide whether a given component fits his overall design?

Designer takes component for granted.

The selection of an existing component is related to the selection of a **design heuristic** – defined as a principle, procedure or other device that contributes to reduction in the search for a satisfactory solution. A heuristic may name or imply specific components, or kits of components. Alternatively, heuristics may involve something much more abstract, such as what software engineers commonly call patterns and frameworks.

There is a social process whereby heuristics become embedded in standard design practice, and are taken for granted by the majority of practising designers. In such situations, the few analysts or designers who can keep a critical distance from these heuristics, and are then able to challenge them where appropriate, can get themselves a reputation for creativity, although this is creativity in a fairly narrow sense.

> Q   Can you think of any examples of creativity in this sense?

In some cases, the use of a specific component has become universal, and it doesn't even occur to the designer to question the use of this component. Perhaps the designer makes a conscious choice of component, but only from a very narrow range of similar components, sharing a common pattern or style. The pattern or style can then be regarded as a given. Sometimes these unquestioned design assumptions can only be detected with hindsight, after defects in the design have become apparent, or after a particularly innovative designer has demonstrated an alternative design.

> Q   What patterns or styles of business relationship or contract are now universally accepted? What patterns or styles of software design?
>
> Q   What patterns or styles had a period of universal acceptance, but are now regarded as flawed, limited, or obsolete?

Minor components that take over the show.

In the conventional view of technological development, the designer establishes a mapping between a set of demands (usually known as The Requirements) and a set of components or services that collectively satisfy the demands (usually known as The Solution).

But the design logic of component-based development isn't compatible with the research logic of technology breakthrough. In many leading edge projects, especially where there is a research element as well as a development element, this is not the case. The Solution often turns out to require several components that haven't been invented yet, although engineers are typically confident that they can develop leading edge technological devices, given time and budget. The components that don't yet exist create "holes" or "attractors" in the design structure, with a distorting effect on the project as a whole.

In a brilliant and detailed case study of a French R&D project called Aramis, Bruno Latour describes how the social and technological worlds of research and development interact in very complex and interesting ways. As one of the many threads of the Aramis story, Latour describes how Aramis demands the invention of a new type of electric motor. The variable-reluctance motor is invented, and then this invention starts to be cited as one of the beneficial spin-offs of the project as a whole, although when pressed nobody can think of any other use for this motor. The design of Aramis now revolves around this motor; having gone to the trouble to invent it, the project seems to have no choice but to use it. The use of this component becomes a design goal or design constraint, instead of a design option.

Do you have any experience of a single component dominating and distorting the entire solution? What was it about the component that gave it this power? What were the overall effects on the project or solution?

Complex systems and artefacts can be explained by decomposing them into components.

Decomposition or reductive analysis provides an important type of explanation – although it's not the only type. In this section, we'll explore a couple of contrasting examples.

 What are the advantages of this type of explanation? What are its limitations? Which phenomena can best be explained in this way? Are there phenomena that cannot be explained in this way?

Even complex financial products, such as forwards, futures, swaps and options, can be built from simple components.

In this section, we provide a brief summary of a classic 1987 paper by the financial engineering guru Charles Smithson.

Smithson showed how a wide variety of financial risk management products, involving hedges of various kinds against interest rate and exchange rate fluctuations, could be composed from a small number of simple building blocks.

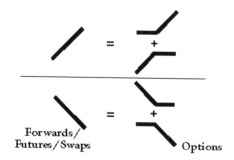

Figure 1.2: Smithson's "Instruction Manual".

Smithson describes Figure 1.2 as the "instruction manual" for what he calls his box of financial building blocks, and he adopts an avuncular tone, as if he was about to explain something to a fond nephew.

"A quick look shows that though there can be many pieces in the box, there are only six basic shapes to concern yourself with. The straight pieces come in three colors; we know we can obtain a forward payoff profile either with forwards (the red ones), futures (the yellow ones), or swaps (the blue ones). The kinked pieces are all the same color (white) because options can be combined to replicate a forward, a future, or a swap."

Got that? The fact that the diagrams are all in black and white (at least in the Internet version of the paper) gives this explanation a surreal quality. But we're not going to explore the financial aspects of this example here so don't worry about the details. There are just a couple of general points we need to look at.

One of the interesting things about this example is the fact that the decomposition of financial products into building blocks represents a post hoc rationalization of financial engineering. These complex deals were being widely traded, with considerable diversity and confusion of jargon, some while before Smithson demonstrated that they could be constructed from simple building blocks.

Smithson's analytical work introduced a standard conceptual framework to the field, with three benefits to financial engineers. The framework gave them a common language to describe what they were doing; it gave them an apparently sound basis for calculating and confirming the risks and rewards of existing complex products; and it set them off on a search for new ways of composing the building blocks to create new products.

At the time of writing, many financial institutions are experiencing some problems in the IT systems supporting these financial products. The connections between the financial building blocks are not reflected in the IT systems, with the result that there is little or no product cohesion, no common terminology or underlying model, and the information and systems themselves are fragmented.

> Q   Who do you imagine might be troubled by this situation? Who are the stakeholders?

Researchers at Loughborough University are currently developing software components that correspond to Smithson's financial building blocks. Their work will provide an interesting bridge between the financial engineering world and the software engineering world.

People explain how the brain works in terms of interconnected "components".

In this section, we provide a brief summary of relevant work, much of which has been done within the artificial intelligence community, by such people as Marvin Minsky and Jerry Fodor. This links to the discussion on organizational intelligence later in the book.

Let's start with a well-known observation about mental ability. In 1956, George Miller published a paper in which he claimed a fairly constant limit on the number of unrelated things that a person could remember in one go: seven plus or minus two.

The natural way to explain this phenomenon is to imagine some "component" within the brain that has a limited capacity. Put very crudely, it is as if there is a box in your head that you use for these kinds of tasks, and it has a fixed number of compartments: seven plus or minus two.

> Q   From an engineering perspective, there are some obvious ways of improving a system whose behaviour is constrained by the limited capacity of a particular component. What might an engineer suggest as a way of overcoming Miller's limit? What problems can you see with the engineering approach in this situation?

This way of picturing the workings of the brain is a very ancient one. In the Theatetus, Socrates compares the brain to a birdcage, and items of knowledge to the birds. Knowledge is trapped in the brain, much in the same way that birds are trapped in an aviary. There are many other theories of mental functioning that describe the brain in terms of a model of interconnected components. For example, Freud developed several different models in the course of his research. One of the aspects of mental functioning that particularly interested Freud was the way sense-perceptions were processed. Freud described this in terms of several unconscious mental processes, which he called condensation, displacement, representation and symbolization, and Freud's followers often draw pictures in which these processes are carried out as if by a series of filters, positioned between the sense organs and the conscious portions of the brain.

> Q   Do you think this is a suitable metaphor for the flow of knowledge through an organization? What kinds of organization and information models does this metaphor suggest?

Other lines of research initiated by Freud are also still pursued today. Another interesting idea is that mental function can be understood as a set of what psychoanalysts call "object relations". (Note: this use of the term "object" has no immediate connection to the software engineering use of the term "object".)

In one simple and popular version of object-relations theory, each person is supposed to contain a Parent, an Adult and a Child, each with a different pattern of behaviour and interaction. An interaction (or "game") between two people can then be characterized as any combination of these: thus Parent–Child or Adult–Adult.

There are many other, more sophisticated and subtle versions of object-relations theory, as well as many other schools of psychoanalysis. What they all have in common is an attempt to explain psychological phenomena in terms of some internal mental divisions, a fractured identity or divided subject, and to offer some therapy that helps people understand and cope with these fractures and divisions. Indeed, some schools talk as if it were possible to heal the mind, to glue the fractures back into a single integrated whole, although other schools dismiss this as inappropriate or unrealistic.

It is sometimes helpful to think of organizations in similar terms. A business process or enterprise can often be perceived as fractured. A pseudo-therapeutic intervention may be designed to "heal" such fractures, in order to achieve a more "integrated" enterprise. Alternatively, each fracture can be established (with some redesign and realignment) as an autonomous entity or properly constituted component. (Either type of intervention demands considerable skill and sensitivity, usually from an external consultant.)

Sometimes a business model can have a direct therapeutic effect in this sense, simply by clearly articulating the structure of the business. The possibility of this effect has important implications for the business analyst or systems analyst within the IT function.

 What kinds of fracture are visible from an IT perspective, or may be discovered from a business modelling exercise led by IT personnel? What cannot be seen from such models?

Is the brain like a computer?

Conceptual models and metaphors of brain functioning have changed almost as often as the fashionable technologies have changed. For example, at one stage, Freud talked about the brain as if it followed the laws of hydraulics, while his follower, the French psychoanalyst Jacques Lacan, briefly explored cybernetic theories of the mind. It's probably a long time since anybody took the hydraulic theory of the brain literally, although we still speak loosely and metaphorically of pressure and release. Cybernetic theories are still popular in some circles.

After the Second World War, the computer started to proliferate in academic and commercial life. The new science of cybernetics sprang up, with many leading thinkers of the time participating in a series of conferences known as the Macy conferences. A range of people, from science fiction writers to serious researchers, started to explore the notion that the brain might resemble a computer, or vice versa.

Looking back on this notion nearly fifty years later, it seems quite incredible that they should have taken it seriously. After all, the computers we have today are incomparably more powerful and sophisticated than the crude and bulky machines of the post-war period – and we seem further than ever from the vision of a genuinely artificial brain.

As an aside, it may be observed that we often overrate the quality or significance of the latest technology. There is a Sherlock Holmes story, written in the 1920s, in which a criminal mistakes the sound of a gramophone for the sound of a real violin. Accustomed as we are today to digital and Dolby®, we find it incredible that anyone could have been fooled by an old-fashioned 78 rpm record-player. And yet Conan Doyle took the technology seriously enough to base a story on it.

What was established fairly quickly in the post-war period, and extensively discussed at the Macy conferences, was that brains were not actually structured in the same way that computers were then structured. Early computers were based on pioneering mathematical work by Alan Turing and John von Neumann, among others. For many decades, the science of computation was dominated by an abstract and imaginary machine known as a Turing machine, and by a sequential processing architecture named after von Neumann.

Brains differ from such computers in several important respects. They do not follow fixed rules, they do not store information in precise locations, and they do not process information sequentially in a central processing unit.

As researchers tried to build machines that could replicate some elements of human intelligence, they started to gain a greater respect for the complexity and depth of human intelligence. Even the clumsy physical and verbal manoeuvres of a baby turned out to require previously unrecognized levels of intelligence, which no artificial machine could emulate.

Thus in a strange way, the hypothesis "brain=computer" may have served science and mankind well. In attempting to prove this hypothesis, computer scientists and psychologists have pushed forward our understanding of both computers and brains. We can now see – perhaps much more clearly than ever before – many differences between computers and brains.

But the battle is not over. If we now believe that brains are not like the early computers, we may still suppose that they are like some other form of computer. And so the whole research programme begins again.

At the cellular level, it seems as if the brain is physically constructed from a set of neurones. This is a form of building block at the smallest level. Can we construct artificial systems from such building blocks, so that intelligence somehow emerges from the interaction of vast numbers of them? This research question leads to radically different computer architectures, based on cellular automata, parallel processing and so-called neural nets. (Ironically, some of these "computers" don't really exist; they are simulated by incredibly fast von-Neumann machines. But that's another layer of complexity on our story.) In Chapter 2, we shall take a brief look at some of the latest experiments in massively parallel computing, including IBM's Blue Gene project.

At an intermediate level, some researchers have tried to identify cognitive components that can collaborate to produce recognizable forms of intelligence. In *The Society of Mind*, Marvin Minsky uses the building block approach to plug together a series of independent mental agents, each responsible for a different aspect of mental functioning.

In this section, we have seen several different ways of accounting for the mental activity of the brain. What these ways have in common is an attempt to decompose mental functioning into building blocks or modules, which operate in parallel.

Increasingly, IT solutions are constructed from software components.

Software componentry is an industry phenomenon.

There has been a significant growth in software componentry in recent years. This is sometimes known as component-based software engineering (CBSE), or component-based development (CBD). Major software companies, including Microsoft, IBM and Sun, are fully committed to what they call software components, both for building their own software products, and for providing capability to other software factories.

Some readers may still think of IBM as predominantly a hardware company. But as hardware becomes an increasingly cheap commodity, IBM and other manufacturers have shifted their focus onto software. And Sun, once an obscure hardware company, is now best known for its role in creating the Java programming language. In Chapter 3, we shall see the logic for this shift.

The software industry has experienced similar bandwagons in the past, with other technologies, and the path being trod with componentry follows a familiar pattern. The software industry has a tendency to fall into what Borgmann calls the **Device Paradigm**: viewing any new technology exclusively as a kind of device or gadget, and evaluating the technical features and powers of this device, without having any other perspective.

Role of telecommunications companies.

While much of the attention about component-based development has focused upon the activity of traditional IT companies, a fair share of the original thinking stems from the telecommunications world. The telecoms companies have done a lot of the groundwork for the service-based economy, and may soon be taking the leadership of CBSE away from the triumvirate of Microsoft, IBM and Sun.

Many years ago, some computer visionaries preached the convergence of computing and telecoms, to form a composite subject to be called IT (information technology). For a long time, however, the computer side of the equation dominated the field, IT became synonymous with computing, and the telecoms side was forgotten. (More recently, some purists have tried to reassert this convergence through the acronym ICT – information and communication technology – but this has failed to take hold except in some academic and government circles.)

Once upon a time, computer entrepreneurs grew rich developing spin-offs from HP or crumbs from IBM's table. And, for a while, it seemed as if every new idea in the IT world could be traced back to some work at Xerox Labs.

But let's look at what was happening behind the scenes during the 1990s. The World Wide Web appeared, apparently from nowhere. Concepts such as distribution and federation are widely used, in business processes as well as technology. CORBA, while now technically challenged and bypassed by other products and proprietary standards, nonetheless triggered a significant mindset change in distributed software engineering. These weren't invented by Microsoft or Sun, nor even IBM and Xerox. It was the telecoms companies that funded this work. Now it's Bell Labs (part of Lucent) that everyone seems to wants to steal ideas from.

Many people view componentry as an engineering tool.

Some of the major players in the software industry are promoting componentry to the rest of the software industry as a radically new approach to the design, construction, implementation and evolution of software applications.

Several strong claims are made about the potential benefits of a component-based approach to software. Software applications may be assembled from components from a variety of sources; the components themselves may be written in several different programming languages and run on several different platforms. Above all, components may be extracted from existing systems (the so-called legacy systems), enabling a quasi-evolutionary transformation of legacy software.

Just as the vendors and early adopters of componentry promote its benefits as if it were a new kind of engineering tool, so the late adopters resist these arguments on the same basis. The strong claims of the champions of componentry prompt a range of negative or sceptical reactions, both sides apparently accepting the technological view of componentry as some kind of engineering tool.

Thus some people claim that this tool is nothing new, that it is practically the same as the tool they are already using. Some people find fault with the tool, or claim that they are not ready to use it, for a variety of reasons. Some people try to measure the tool, or record its effects. Some people try to classify situations where the tool should be used, and situations where it should not or cannot be used. Some people grasp it with enthusiasm, or perhaps see it as yet another opportunity to reassess and redefine their software processes. Some people go off and invent something else, rather than suffer the indignity of using this particular tool ("Not Invented Here").

Q   Does every software innovation prompt all these reactions?

What is common to all these reactions is that they all regard componentry as a tool, as something an engineer might use to solve a particular range of engineering problems, and fail to view componentry from any other perspective. In Borgmann's terms, they all succumb to the Device Paradigm.

An equally valid perspective is to view componentry as an ecological phenomenon.

If we look at populations of software, rather than specific software artefacts, it is possible to view technological innovations in an entirely different way. From the ecological perspective, componentry is not a tool that engineers consciously decide to deploy, but a trend that may be detected spreading through a population.

The more that a particular component is thought to be useful, the more it will find its way to a range of settings – and it doesn't make any difference whether people are consciously pushing and pulling components for the sake of componentry, or merely making ad hoc choices. The spread of componentry results from a large number of these small decisions put together.

The ecological perspective removes the engineer (and the engineering project) from centre stage. Perhaps for this reason, engineers (even in universities) prefer not to view things from this perspective.

Of course, the spread of software components (whatever they are) and associated matter through a software population may be strongly linked with the rational intentions of some software engineers. However, such linkage is the stuff of intellectual speculation and academic research, and should not be taken for granted. In any case, there are other possible explanations.

To take an example that we can discuss without upsetting the sensitivities of software engineers, let us consider the spread of a software virus through a population. Many software engineers will themselves have been victims of a software virus; in any case, most will prefer to identify with the victims rather than the perpetrators of such viruses.

It is easy to see that the spread of a software virus depends not only on the deliberate actions of the virus creator, but also on the unwitting actions of large numbers of software users, who inadvertently infect themselves and their friends. The spread of a virus is therefore an outcome that emerges from a large number of mostly unintended actions.

Software engineers should be willing to accept that bad outcomes may be the result of accident or malice, and not just incompetence. Some may also be willing to acknowledge that good outcomes may be the result of fortune or providence. But many may still wish to claim that all good outcomes are the result of their own cleverness and diligence. (This distinction is only possible in the first place because software engineers presume to know which are the good outcomes and which are the bad ones.)

If you're interested, as I am, in technology transfer, then you'll want to know the factors that will affect the speed of this move towards software componentry. (We'll find some clues later in the book.) Different sectors of the software industry will move at different speeds, and these differences may well have a lasting effect on the shape of the software industry. Although we may predict that technology will introduce greater role differentiation, we don't yet know exactly what form this will take here.

> Q What responsibilities do you expect to be taken by suppliers or intermediaries? And what responsibilities do you expect to be taken by third parties? What factors will determine this distribution of responsibilities?

The software components market can be viewed ecologically, as an ecosystem. From this perspective, it doesn't matter how many companies decide it would be a nice idea to sell a few components, how many companies are reassured by complicated intellectual property safeguards, how many companies spend money on advertising and PR. What matters is that some companies will be extremely successful with a component-based strategy, and these are the companies that are likely to survive and thrive in the new software economy. We'll come back to this point in Chapter 3, where we'll describe the software market not as a single ecosystem but as four separate but connected ecosystems.

CBD has notable outcomes – or does it?

In earlier epochs of the software industry, there were many programmers who produced well-structured programs without consciously following Structured Programming methods, and many systems designers who produced well-structured systems without consciously following Structured Design methods. And there were also many people who produced poor structures despite using the best methods. There were also many software artefacts that were initially well-structured, but which degraded fairly quickly as they were "improved".

And some people pick up someone else's component because they recognise it as having a clean interface for the purpose they desire. So the clarity of the component – whether deliberate or inadvertent – increases its survival and propagation. We'll come back to this in Chapter 3.

The fact that a project declares allegiance to a particular method is no guarantee that the method will be successfully used. Some projects that attempt to follow a component-oriented approach may fail to deliver clean components with good quality interfaces, for a variety of reasons. Meanwhile some projects may deliver clean components with good quality interfaces, but without having consciously followed a component-oriented approach. Some people choose an articulation that works, and some miss the mark – but they may only find out later what works and what doesn't.

Software researchers can assess software artefacts, in terms of the degree of component-like structures within the artefacts, and the presence of clean interfaces and other recognized patterns. There is a growing body of academic research, based not only on single snapshots at a single point of time, but also on longitudinal studies.

 What can be learned from a single snapshot? What can be learned from a series of snapshots, with no direct knowledge of what happens between the snapshots? How can the ecology of components be studied?

Full understanding of software evolution needs knowledge of the spread and survival of successful software structures, and the gradual elimination of unsuccessful structures. In Chapter 3, we shall explore the hypothesis that software components with certain characteristics have a competitive advantage, and this advantage does not depend on whether these characteristics were deliberately planned by the software designers.

We also need to explore the hypothesis that certain system architectures have a competitive advantage. The evolutionary perspective taken by this book leads to a substantial revision of traditional expectations of technical elegance and quality.

 Can you think of any situations where a technically superior product was wiped out by a technically inferior competitor? Have you experienced any such situation personally?

There are some well-documented situations where technical factors have been swamped by market factors, but this is an area where little systematic research has been done.

Of course any technologist will acknowledge that technically superior products may sometimes be rejected by an ignorant market. But when one views these trends from an evolutionary perspective, it is tempting to go much further, and experiment with the subversive idea that technological notions of technical superiority are almost completely irrelevant to anything, and have practically no real effect on the market.

The next step is to construct a whole business from building blocks.

There is a growing market in business services.

The Growth of Software Rental – Back to the Bureaux?

As I write, there are continuing attempts, with differing degrees of success, to create a market for Application Service Provision (ASP). These attempts have been triggered by various considerations.

On the supply side, several suppliers of large expensive software packages, such as Enterprise Resource Planning (ERP), have found it increasingly difficult to find new customers prepared to undergo large and expensive package implementations. These suppliers recognized that if they could make their products available in the form of outsourced application services, this would substantially expand the number of potential customers. Assuming reasonable levels of customer retention, this approach would hopefully also provide a much longer and steadier revenue stream.

And when the package suppliers themselves are not willing to enter the ASP market, third parties are clearly ready to take up the opportunity, provided that they can negotiate a good deal with the software copyright owners.

On the demand side, many purchasing organizations are willing to pay a significantly larger cost over the expected lifetime of product use, rather than incur the bulk of the costs as an initial investment. This approach seems to shift much of the risk onto the supplier, especially if an organization can discontinue using the service at relatively short notice.

The Fidessa application package is used by banks for equity trading. Major investment banks typically install the software at their own site, but smaller banks can rent the software over a network, thus saving a large initial investment.

Royalblue, the maker of Fidessa as well as other financial and helpdesk software, has increased sales by 42% in the past six months, mainly as a result of the trend towards software rental, which has helped it tap into new markets.

Case 1.2: Fidessa.

It is natural to compare ASP with the computer bureau services that proliferated in the 1960s and 1970s. Bearing in mind the performance difficulties experienced with many of these bureaux, some analysts have issued warnings about the capacity of the new ASPs and their ability to deliver required service levels. In fact, although it's clearly important to specify, negotiate and monitor service levels, there is no reason to suppose that an external service provider would be any less powerful or reliable than an inhouse solution. Hardware is surely no longer the major cost factor, and the ASPs are often closer to the Internet hubs than their customers. And for web-based services, where demand levels may fluctuate enormously, a specialist service provider may be better able to procure extra capacity at short notice.

(This highlights one of the key differences between applications and services. Services make use of shared resource that remain in the ownership and control of the provider, not the user. Therefore ownership protection and capacity planning need to be considered carefully when making service engineering decisions – indeed, these considerations can affect the order in which the engineering decisions should be made.)

A much more serious inhibitor for the ASP market has been the clumsy footprint of many of the services, whose scope – if not the actual software – is typically based on the legacy of an existing application package. Many user organizations have experienced difficulties with wide integration, even with specialist support, and this is one of the reasons why ASPs have so far failed to dominate the market. (It's not the only reason, as we shall see later.)

In some sectors of the software market, however, service provision has been extremely successful, especially where the service has been tightly scoped. Even if the ASPs manage to reinvent themselves, the flexibility and choice they can offer may remain markedly inferior to anyone who can offer independent sets of services.

SCMdialtone is an Internet-based software service that exposes business components for real-time supply chain management.

Behind SCMdialtone is a collection of business objects that do everything from managing customers and item part numbers to calculating (in real time) the production and procurement plans that will replenish stock based on the day's sales. These business objects are invoked on the service host using the simple object access protocol (SOAP).

Central to the SCMdialtone business model is the notion of transaction-based billing ("microbilling"). The service is designed to support very high volumes of low-cost transactions, via a network of franchised datacentres.

SCMdialtone is targeted at vertical B2B hubs and system integrators, as well as end-user organizations.

Case 1.3: SCM Dialtone.

Back Office.

A number of financial institutions have been looking at Back Office as a potential ASP or business service. Either they might outsource Back Office to someone else, or they might provide Back Office as a service to other finance companies. However, it turns out that Back Office is not a meaningful service in its own right, but may be a collection of loosely coupled services, provided by multiple companies.

In Chapter 4, we'll look more closely at the split between "front office" and "back office". For the present, let's just note that people often talk about "The Back Office" as if this term had the same meaning everywhere, in all financial organizations, equally for paper-based and electronically mediated processing. Back Office is apparently the name of a universal service, and a finance company might consider sharing a single Back Office between several Front Offices, outsourcing Back Office to a generic Back Office service provider, or becoming a Back Office provider to other companies.

But as soon as you look at the detail, the interface between Front Office and Back Office turns out to vary significantly from place to place. It's certainly possible to share a single Back Office between two Front Offices, or conversely to distribute the support for a single Front Office between two Back Offices, but it's by no means a trivial exercise.

Thus instead of regarding Back Office as the name of a service provided to Front Offices across a well-defined interface, it may be more appropriate to regard it as the umbrella name for a loosely packaged set of services, which may be assembled from different sources.

Telecommunications companies traditionally maintained a similar division – the Back Office was split off from the technologically important domain of delivering connectivity, and included such lesser functions as support, administration, billing and management systems. However, since the customer relationship management sits with the Back Office functions, the emphasis has now been reversed, and it is often the Back Office systems that are now regarded as strategic.

Manufacturing

Another structural metaphor that is commonly found in the financial industry is manufacturing. (We might want to regard this as a business pattern or framework.)

A recent merger between two banks used a form of component-based business to hasten the integration. A Manufacturing Division was created as a common platform, providing services to both of the retail brands, which were left separate and intact to pursue revenue growth. This is an attractive form of **articulation**.

In this situation, component-based business is being deployed as a cost-saving measure, not a revenue generating measure. This restriction has some advantages and some disadvantages. It reduces the risk of the integration programme, and allows the managers to concentrate on either one thing or the other. But some business opportunities will be missed – notably in the mass customization and connectivity stakes.

B2B Exchanges.

Early B2B initiatives were often naive. Ambitious start-ups claiming that they could save billions in procurement costs for big corporates, taking a large cut of the savings for themselves. Of course, the big corporates quickly realized that they could do this for themselves, and were not going to hand over the savings to third parties. Many of the early initiatives have been dominated by the big corporates, although there remains a role for independent third parties to provide well-focused B2B services, based on specific technical and business capabilities.

Enter a new player: the regulator. B2B marketplaces may sometimes increase competition, cutting transaction costs, reducing barriers to entry, and leading to increased choice, reduced prices and better inventory management. But when dominated by a cartel of big players, it can be an anti-competitive force. US regulators have been reviewing several new ventures, notably Covisint, the auto exchange formed by DaimlerChrysler, Ford and General Motors, supported by Oracle and CommerceOne. Architectural and technological issues – such as global integration and market transparency – will overlap with regulatory issues, and this may create additional roles for smart and independent service providers.

New Roles.

In general, technological progress typically results in an increase in the number of separate players, and a creation of new niche roles. This is particularly evident in the telecommunications sector, thanks to a combination of deregulation and other factors to which we shall return below. Another widely studied example of role proliferation is the introduction of electronic tax filing in the United States (Case 2.4).

Of course, a proliferation of roles doesn't necessarily mean a proliferation in the number of independent players within a market, as a large organization can take a strategic decision to play multiple roles, or to enter strategic alliances with partners playing complementary roles. However, even when many roles are played by a single organization, there is still a strong business argument as well as increasing technical support for configuring this organization as a federation of explicitly collaborating service providers, rather than as an old-fashioned tightly coupled monolith.

Since 1990, US taxpayers have been able to submit their tax returns electronically.

The introduction of electronic tax filing in the US has resulted in a considerable increase in the number of separately identified roles within the system – some necessary for the electronic system to work at all, and some new commercial and professional opportunities generated by the system.

Prior roles		
	°	tax payer
	°	return preparer
	°	mail carrier
	°	banking service
	°	Inland Revenue Service
	°	retailer
Required new roles	°	electronic filer
	°	communications network provider
	°	software vendor
Additional opportunities	°	information broker
	°	consumer credit provider
	°	tax planner
	°	investment banker

Case 2.4: Electronic Tax Filing.

Business Services.

In the future, outsourced services are more likely to be business services than application services. This is because this places the commercial costs and risks together with the operational responsibility.

Suppose I represent an insurance company, and I use a component-based service from another company to help me perform the underwriting. Don't I need to know the algorithm that the other company is using? Suppose that the algorithm is based on factors that I don't believe in, such as astrology? Suppose that the algorithm neglects factors that I believe to be important, such as genetics or genomics? Am I not accepting a huge risk by allowing another company to define an algorithm that is central to my business?

There are three main attitudes to this risk. One attitude, commonly found among civil servants, lawyers and software engineers, is to break encapsulation, crawl all over the algorithm in advance, and spend months testing the algorithm across a large database of test cases. If and when the algorithm is finally accepted and installed, such people will insist on proper authorization (with extensive retesting) before the smallest detail of the algorithm can be changed. The second attitude is denial: impatient businessmen and politicians simply ignore the warnings and delays of the first group.

There is a third approach: which is to use the forces of competition as a quality control mechanism. Instead of insisting that we find and maintain a single perfect algorithm, or kidding ourselves that we've already achieved this, we deliberately build a system that sets up several algorithms for competitive field-testing, a system that is sufficiently robust to withstand failure of any one algorithm.

The most direct mechanism is a straight commercial one. If the company operating the underwriting algorithm also bears all or some of the underwriting risk, then its commercial success should be directly linked to the "correctness" of the algorithm.

Where this kind of direct mechanism is not available, then we're looking for feedback mechanisms that simulate this, as closely as possible. Just as the survival of the company using these underwriting services may depend on having access to several competing services, so the survival of the underwriting services themselves may depend on being used by several different insurance companies, with different customer profiles and success criteria. (This reduces the risk that all the customers for your service disappear at the same time, and gives you a better chance to fix problems.)

The bottom line is that I'm buying an underwriting service rather than an underwriting calculation service, a business service rather than an application service. ASPs will have to rebrand themselves yet again, and present themselves as genuine business process outsourcerers.

It follows from this argument that we should focus on business components that deliver business services, rather than merely information or application services.

Alterna Technologies is a Canadian company providing corporate treasury services via a hosted virtual shared service centre in Dublin. Bulk payments are formatted on behalf of customers, and sent to one or more banks for processing.

Benefits to customers include the ability to use the web to access information about their transactions. The service also offers a degree of independence from regular banking providers.

Case 1.5: Alterna Technologies.

Policy Management.

Technologies to support the management of the enterprise as a network of services are likely to emerge from the telecommunications industry, through the concept of **policy management**. Telecoms uses software intelligence in the form of a policy server to manage network services using rules. Policy servers understand the rules by which the network manager describes the behaviour of the network, the topology of the network, and the behaviour of the devices that constitute the network. Using business-related information from the corporate information database, the policy server then configures the devices in the network so that the desired behaviour can be implemented.

Strategic Considerations.

Business processes are traditionally understood as value chains; the process is decomposed into a series of steps, each of which adds some value to the whole. Some methods of business process analysis go slightly further than this, and divide processes into value-adding and enabling. Many early outsourcing initiatives focused on the so-called enabling processes; however, modern business process automation typically also considers outsourcing of the value-adding steps of the process.

This approach works reasonably well in slow-moving businesses, where the value chain doesn't change very much. For many industry sectors, even the conversion of a business process into an e-business process may not radically affect the way the value chain is understood. An Internet bank receives deposits and makes payments, charges or pays interest, pretty much like a traditional bank. Even when the process goes wrong, it still goes wrong in recognizable ways.

In these businesses, the likely services will correspond to the smallest meaningful steps in the value chain – you may wish to regard these as business objects or elementary processes, depending on your background. The likely service providers will be those companies that control the relevant resources and can deploy the necessary capabilities most cost-effectively across the largest domain.

However, in high technology and high service industries, including telecoms, the basis of competition is rather different. We have already seen how the strategic emphasis in telecoms has been reversed: from connectivity to customer relationship management. Service providers are not competing to provide specific services within a fixed and well-understood business process, but competing to exert design control over the way the business process itself is configured.

Overall, the critical success factors for both providers and procurers in the emerging market for business services are the scoping and integration of these services. In this book we shall look at these factors from a number of different perspectives.

A new and thriving business can be completely constructed (plugged together) from off-the-shelf "components".

One demonstration of this principle is the speed with which aggressive companies are able to develop an entirely new business. Such companies can plug a new business together in a very short time, and enter industries where they have no previous track record.

In the UK, there are two strong role models for this kind of activity: Tesco and Virgin. Tesco, originally a grocery chain, currently the market leader among UK supermarkets, is now operating as an ISP and a bank, among other things. Virgin, once a record company, now includes an airline, a railway company, and an insurance company, as well as a radio station. Similar examples can be found in many other countries. Grocery chains such as Albert Heijn in the Netherlands, and Safeway in the USA are following Tesco's lead.

There's considerable ambiguity of identity here, as indicated in Figure 1.3. Can we really regard Tesco as all of these things – a grocer, an ISP, a bank, a travel agent? The company name "Tesco" is being attached, not to a traditional business organization, but to a network of alliances and supply chains, under a common brand name. The identity of a modern (or post-modern) company is increasingly complicated. Perhaps part of the dynamism of an entity like Tesco is that it is constantly redefining its identity.

The consequences of this ambiguous identity may not be lost on the customers. Like many organizations, especially airlines and retail chains, Tesco distributes so-called loyalty cards to its customers. I have accepted such a card myself, which gives Tesco the right to identify me as a "loyal" customer of theirs, whatever that means. But how do I identify Tesco? Who exactly is the Tesco that I am supposedly being loyal to?

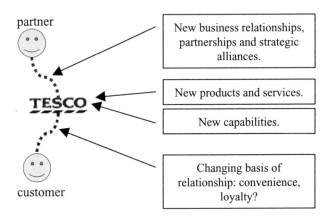

Figure 1.3: Changing identity – company or brand?

This apparently abstract question has direct practical consequences. For example, I may expect to receive loyalty reward points from every transaction that I perceive as belonging to Tesco. But some of these transactions may be operated by independent franchises, who are merely renting space and other services from Tesco, and don't participate in the loyalty reward scheme.

To what extent do you think it's a good idea for a complex grouping of companies to present itself to customers as a seamless whole? What are the consequences of not doing so? What is required – from a business point of view and from an IT point of view – to achieve this?

Diversification.

Strategic diversification has gone in and out of fashion among management gurus. In the old days, diversification was achieved by acquisition of diverse businesses, and it often took years before an acquired business was brought under the parent company's brand name, if at all. Tesco and Virgin appear to be achieving the strategic benefits of diversification without significant acquisition costs, and with much shorter lead times, through strategic partnerships and joint ventures. We can call this **virtual diversification**.

In this strategy, these businesses are not operated or controlled by Tesco and Virgin alone. They are usually managed jointly with other partners, operating under a Tesco or Virgin brand name. In most cases, these partners are reusing capabilities and systems already developed elsewhere.

 Can you name any other companies that are following a strategy of virtual diversification? Would your organization be capable of this strategy?

Under a strategy of virtual diversification, the building blocks for a new business start-up include:

➢ business relationships
➢ business processes
➢ packaged business expertise
➢ available software components.

Q If amazon.com or freeserve.co.uk wanted to start a banking service, what would they need?

Q If Microsoft or AOL or Tesco or Virgin wanted to enter (and dominate) your industry, what would they need? And what would your organization need in order to respond effectively to such a threat?

An existing business can be deconstructed into separately articulated "components".

A well-known example of process change is provided by the US retail chain Wal-Mart, which transformed its business relationships as follows. Goods were received from suppliers and displayed on the shelves in the retail store. But instead of the goods belonging to the retail organization, ownership remained with the suppliers. Wal-Mart did not pay the supplier until the goods had been purchased by a customer.

Before	After
° We pay for goods when we receive them from suppliers.	° We pay for goods when a customer buys them.
° If nobody buys them, it's our problem.	° If nobody buys them, it's the supplier's problem.

Table 1.1: Transformation in Wal-Mart's business.

> Q What are the benefits of this change to Wal-Mart?
>
> Q Are there any benefits to suppliers? Why would suppliers agree to bear the costs and risks of retail inventory?

Note that this transformed process involves the same process steps or components, but in a different sequence.

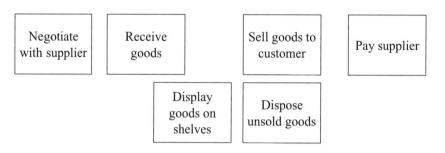

Figure 1.4: Wal-Mart process components.

> Q Draw two flow diagrams to show the difference between Before and After, showing different configurations of the same process components.

It is reported that the IT costs of this transformation were relatively small, as the applications were already well designed and well integrated, and could therefore be substantially reused to support the new business requirements.

Business extensions can often be achieved by plugging in extra capability.

E-commerce.

E-commerce is currently the most widespread and popular example of the extension of business into new markets or channels-to-market. Within the past year or so, nearly all the large traditional retailers, as well as many small ones, have established a website from which a selection of goods can be ordered. Most of these firms still regard these "virtual" services as supplementary to their main business, which depends on "real" people paying "real" visits to "real" stores. At the same time, many other service providers are adding on-line versions of their services to their existing provision.

Piggy-back tactics.

In many cases, new services are piggy-backed on existing processes and resources. One major retailer currently satisfies on-line orders by employing people to pick the requested goods from the nearest store.

From a business point of view, it seems wonderful to be able to add new services by reusing existing business processes and resources. This is a quick and apparently cheap way to deliver greater added-value to your existing customers, and perhaps also to gain new customers.

However, there are important limitations to the piggy-backing approach. Such solutions are inherently small-scale. If the demand takes off, before the capabilities can be scaled up, there is a strong risk that the service provision may collapse, leaving disappointed, frustrated or angry customers.

From an Information Technology perspective, these business extensions are often extremely challenging. Many IT departments are currently struggling to provide reliable and robust Internet access to legacy computer systems, and to provide properly integrated information and system services to the business. We shall return to the IT response to these challenges in Chapter 5.

But most e-commerce attempts are rubbish, aren't they?

At present, there are loads of new e-commerce sites, and many of them – perhaps most of them – are poorly thought through, and poorly executed.

What do you see as the main weaknesses of the e-commerce sites you have visited?   What is your experience of e-commerce generally?   Are you impressed? But are you sometimes impressed?

Perhaps only a handful of e-commerce companies are supremely successful. There is already a huge gap opened up, between the incompetent and frustrating attempts of the many, and the smooth service of the few.

If we take an ecological view of the e-commerce market, we can choose to see this, not as a sign that the technology is immature, but as a healthy sign of competition. It doesn't matter how many companies decide to enter the e-commerce game, it doesn't matter if most of them do it very badly, because the end result is already known: a small number of companies will dominate.

Best practices and business patterns can be regarded as components.

One of the characteristics of an excellent company is the ability to identify and share best practices across the organization.

It is said that when Xerox started to distribute colour photocopiers in Europe, it found that the French sales force was far more successful than the sales force in any other country. For a short period, the French sales accounted for about half the total European sales. This prompted a careful analysis of the components of the French sales success. Could any of these components be taken out of the French context and used in other countries for selling colour photocopiers? Could any of these components be used to improve operations in general? This analysis identified a number of factors, which were then regarded as candidates for dissemination across Europe as best practices. These included a particularly effective training programme for the sales force, and a particularly effective marketing information system.

Such best practices can then be packaged as components for dissemination. Sometimes a software component already forms an essential part of the best practice itself. In other cases, a best practice can be embedded into a software component, which then serves as a delivery mechanism for the practice to be disseminated. Even if software components are not involved, the work practices can still be regarded as clerical components.

 What are the potential advantages of using software components to deliver best practices across an organization?   What are the potential disadvantages?   Which of these advantages and disadvantages are applicable to your organization?

The cost equation for business demands the reuse of building blocks.

In business almost everywhere, the operating costs are going down, or being pushed and squeezed down. This is obviously true of information processing and communication costs, and this in turn brings down other intangible and administrative costs. It is often also true for the production costs of physical items, as productivity increases.

 How is the balance of costs shifting in your industry? How do you expect it to shift in future?

But if the operating costs are going down, the design costs are going up. A single transaction may cost practically nothing, but a company must first devote considerable energy to the design of this transaction. This usually requires intellectual input, as well as considerable negotiation with other parties. Design costs include costs of quality – making sure the transaction is right first time.

To put this another way, the first transaction may cost millions, while the second and subsequent transactions only cost fractions of a cent each. This cost structure is perhaps already familiar for word processing software or Hollywood films – the original is hugely expensive, but it costs practically nothing to make duplicate copies. This cost structure can now be found in many other industries, including financial services, retail, telecoms and other utilities.

As design becomes one of the predominant cost factors, and also the key strategic differentiator, we should also expect it to become a focus of management attention, although many industries haven't yet made this switch.

 How much management attention is devoted to the design phase in your industry? How do you imagine this will change in future?

This cost equation sets up a strong motivation for businessmen to design their businesses in the form of reusable building blocks. If you've spent millions designing a banking transaction, or a retail alliance, or a supply chain, you want to be able to exploit this design to the full.

What is the role for IT in facilitating the componentry of business?

We need a word for the trend described here: the greater articulation of a system into separately articulated components. In this book, I shall use the word **componentry**. This is a deliberate extension of the traditional use of the word to mean a simple collection of components, but I think it is justified by the extreme ugliness of the word "componentization".

Given that both business and IT are heading towards greater componentry, businessmen and engineers alike might expect to take advantage of this. IT practitioners reading this book may want to consider how componentry in IT can support componentry in business. This book suggests the principle that IT should focus on the provision of software components and interfaces to support business building blocks and relationships. This is a significant change in emphasis from previous approaches to business–IT requirements and business–IT alignment, and redirects attention away from the traditional IT focus on data structures and process flows.

Against componentry.

In this section, before we get carried away into thinking that everything can and should be decomposed into components, we need to review some past failures and ongoing misconceptions.

Can we decompose work into simple tasks?

The decomposition of work, leading to the specialization of tasks, has been preached by economists since Adam Smith, as a means to achieving economies of scale. This was an important feature of the traditional production line style of manufacturing, pioneered by Henry Ford, and parodied by Charlie Chaplin in the film Modern Times. This style, together with related attitudes towards employment and work, has now come to be known as Fordism. Fordism is closely related to Taylorism, named after Frederick Winslow Taylor, an early management consultant and guru.

The arguments against Fordism and Taylorism, both economic and ethical, have been widely rehearsed elsewhere, and I don't want to dwell on them here. In some ways, the arguments may appear to have been overtaken by technological progress. Machines have now largely replaced mankind on the production line itself, and perform nearly all the trivial, repetitive and mind-numbing tasks. People are employed mainly to look after the machines and keep the line running smoothly. This change has not occurred for humanitarian reasons, but because in most cases, machines can perform the production tasks more cheaply and reliably. Many boring factory jobs do remain, but these are usually fiddly or intricate, and either "not worth automating" or "too complex to automate".

Following Adam Smith, we might imagine a production line consisting of specialized machines or robots, each performing a small addition or transformation to the end-product. But most automated production is not configured in this way – it would be too expensive and too inflexible. Instead, flexible machine tools and computer-controlled machines are used to perform a range of production tasks. Thus in many industries, the Fordist style of manufacturing seems to be out of fashion, regardless of whether the actual production work is done by people or machines.

> Q What's wrong with task specialization? Why doesn't it always lead to economies of scale?

Can we decompose information or knowledge into simple facts?

Some readers may have been lucky enough to have had a physics teacher at school who appreciated the natural drama built into the science curriculum. That sense of surprise when you put two pinholes in a card and found out that this didn't always mean you got twice as much light through. The struggle to make sense of this phenomenon, not in terms of particles, but in terms of waves.

Today, most information scientists think of information as composed of particles. Information can be decomposed into elementary units of meaning, called facts. These units of meaning, these semantic atoms, may be expressed in a formal notation, stored in a normalized database, and processed using a formal calculus.

It's about time that information science woke up to the phenomenon of information interference. If I buy two newspapers, does that mean I get twice as much information? Of course not. And if an organization receives two different messages on the same subject from different sources, they may sometimes reinforce one another, sometimes cancel one another out, among other possibilities.

Now I'm not saying this means we need a wave theory of information, as well as or instead of our traditional particle theory. (It's perhaps worth noting here that modern physics is now moving away from the wave-particle dichotomy.) But information interference and other related phenomena call into question the idea that information can be decomposed into separate parcels.

When we look at knowledge management, the situation is more complex still. Since mediaeval times, administrators have tried to classify knowledge into different fields and disciplines, and introduce and enforce specialist disciplines. And we can see the progress of knowledge as a succession of established facts – what the French sociologist Bruno Latour calls "black boxes". Once established, these black boxes can be used elsewhere, as building blocks for later work, without needing to be re-examined or re-tested. Latour's work concentrates on science and technology, and provides an elegant and well-documented commentary on research and development in these fields; similar principles could be applied in other fields of knowledge, including organizational knowledge and business intelligence.

I'm hoping to write a separate book on the difficulties of the artificial decomposition of knowledge. This has implications for knowledge-based enterprises and knowledge management as well as for management information and decision-support systems.

Components are not a choice. They represent a new game.

Some people are trying to evaluate the benefits of components, as if they could decide whether to embrace components or not, as if there was a real choice. (Componentry itself serving as a component of your business or technological strategy.)

Maybe components are going to benefit you, maybe they're not. Maybe business components are going to benefit you, maybe they're not. This book doesn't aim to sell the benefits of components, or anything else. The argument of this book is that business and IT are jointly starting to play a new game, with different rules. Whether you like it or not.

It was at Rugby School that football (soccer) developed a variant now known as Rugby Football. But imagine a Rugby schoolboy saying: "I'm not going to pick up the ball. I'm just going to kick it, like my father and grandfather before me. I'm sure this handling is just a fad, and then we'll settle back down to good old kicking." Software professionals are currently saying similar things about CBSE and other software industry trends. Meanwhile, many businessmen are saying similar things about such business trends as e-commerce and e-business.

If you want to stay in the game, you have to understand that the rules have changed, are changing, and will continue to change. The purpose of this book is to help you understand the new game, and play your own corner with a little more knowledge and skill.

Of course, if you have enough power, proximity and interest, you may try to change the rules of the game, or at least influence them. Changing the rules of the game is itself another game. There are some powerful players in the software industry, in the telecommunications industry and elsewhere. But in that game, most of us are only interested spectators.

Recap.

In this chapter, we've reviewed some of the ways that people use building blocks to make sense of their world and the things in it, to construct and reconstruct artefacts, and to construct and reconstruct their world. Sometimes these building blocks are in the model used to understand the world; sometimes they appear to be in the world; and sometimes the line between model and world gets blurred.

In order to understand complex systems, we typically try to analyse them, to decompose them into subsystems, which we can then try to understand semi-independently of one another. For centuries, scientists have used this approach on such complex systems as the human brain, and human society, and have used prevailing technologies to provide metaphors for these systems. Over the past fifty years, computer technology has provided a rich source of metaphor, from simple calculating machines to global distributed communications systems. The attempt by successive generations of researchers in various disciplines to explore these analogies, and to discover the building blocks of the brain and of society, has led to an enhanced appreciation of the complexity of these entities. Despite centuries of meditation, analysis and positive thinking, we are still surrounded by fractured personalities and fractured societies. And despite impressive breakthroughs in computing and artificial intelligence, we seem as far away as ever from the vision of replicating human intelligence into a man-made device, or using machines to solve any social problem. Thank God for that, some will say.

From the manufacturing examples, including the bicycle and the gun, we saw the economic force behind the use of components, and how the use of components may enable economies of scale, not only in mass production, but also in tailoring and repair. The example of the gun also reminded us of the importance of standard connections between interchangeable parts, and how this entailed a notion of tolerance, or good-enough fit.

The examples of the car lights and the computer power switch showed us how production from components doesn't always lead to ease of repair. Ease of repair depends on a number of other factors, including the way that a product is configured into components in the first place, and the way the manufacturing process keeps track of these components. These factors may often be based on convenience or profit for the producer, rather than convenience or cost saving for the consumer or repair shop. They may also be a consequence of sheer thoughtlessness or incompetence on the part of the producer or repair shop.

The use of building blocks in manufacturing changes the product in some important ways, but perhaps more importantly, it changes the production process. Key processes, including design, assembly, testing and repair, are focused on the building blocks. This component focus has a number of side effects, some of them perhaps unwelcome to some people. Furthermore, the production process itself can now be configured in new ways, as we saw from the bicycle industry. This in turn leads naturally to the idea that whole businesses can be configured and reconfigured in new ways, as well as the software systems to support these businesses and business processes.

This trend may be regarded as liberating or not, depending on your point of view. Today's companies have more ways than ever of making money, but only if they plug themselves into the global economy, where they become components of something much larger, and out of the control of their own managers.

This chapter has tried to demonstrate that the game has a new set of rules. In the remainder of the book, we shall look at ways to play this game, and to adapt yourself and your company to the game.

2. Systems Constructed from Building Blocks

In the previous chapter, we explored the growing importance of building blocks in understanding, constructing and reconstructing various types of system, including business organizations and software architectures.

But we don't actually want building blocks – we want whole systems: business organizations, supply chains, software architectures, market configurations. And we want these systems to have certain properties. Above all, we usually want these systems to have some ongoing viability – in other words, to survive. Above a certain level of complexity, systems typically have some self-management ability, which includes some degree of self-preservation.

For the purposes of this book, we have chosen to explore two contrasting system properties: **intelligence** and **character**. Under a fairly wide range of conditions, systems possessing these properties in appropriate degrees are likely to be better able to deliver value to their stakeholders and also maintain their own integrity and survival. These properties are therefore commonly thought to be worth something; considerable energies are expended to enhance aspects of systems that are related to either intelligence or character

Like many other interesting and desirable system properties, the intelligence or character of a system is not a simple function of the intelligence and character of its component parts. Intelligence in a component connects to intelligence in the larger system in subtle and sometimes counter-intuitive ways – and the same is true of character. These are emergent properties of the whole system, depending substantially on the way the whole system is articulated, and on the wiring between the components. Thus when systems are constructed from building blocks, or deconstructed into building blocks, this has a substantial impact on both the intelligence and the character of the whole system.

A neat (but misleading) equation: tightly coupled systems tend to be better adapted, loosely coupled systems tend to be more adaptable. (As we shall see in Chapter 5, there are serious difficulties with the management of change in loosely coupled systems which undermine this equation.) Intelligence and character are related to adaptability – but in different ways. Both characteristics are impaired by excessively tight ("uptight") or excessively loose coupling.

System thinking also needs to be applied to individual components. Properties that are commonly attributed to individual components – including flexibility and trust – can be *seen to be dependent on the broader system. An artefact can be flexible and trustworthy in one operating context, and not in another.*

There are some common patterns of system success.

System success is subjective.

People talk endlessly about systems, in a wide variety of situations, but we are not always clear what we are talking about. Perhaps we are never entirely clear. But we still manage to understand one another, good enough for most purposes, albeit often only after a bit of a struggle.

Formal languages, models and notations have frequently been proposed to enable complete and consistent descriptions of systems. These formal languages always omit something important. (Sometimes it's precisely what they omit that is most important.)

We select systems to talk about that are meaningful and important to people. All such systems have both social and technological aspects, although these aspects are sometimes obscured by the way we talk about them.

All description of these systems (including identity and scope) is dependent on the **observer** and the **observation process**. The observer is always an active participant, at one level, and the participants are all observers – although they may not always perceive the same system. Perceptions and descriptions may differ widely.

People attach **intentions** to systems, and make **demands** from systems. People attach value to certain perceived properties of systems, and they are often eager to take action to change certain systems properties, or to create systems that possess desirable properties. Any intervention in a system relies on a **stakeholder**, or community of stakeholders, with a particular attitude and purpose. In many cases – perhaps most – there are perceived conflicts between stakeholders.

For a system to fulfil some intentions, it needs to **survive** for some definite or indefinite duration. Survival means maintaining the identity and integrity of the system, in some sense, from some point of view. Complex systems often devote considerable energies to survival – apparently for its own sake. However, there is often a tension between identity and survival.

Thus whenever we talk about systems, and the success of systems, there are some essential elements that are implicit, including values, observer, stakeholder, perspective, purpose and scope. We do not always make these elements explicit, but they're always there.

But system success still means something.

Despite the evident fact that people have conflicting intentions and values, and widely diverse perceptions and beliefs, it still seems to makes sense to talk about the success of systems, as long as we remember that this means success from some perspective, against some set of values and intentions, as perceived by an interested party.

People are interested in the power, flexibility, effectiveness and survival of systems of all kinds. A successful system delivers ongoing value to its owners and other stakeholders.

There is a cluster of interrelated properties, which can be used for describing and characterizing complex systems. Systems may be said to have power, flexibility and effectiveness, relative to some set of intentions, in some context. Some complex systems may be said to be self-conscious or rational, in some sense. Systems may survive, or have a certain prognosis of survival under certain circumstances. These characteristics are almost certainly connected. Investigate one, and you are implicitly investigating the rest. Alter one, and you will inevitably alter the others.

Most or all of these characteristics are relevant to system owners and stakeholders, as well as to independent observers. System owners usually want their systems to survive, at least until some set of intentions is fulfilled. Many systems are intended to survive indefinitely – this certainly applies to most organizations. And system owners and stakeholders want their own intentions to be furthered by the system, as long as the system survives.

Q Under what circumstances should an organization or institution have a limited life? Under what circumstances should a business process or service have a limited life?

Q Under what circumstances does a system have a limited life? Under what circumstances is a software artefact intended to have a limited life?

We can identify four factors that appear to have an influence on success. These are shown in Table 2.1.

Intelligence	Mental ability. Behaviour in relation to knowledge, complexity and change.
Character	Moral and social qualities. Behaviour in relation to oneself and others.
Beauty	Physical appearance and style. How one is favoured by other people.
Luck	How one is favoured by Chance or Providence.

Table 2.1: Generic Success Factors.

Q Do you think that there is any correlation or causal relationship between these factors? Do intelligent people tend to be more beautiful or lucky than unintelligent people – or the converse? Do intelligent people make better use of their assets – including beauty or luck? If not, why not?

Q Do you think that organizations or other social systems can be beautiful or lucky? Do you think that software components or other artefacts can be beautiful or lucky? Do you think this helps?

In this book, I am going to focus on intelligence and character. This choice is based on my belief that these properties are interesting in their own right, as well as connected in interesting ways to a cluster of other important system properties.

However, I don't propose to laboriously demonstrate these connections at every turn. Much of what I have to say about intelligence, and ways of enhancing system intelligence, will apply equally to other valued system properties, including effectiveness and survival.

Intelligence and character are desirable properties of systems.

Intelligence is a recognizable property of systems.

Just like people, an organization may behave in intelligent or unintelligent ways. And, as we shall see later on, the collective intelligence of the organization often bears little relationship to the individual intelligence of the people in the organization.

Most observers can probably think of organizations that have appeared oblivious to its environment, made the same errors over and over again, and displayed no ability to remember or learn. Many of these organizations have already collapsed; many yet survive through political intervention or clinging to some fortuitous monopoly.

When we find this kind of behaviour in people, we may take it as evidence of crass stupidity, and so it seems reasonable to describe organizations the same way. Unintelligent organizations fail to detect even the most obvious signals of change in their environment, and they fail to respond appropriately – if at all – to the most insistent demands from their stakeholders. They learn slowly, making the same mistakes repeatedly without any insight or understanding.

> Q Think of some organizations that have collapsed. Could the symptoms of unintelligence have been detected in advance? Could a greater degree of organizational intelligence have saved them? If so, how?
>
> Q Think of some organizations that currently survive, despite symptoms of extreme unintelligence. On what does their survival depend? How long do you imagine they might survive?
>
> Q Do you think that the lack of intelligence may be somehow caused by the same factors that allow the organization to survive?

Other organizations are alert to changing circumstances, react creatively to new threats and opportunities, are constantly learning from their own experiences and from the mistakes of their competitors. These organizations display the same qualities that we can recognize in intelligent people: an eager and receptive curiosity, a consistent but flexible set of responses, and an ability to learn quickly.

It seems appropriate to refer to this difference as a difference in organizational intelligence.

> Q Think of some organizations that have survived adversity, against the odds. Do you think this was sheer luck, or were there some elements of organizational intelligence that helped?

Intelligence is worth something.

Intelligence is assigned a positive value, according to many popular value systems.

It seems reasonable to work on the basis that organizational intelligence has a positive value. An intelligent organization is likely to be more successful in the short term, and have greater prospects for survival and growth in the longer term. Staff morale is likely to be better, and the individual employees will themselves have greater opportunities for personal growth and fulfilment. In the broader socio-economic system, intelligent organizations will create more wealth – not merely economic wealth but in human potential.

Do organizations pay for maintaining intelligence or is it free?

Intelligence has a cost – it uses energy and resources that might be devoted to something else. There may be situations where the cost of intelligence is greater than the benefits.

Organizations facing a flat and unchanging environment may not need much intelligence, but organizations facing diverse and turbulent environments may need much higher degrees of intelligence. To the extent that organizational intelligence costs something to develop and maintain, this investment may be justified in the latter case, but not in the former case.

But there is a widespread belief that there is a universal trend away from flat and unchanging environments towards diverse and turbulent ones, and this seems to entail a greater overall need for organizational intelligence.

 Do you think that there will always be some situations where organizational intelligence is not required? Do you think that there are some situations where organizational intelligence may be a disadvantage?

Is there really a universal trend away from flat and unchanging environments towards diverse and turbulent ones? The belief in accelerating technological and social change is taken as an unquestioned assumption for many writings on business and technology. Where evidence for this trend is offered, it is usually based on fairly superficial or narrow metrics, such as the growing number of patents, or on selected anecdotes; and the argument has little or no historical perspective. After all, there have been many other epochs in history when people thought the established order was breaking down, and exaggerated the turbulence to come. And modern life is in many ways safer and more predictable than in the past.

Q Do you think that there are some aspects of modern business life that are becoming more predictable and controlled?

Intelligence is an emergent property of a system.

Intelligence must be taken in the context of a system.

An organization is a sociotechnical system, and may be composed of many interoperating systems, each containing some intelligence. Thus the human intelligence of many employees is combined with the artificial intelligence of machines, contained in intelligent buildings, and distributed through intelligent cyberspace.

People and computers alike display intelligent behaviour in some contexts, and not in others. People and computers alike depend on a complex support network. A person's ability to solve certain puzzles depends on various cultural factors. A computer's ability to beat a grandmaster at chess depends on a team of chess experts and skilled programmers.

In a recent article in the New York Review, John Searle makes the point that when computers can beat grandmasters at chess, this does not prove that computers are now more intelligent than humans. "The real competition was not between Kasparov and the machine, but between Kasparov and a team of engineers and programmers." [New York Review of Books, Vol xlvi number 6, April 8th 1999]

As in Formula One racing, where the driver takes the credit for the work of a team, so the chess computer Deep Blue took the credit for the work of a well-coordinated team of people and other machines. A Formula One driver does not need to be a creative thinker – that falls to other members of the team – but must have incredibly fast reactions. The same is true of a computer.

This discussion leads us to view intelligence as a property of a larger system – the whole team. It is a property that is only manifest when the team is working as a team – in other words it is an emergent property.

The intelligence of a system is not a simple arithmetic function of the intelligence of the subsystems. A lot of intelligent pieces doesn't add up to an intelligent organization.

To make an intelligent organization, it isn't enough to recruit the brightest people, locate them in state-of-the-art office buildings, and provide them with the smartest computer tools and networks. Super-intelligent individuals are often poor at talking to one another and sharing knowledge, let alone coordinating their work effectively. Each individual may only make a given mistake once, but if the people don't talk to each other, the same mistake can be repeated hundreds of times without any organizational learning.

And even if an organization is collectively oblivious to major threats and opportunities in its environment, that doesn't mean that the individual employees are unaware of these threats and opportunities. Intelligent people get very frustrated and demotivated in stupid organizations; they can see what is happening, and they can often see what needs to be done, but they don't have adequate channels of communication or action.

Organizational intelligence is what systems thinkers call an emergent property – it is an attribute of the whole system, not of the individual parts. What matters most is how the parts of the organization are put together.

A stupid organization can be composed of apparently intelligent people.

Most universities conform to this pattern. The cleverer the professors, the worse it gets.

> Q If you have any recent experience of university organizations, does your experience confirm this hypothesis? What do you think happens?

An intelligent system can be composed of unintelligent components.

Colonies of insects (ants or bees) display intelligence at the level of the colony. An individual insect has a tiny brain, but the collective behaviour of the whole colony is something else.

There are many delightful tales of insect colonies outwitting human beings. My favourite one concerns some researchers who wanted to find out the distance that bees could travel, so they experimented with placing artificial sources of sugar further and further from the hive. Each time they moved the sugar, a few bees watched and then flew back to the hive to report the new location. But one day, they arrived at the site to move the sugar, and there were no bees around at all. Well, they decided to move the sugar anyway, according to their predetermined research plan – and there were the bees at the new location, waiting for them!

There's another version of this story, where some picnickers disturb some ants or wasps or something, trek across country to escape them, take a long route back to the car, and find the insects waiting for them there. Many of these stories may be apocryphal, but the fact is that we do find them plausible.

Out of control – embrace the swarm.

The emergence of intelligence from large numbers of unintelligent or uncontrolled interactions can be found in a wide variety of domains.

Some writers are now proposing this as a management principle or heuristic. Tom Peters is well known for making provocative and paradoxical statements about control; and Kevin Kelly, who has previously documented "Out of Control" complex systems including biological, social and technological ones, has more recently applied similar thinking to the business domain.

Kelly makes the biological analogy explicit when he names one of his proposed strategies "Embrace the Swarm". He illustrates this with an example of a cement delivery company, summarized in Table 2.2, which shows how the uncontrolled interactions of a fleet of intelligent and autonomous drivers produced a much better outcome than had previously been achieved by central control.

Before	After
Cement delivery controlled centrally	Cement delivery left to drivers
Rigid delivery schedules fixed in advance	Drivers given full information and authority
Traffic delays, poor roads, unreliable third parties	On-time delivery rate = 98%
On-time delivery rate <35%	

Table 2.2: "Embrace the Swarm".

> Q Do you have any experience of distribution and decentralization resulting in such dramatic improvements? Do you have any experience of distribution and decentralization making things worse?

When intelligent components are successfully combined, they can achieve wonders.

Earlier in this chapter, we looked at Deep Blue, the IBM supercomputer that beat Gary Kasparov at chess. As I'm writing this (December 1999), IBM has started work on a sequel to Deep Blue, called Blue Gene. The plan is for a computer system composed of around a thousand circuit boards, each containing 64 of the most powerful chips available, all working in parallel. The system as a whole will be around a million times as fast as a normal desktop computer, vintage 1999. The project is estimated to take 4-5 years, and to cost $100 million.

Blue Gene's task is to simulate the building of proteins in the body, and to calculate how proteins fold themselves. They reckon the calculations will take this computer a year for a typical protein. (The body itself does the calculations in a fraction of a second, but that's another story.)

> Q In what sense can Blue Gene be regarded as intelligent? What do you think this example shows?

Identity may be distributed over many components.

In any case, there are some problems with identity, both of people and of computers. Common sense notions of consciousness and free will are undermined by both psychoanalysis and hypnotism. As we saw in Chapter 1, things seem increasingly disembodied and fragmented – we are increasingly led to see our artefacts and ourselves as loosely coupled components. And it's often easier to see the parts (or part-objects) than to see the wholes.

A person is not just a mass of organic material, but also a mass of characteristic ideas, thoughts and feelings, expressed in words or acted out, distributed across diaries and letters, or captured in the memories and interpretations of other people. My name is held on countless databases, with various fragments of information about me, and embossed on several pieces of plastic card. No doubt much of this information is incorrect, incomplete or out of date.

What appears to be a self-contained computer may be merely a facade, providing access to a distributed network of other machines and systems.

Intelligence needs to be off-set by character.

Character refers to the ability of an entity to relate productively and authentically to other entities.

If we're interested in what a person can achieve in isolation, then intelligence may be an important factor. But if we're interested in what a person can achieve in collaboration with others, then character may be just as important.

In particular, leadership is usually regarded as a question of character rather than intelligence. The leader doesn't have to be the most visibly intelligent person on the team.

When we look at the outstanding leaders in history – people like George Washington and Nelson Mandela – what we see first and foremost is a strong and attractive character. Even when surrounded by such intelligent and forceful men as Franklin and Jefferson, Madison and Hamilton, Washington was regarded by his peers as the natural leader.

Character relates to desire.

J.S. Mill defined character as follows: "A person whose desires and impulses are his own–are the expression of his own nature, as it has been developed and modified by his own culture–is said to have a character. One whose desires and impulses are not his own, has no character, no more than a steam-engine has a character." [On Liberty, 1859]

A number of thinkers, from Spinoza to Lacan, have seen desire as the essence of man. According to Lacan, a leading French psychoanalyst, the aim of psychoanalysis is to lead the analysand to recognize the truth about his desire. Psychoanalysis can therefore be seen as helping people to develop character in Mill's sense.

A traditional education (as in English public schools) always valued character higher than intelligence. (And perhaps they had a point.)

At least as taught in schools, intelligence is largely to do with what a child can achieve on its own, and is tested for each child in isolation. Collaboration between children during tests and exams is regarded as cheating.

In contrast, character has to do with the behaviour of the child in social situations – in the playground or the sports field. Healthy collaboration, direct competition, responsible behaviour, standing firm against bullying. Even such apparently private matters as concentration or self-esteem have strong links with social behaviour.

To some readers, this discussion might sound as if it only applies to boys' schools. But traditional girls' schools also valued character above intelligence, although perhaps for different reasons.

 Do you think Good Character still means something different for girls and boys?

Do we have to make the choice between character and intelligence? Can't we have both?

Intelligence without character tends to disrupt the larger system. Intelligence with character tends to enhance the larger system.

There are certainly people who have both character and intelligence. But it's often difficult to spot them. Because it is usually the people without character that want to draw attention to their intelligence, and the people without intelligence that want to draw attention to their character.

Character is a recognizable property of various entities.

Sometimes a highly intelligent person can fail to make much of an impression on a situation. The quality of making-an-impression is one aspect of something that is usually called personality or character. In Chapter 3, we'll see how this property might apply to business components.

Kevin Kelly argues that the only factor becoming scarce in a world of abundance is human attention. Character is, among other things, the ability to command and retain attention. This is something that business organizations need. It is also something that software artefacts – or indeed any technological artefacts – need. If your customers and users can't find you, or if something else attracts their attention first, they won't use you.

Earlier in the chapter, we extended the notion of intelligence from humans and animals to a range of other entities, including technological artefacts and business organizations. Now we're going to attempt the same thing with the notion of character. Does it make sense to discuss the character of business organizations or software architectures?

There is a precedent for this discussion. Some management consultants with a psychoanalytic bent have tried to show that organizations as well as people can manifest such pathological conditions as Narcissism and Paranoia.

Often one of the most important assets of a modern business is its brand. The character of the brand is crucial, as it affects the trust placed in the brand by customers. We can regard trust, like attention, as a scarce resource.

As we saw in Chapter 1, there are some large companies that are using partnerships and alliances to take on an increasingly broad range of products and services under an existing brand name – in the UK, Tesco and Virgin are two major examples of this. This is a bold strategy, and a risky one, as it binds together the fate of otherwise independent products and services. If a brand name suffers a public relations setback in relation to one product or service, this may affect other products and services using the same brand.

> Q How significant do you think this is in practice? Imagine a fictional company called Taurus, which owns a railway company and an insurance company, among other things. Do the perceived problems of Taurus Railways affect the commercial prospects for Taurus Insurance?

For a brand to have character, it needs to have positive public awareness. It also needs to have clarity, and a consistent set of brand values. This means that customers know what to expect from the brand, in terms of product quality, customer service and so on. It also means that people supporting the brand (whether your own staff or third parties) know how to deliver these values consistently.

In a large insurance company I recently worked with, the corporate brand was explicitly equated with the attitudes of customer-facing staff. Posters on the office walls, and in the staff canteen, declared: "You are the Brand". (Such a poster campaign is an interesting communication exercise in its own right – if it is interpreted as exhortation or wishful thinking, rather than as reinforcement and reminder of an existing fact, then the brand may be nothing more than a series of attempts to communicate it.)

Some of the best-known global brand names – soft drinks and cigarettes, fast food, credit cards – are delivered by complex global networks of partners and franchisees. Let's use Coca-Cola as an example, although the same is true of many other global brands. What matters for the overall management of the Coca-Cola brand is not the Coca-Cola company itself, but the larger Coke organization – you might call it a virtual organization – including independent bottling plants in nearly every "civilized" country.

It is the character of the larger, virtual organization that needs to be considered. (We'll come back to this later in the chapter, when we look at the ability of these virtual organizations to handle product recalls.)

> Q Is it possible for a brand to have character, if the organization owning the brand lacks character?
>
> Q If the brand is supported by a complex global network of partners and franchisees, does this represent a risk to the character of the brand?

The brand defines the level of granularity at which the consumer makes a character judgement. The consumer is only capable of making a finite number of judgements, and needs some mechanism to lump these judgements together. The brand provides a way of doing this.

Intelligence in the purchasing system may increase the maximum number of judgements of which the system is capable, or enable judgements at a finer level of granularity. Of course, we may be interested both in the intelligence of individual customers, and in the (emergent) intelligence of the market as a whole.

Character has five key elements.

Character can be conceptually divided into five elements as shown in Table 2.3, although these elements are tightly knit together in practice.

Standing out	Making an impression. Having a strong image.
Clarity	Decisiveness. Making up one's mind – and sticking to it.
Engagement	Committed engagement with situations. Authenticity. Being there.
Correctness	Sincerity. Legal, decent, honest and truthful.
Integrity	Wholeness. Steadfastness.

Table 2.3: Elements of character.

When we talk about people and other entities possessing character, we're interested in a balanced set of all the elements of character. Sometimes, people can have one or two elements of character, and lack others. A person can be eccentric, determined or stoical, but these qualities are not enough for a well-balanced character.

> Q Which men and women are regarded as character role models? In your opinion, how well-balanced are their characters?

Character can develop.

As we saw earlier, schools traditionally valued character more than intelligence.

However, to the extent that character means standing out, many schools are highly ambivalent about this. Teachers want children to stand out only when this is convenient in the school situation. In many contexts, standing out is not regarded as an admirable quality but as a Problem.

Many highly intelligent people only start to develop character later in life, after a series of failed relationships and engagements with other people. Perhaps the more intelligent you are, the longer it takes to develop a decent character.

Many of Shakespeare's plays involve the slow development of the protagonist's character. For example, the two parts of Henry IV show the development of Prince Hal from an irresponsible youth to a perfect King; and most of the tragedies explore the gradual unfolding of a fatal flaw in the protagonist's character. Some critics see Shakespeare as the foremost analyst of character, largely based on the deep psychological insights contained in these tragedies.

Q Do you think the character of Microsoft or IBM has changed over time?

Q Can you think of any business organizations whose character has improved over time? What about organizations whose character has worsened over time? Which phenomenon do you think is more common?

Q In what ways can the character of a product, service or brand develop over time (for better or worse)?

Character depends on context.

We saw earlier that intelligence is an emergent property of a system. A complex system may possess intelligence, even though none of the components possess intelligence.

With character, the situation is a little different. Let's think about the composition of teams of people. A team composed entirely of weak people is likely to be a weak team. It seems reasonable to suppose that character cannot be present in the whole system, unless there is character in the components. This is an important hypothesis, and we shall need to return to it in Chapter 3.

> Q Does your experience of people and teams confirm this hypothesis? How do
> you think it applies to other kinds of system, such as technical systems?

On the other hand, a team composed entirely of strong characters isn't always a strong team. Character in the components may be a necessary condition for character in the whole system, but it's certainly not sufficient.

> Q Does your experience of people and teams confirm this hypothesis? How do
> you think it applies to other kinds of system, such as technical systems?

So if we're interested in the character of the whole system, we need to look both at the character of the components, and at the way these components are joined together.

One thing character can do is to use character in others to open up a broader perspective than was ever available to the individual. Character works in and through relationships.

There is a substantial literature on the effectiveness of groups and teams. There is also a substantial literature on technical architectures, especially in computer hardware and software. However, these literatures inhabit different worlds, and some readers may find the attempt to bridge these worlds to be controversial.

Character should not depend overly on context.

We have seen that intelligence is dependent upon context, to a much greater degree than we usually acknowledge. However, an important point about character is that it should not be so dependent on context. Indeed, character-building exercises often involve taking people out of their normal context. And whereas intelligent people are sometimes only able to interact seriously with other people whom they regard as equally intelligent, character typically involves the ability to interact with a wide range of different people, of different intelligences, characters and backgrounds.

Some systems lack intelligence, character or both.

In some cases, it's easier to see something when it's not there.

Like many things, intelligence and character can often be recognized by their lack. There are common symptoms and patterns, which have been explored by novelists and playwrights for centuries.

As we said earlier, psychoanalysts and other therapists pay attention to the barriers to intelligence and creativity, and to the defects in a client's character. They often want to find out how these barriers and defects originated, and what function they now serve for the client, in the hope that this knowledge will help alleviate or eliminate the symptoms by attacking the root causes.

One technique is to look at the hidden repetitions in a person's behaviour and relationships. This follows the principle that stupidity is not making errors, stupidity is repeating them. Similarly, managers and consultants can look at the barriers to intelligence and creativity in organizations. Here too, stupidity manifests itself in a repetition of some kind. Each organization has its own particular form of stupidity – it is up to the consultant (or the above-average manager) to recognize the ways that stupidity manifests itself and to find a way of doing something about it.

> Q Which forms of stupidity are apparent in your organization, or in organizations you are familiar with? Can you identify underlying causes? How has the organization managed to preserve its way of being stupid, despite repeated attempts to teach it new tricks?

Repetition and flatness.

As just mentioned, a common symptom of lack of intelligence is **repetition**, in one form or another. Repetition involves a standard or habitual pattern of response to an event, instead of a reflective (perhaps more intelligent, perhaps more appropriate) response. In some cases, the person or organization may be unable to recognize the pattern without external help.

Repetition can often be explained by postulating a component that survives regardless of the fact that it may be damaging to the larger system. Repetition often aims at the preservation of some local success, which can only be perceived as problematic when taking a larger or longer-term or other context.

Lack of character can result in a kind of flatness, which can sometimes be regarded as a form of repetition. But flatness can also indicate a lack of intelligence.

Here's an example, from a small consultancy I once worked for – let's call it James Martin Associates. At the back of the office was a small library, containing a few books as well as copies of reports written for clients. These reports were loosely bound in ring binders, in a variety of styles, sizes and colours. Some people thought this looked untidy, but nobody did anything about it. The number of reports grew, and the library got more and more untidy.

One day, a secretary decided to take the initiative. She procured a large box of identical ring binders, and transferred all the reports into these binders. Each binder had a small sticky label, with the name of the report and a catalogue number. The library now looked extremely tidy.

The trouble was, people stopped using the library. Whereas before, they could find the report they wanted because each report had a distinctive appearance, now they needed to search through a catalogue and several identical-looking shelves to find what they wanted. The library had become flat and homogeneous, and lost its character; and the individual reports had lost their character and become clones.

This impaired the intelligence of the whole system. Given that the library represented an important component of the memory of the organization, the flatness of the library reduced the effectiveness of the organization's memory.

This is a common difficulty with corporate libraries, whether physical or on-line. Lots of companies have put large amounts of investment into electronic knowledge-bases or so-called Intranets, but these typically lack character, and fail to contribute usefully to the intelligence of the whole system.

 What experience do you have of corporate libraries, knowledge-bases or Intranets? Did they have much character? Did they contribute usefully to the whole?

Legacy computer systems lack intelligence.

Another way that a system may manifest a lack of intelligence is by resisting necessary change. (Obviously there may be different opinions about the necessity of a given set of changes, leading to different assessments of the system's intelligence or resistance.) A system (or other sociotechnical artefact) that is perceived as resistant is often branded as **legacy**.

To assess whether any artefact deserves this label, we need to look at the alignment between the artefact on the one hand, and a set of intentions (or requirements) on the other hand. The intentions for this artefact have shifted, and the artefact is now perceived as out of alignment with these intentions. Obviously alignment is not a simple Yes/No. Few if any artefacts are perfectly matched to the users' intentions, even when first developed. And all legacy systems, if they are still in use at all, can be presumed to satisfy some requirements. A system is more or less aligned, adequately or inadequately, relative to a specific set of intentions. But which intentions, and whose?

Before we can criticize an artefact for failing to meet its needs, we must make a judgement about what its needs are – in other words, of all the requirements and desires of all the users, which ones naturally belong to this specific artefact?

Here's an example. In the finance sector, the launch of a new financial product usually generates some new requirements on IT systems. These could either be regarded as additional requirements for existing (legacy) systems, or as requirements for new systems that would operate in parallel with the existing systems.

Another example: Many billing systems still in operation were designed and built before the advent of direct debit. Instead of modifying the billing system itself to support direct debits, a separate direct debit system was built.

In practice, the judgement as to whether to extend/modify an existing system, or to build a new system, depends largely on a perception of the ability of the existing legacy system to accommodate some or all of the new requirements. Or perhaps the ability of a given team of software engineers to make this accommodation.

This judgement also depends on how the legacy system is perceived – its identity. When an organization tries to accommodate something new, there is a question where it is going to belong within the organization. Which manager, or which department, is going to take responsibility for it? Whose budget is going to pay for it? Sometimes these questions are easy, or even trivial to answer, but sometimes there is a difference of opinion, resolved by debate between peers, or escalation to a higher level of management.

The evolution debate needs to include a discussion of the evolution of intentions, as well as the evolution of artefacts so that they better satisfy these intentions. Intelligence implies that a sociotechnical system should have the capability to track the environment, to keep in alignment. We'll discuss the management issues of legacy systems in Chapter 5.

Q What does it take for a system to track its environment? Are the situations where this is impossible?

Existing business organizations also lack intelligence.

Theodore Zeldin has recently studied the hotel industry, and is amazed at the amount of unused potential.

"A hotel is not just a place where travellers sleep, but a United Nations in miniature. People from all over the world meet at hotels, though they usually pass each other in silence. A large proportion of hotel staff are foreigners too, keen to learn a new language and discover a new civilization, but they have the most superficial relations with the guests. Hotels could be cultural centres, active intermediaries between the guest and the city, genuine hosts bringing together people who have not met. Hoteliers could use the knowledge of the many students they employ, instead of giving them only menial tasks. If they paid closer attention to their staff's deepest ambitions, they would realize that there were many other services that hotels could provide. But they are restrained by the accountants, who say that firms should concentrate on one core activity to make the best profit." [Theodore Zeldin, "Rethinking Work". *Oxford Today*, Vol 12 No 1, Michaelmas 1999]

Q Think of some ways of harvesting the latent intelligence in such a hotel. (Try to think of both technical mechanisms and social mechanisms.) Do your ideas focus on the people, or on the interactions between people?

Increasing the componentry of a system increases a property called articulation.

We are now going to explore a system property called **articulation**. In this section, I shall define and illustrate this property. In the following section, I shall argue that this property is closed linked to both character and intelligence.

For a simple image of articulation, think of an articulated truck. The cab is separated from the rest of the truck, yet connected to it. This articulation is what enables the driver to manoeuvre the truck around tight corners or delivery bays.

We can define articulation as a system property.

Articulation means both separation of parts and connection of parts – decoupling and recoupling. This is sometimes referred to as loose coupling.

In other contexts, articulation also means clear expression. This gives us a third principle of articulation. Clarity of structure is one of the reasons for producing structural models during the requirements analysis.

In this section, I'm going to illustrate the principles of articulation with a series of examples:

➤ data structure example (credit card)
➤ business objects
➤ workflow example (designer proxy)
➤ business structure and strategy.

The first example is based on something that happened to me a few years ago, when I moved back to the UK after working in the USA. It illustrates a class of problems that I have encountered in just about every financial sector organization I have ever worked with, as well as in other industries.

Let's start by describing the actual situation, which lacked the property that we're calling articulation.

When I moved back to the UK, I wanted to keep my US credit card, but I wanted to pay the bills in sterling rather than US dollars. The credit card company might reasonably regard my change of address as an **event**, and my desire to pay in sterling as a **demand**.

Q Under what circumstances might you expect a company to respond intelligently to such an event, and anticipate such a demand? For example, they might offer to change my billing currency before I've asked for it, or even change it automatically without giving me the option. How often have you experienced such intelligent responses from large companies? How valuable do you think this degree of responsiveness might be to the companies concerned?

It turned out that they couldn't change the billing currency without issuing a new card, with a new number. They had to cancel the old card, and transfer the balance.

Some years later, I discovered the reason for this difficulty. The billing currency was coded into the credit card number itself. In other words, a credit card could never change its billing currency. Furthermore, the company had no way of identifying me, other than by my credit card number. In other words, the customer is regarded as identical to the account.

When carrying out such a change, any useful customer history is almost certainly lost. Even if the old and new accounts are linked, what are the chances that any MIS program or enquiry will trace the link and reconstruct the customer information?

Thus their data structure was as shown in Figure 2.1.

Figure 2.1: Credit card example: data structure without articulation.

Many software engineers, especially those with data modelling training or experience, will recognize the potential improvements of the following data structure. These structural improvements are often expressed in terms of an obscure technical theory known as **normalization**. Instead of using this theory, we characterize these improvements here in terms of articulation: separation and connection.

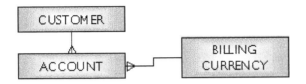

Figure 2.2: Credit card example: data structure with articulation.

This structure is articulated as follows:

➢ separation of customer from account

➢ connection of same customer to many accounts (at the same time, or at different times)

➢ separation of billing currency from credit card number – now we can change billing currency on the same credit card.

Q What advantages do you see in this structure? Do you see any disadvantages?

Q If you are familiar with normalization, or other data modelling techniques, can you achieve the same result using these techniques? Do you think the techniques are equivalent?

Q What would it take for the business to articulate the customer requirement for this flexibility?

Now let's look at articulation in the component domain. Object-oriented software engineers following the object-oriented paradigm will want to design software components around so-called business objects – the "things" that are uppermost in the concerns of business managers. (We might expect that these "things" should also be prominent in the IT systems supporting these managers.)

Business objects are often confused, and the business can benefit from better articulation – connecting and separating. Here are two examples.

Some companies are accustomed to making a conceptual and management separation between PRODUCT and BRAND. The same goods and services are presented to the customer under multiple brand identities. For example, a joint venture between a supermarket and a bank may result in the bank's financial products being sold to customers under the supermarket's brand name.

Or conversely, the same brand identity may be used for more than one product. For example, in the oil industry, the same brand name may be used for a range of slightly different products. The exact petrochemical mixture pumped into cars varies according to the time of year, the state of the oil market, and numerous other factors. Several other industries, including brewing, have different recipes for summer and winter. The customer is not expected to notice the difference.

But some companies have traditionally maintained a one-to-one correspondence between PRODUCT and BRAND. This can turn out to be a significant constraint, especially in IT systems. For example, a financial services company wanted to license its products to a sister company within the same conglomerate. In other words, the sister company would market the products to its own customer base under its own brand name. But the IT systems supporting the products couldn't accommodate this flexibility. Among other things, the billing systems were hard-coded to print a specific brand name at the top of each communication to the customer.

And the constraints were not just from the IT systems. For example, the customer support staff answering the phones didn't know what brand the customer had bought the product under.

From a business perspective, there were three possible outcomes of this lack of articulation:

1. Confusion and dilution of brand identity (loss of clarity).

2. Loss of brand identity – anonymous and unbranded information & services (loss of engagement).

3. Separate capability for each brand – thus restoring one-to-one relationship between brand and product (loss of intelligence).

Another common source of confusion is between CUSTOMER RELATIONSHIP and CUSTOMER INFORMATION. As customer relationship management (CRM) becomes increasingly fashionable, and customer databases are increasingly shared between sister companies or alliance partners, it is increasingly important to make a clear separation between the two business concepts.

Customer information can be easily bought and sold. Customer relationships are not so easy to transfer. It is common to confuse or disconnect these two important business objects.

> Q Do you know any good mechanisms for sharing customer information, while retaining full control of customer relationships?

Here's a third example of articulation, from the world of workflow. In a small company, sales and design staff can work together in small teams. In a larger company, the close coupling between sales and design staff may cause problems, and lead to inflexibility, both in short-term work scheduling and in longer-term work organization. Workflow management systems can help articulate the relationship between sales staff and design staff, using the concept of **proxy** to channel communications effectively in both directions. Instead of sending a design request to a named designer, the sales staff can send a request to a proxy called *<any designer>*.

Finally, similar principles of articulation can be found in managing very large-scale organizations, delivering greater levels of flexibility to corporate strategy. For example, an oil company typically separates "upstream" from "downstream" operations. Another example can be found in the insurance industry, where companies are starting to specialize in either "manufacture" (building insurance products) or "retail" (selling insurance).

For some companies, the primary strategic challenge appears to be **connecting** that which is separated, to deliver the benefits of synergy, economies of scale, and so on, especially following a merger. For other companies, the primary strategic challenge appears to be **separating** that which is connected, to enable more rapid and flexible response to customer demands and market conditions. The principles of articulation aim to keep these two challenges in balance.

The principles of articulation also give us a useful perspective on several questions of business structure and strategy. Enterprise models can help determine whether a given strategy is in balance or out of balance.

Integration	Supply Chain Integration, Vertical Integration, Enterprise Resource Planning (ERP)
Channels	e-commerce, Disintermediation, Reintermediation

Table 2.4: Some key issues of business strategy and structure.

> Q How can you use the principles of articulation to address these key issues?
>
> Q Under what circumstances does construction from building blocks have the effect of increasing articulation? How does this help with these key issues?

Articulation is what legacy systems typically lack.

Typically, one of the main constraints of legacy computer systems, as well as legacy procedures and working practices, is that they lack articulation. This lack of articulation can be experienced in several aspects:

➤ inflexible data structure

➤ inflexible workflow

➤ inflexible business relationships

➤ confused business objects.

The key challenge for managing the evolution of systems is to remove these and other sources of inflexibility.

Articulation can alter both intelligence and character.

Articulated systems can be more flexible and responsive.

The relationship between responsiveness and what we're calling articulation has been studied within management science for several decades. In the 1960s, Emery and Trist developed the idea that the environment makes different levels of demand on the enterprise, and corporate strategy needs to reflect the complexity of these demands. They identified four levels, as shown in Table 2.5.

	Opportunities & threats	Required behaviour
"Placid Randomized"	unchanging undifferentiated	**operational** effectiveness
"Placid Clustered"	unchanging differentiated	**specialist**, to address different clusters of need associated with **professional** skills and institutions
"Disturbed Reactive"	changeable associated with competitors	focus on sustaining the competitive **positions** taken up by the enterprise
"Turbulent Fields"	dynamic arising from the environment itself	dynamic response to environment focus on "**relational**" behaviour

Table 2.5: Demands of Environment.

Following on from this, also in the 1960s, Lawrence and Lorsch developed the idea that an enterprise can cope with variety only as far as this variety is meaningful and coherent, and argued that differentiation of behaviour (viability) needed to be in proportion with integration of differentiated behaviour (identity). Put simply, this meant that organizations faced with complex environments needed greater differentiation among components.

Lawrence and Lorsch were primarily interested in organizations with high differentiation and high integration – in other words, tight coupling. Later writers, such as Karl Weick, have argued that tight coupling may yield high levels of adaptation to a given environment, and thus greater efficiency, but potentially at the expense of adaptability. Loose coupling may be expected to provide greater flexibility, an ability to improvise, and a capability for self-design. Among other things, Weick argues that loose coupling improves the accuracy with which an organization can both perceive trends in the environment and adjust to them. This is well within our notion of intelligence.

Well-articulated systems can be highly stable.

According to their designers, systems based on distributed or parallel operation, such as Blue Gene, the futuristic IBM supercomputer we looked at earlier, can be **self-healing**. This means being able to detect failing components, seal them off, and direct the work elsewhere. It may also mean the ability to automatically repair or replace the faulty components, and bring them back into use, all without interrupting the main task.

> Q What are the limits to this engineered ability to self-heal? What kinds of failures can it cope with? What other kinds of failures are there?

Thus articulation may make a system more robust, more resistant to certain kinds of change, more stable.

> Q What kinds of change would you want your system to resist? How could you possibly answer this first question?

Over-articulated systems are often unstable.

As we saw earlier, a good example of articulation is an articulated lorry. The cab and the container are connected but separate, which gives greater flexibility to the driver, and also to the whole transportation system.

Let's compare this with a private car towing a caravan. Superficially, this seems to have the same structure. But there are some important differences. For one thing, the car is not usually designed to tow a caravan. The motor and brakes may be inadequate, and the mirrors and signals may be poorly positioned. Furthermore, the driver may lack experience towing a caravan, or be out of practice, as many caravans are used infrequently – perhaps only for the summer holidays.

For these and other reasons, caravans are unstable. They sway around, even without much wind, and they have a disproportionate negative impact on the traffic system as a whole.

Personal Computers.

As we saw in Chapter 1, a typical home computer may have dozens of hardware components from different sources – and perhaps thousands of software components. Although in theory this should make repair and upgrade easier, in practice it seems to have the opposite effect. We dare not install something new, in case something else stops working. And we certainly don't dare remove anything, or tidy up the hard disk.

When anything goes wrong, the typical reaction of the support people is to suggest reinstalling everything from scratch. For most of us, this is a daunting prospect, only to be contemplated as a last resort. We may know how to back up documents and other files, but we may not know how to back up the settings and preferences for every software component, and we may not relish the prospect of reconfiguring and resetting everything.

Supply Chains.

Let's have a look at a business example. In Chapter 1, we looked at Wal-Mart, which was able to alter its business process and relationships in radical ways, by reconfiguring a basic set of building blocks. But we can see how this change, with a shift of responsibilities in the supply chain, has had unpredicted secondary consequences.

By putting pressure on suppliers, with low latency, the retailer can indeed improve **short-term** margins and cashflow. But the system (i.e. a set of suppliers plus the retailer) is much less stable. Initially, there is often a shake-out of suppliers. Then, any glitch in production, given the low stockholdings throughout the system, can directly affect the retailer. If the margins are so slight that only a high level of production is profitable, there may be no immediate alternative supplier. The retailer thus has wider issues to trade off against each other. If they drive down costs and inventory too far, they risk disruption to supplies. So we end up with a classic game theory situation, where overall interests may be better served (i.e. a positive sum outcome achieved) if **competition** in the supply chain (for margin etc. between supplier and retailer) is appropriately tempered with **cooperation**. Currently, supply chains are a fruitful area for studying complexity theory in practice, but they are probably just one example of complexity arising in economic (sub)systems – at least in part because of the low latency feedback made possible by IT. This provides a background for the rapid evolution of business models and inter-business relationships that we are seeing today.

Over-articulated systems can be unresponsive.

Product recalls.

When something unexpected happens to a well-known brand name, requiring a product recall, this places unexpected demands on the supply chain. For example, a batch of a drug is mislabelled, or a soft drink is contaminated.

In some situations, the manufacturer has responded promptly and decisively, often getting the whole product taken off supermarket shelves until the exact nature and scope of the problem has been determined, and making clear and honest announcements of the situation to the public. A large short-term expenditure can turn out to be an excellent investment, because when product recalls are managed effectively they can result in a substantial gain in public confidence and thus enhance the value of the brand.

In comparison, there have been some situations that have been marked by fudge and denial. Men in white coats have debated in public whether the level of contamination is sufficient to cause concern, different parties within the supply chain try to blame one another or deny responsibility altogether.

> Q Can you think of recent examples of product recall, or other crisis management? Were they handled well or badly?

What's the critical success factor here? One key difference seems to be the number of separate companies involved. In some cases, too much articulation in the supply chain or market may disable a prompt response to crisis. Each firm concentrates on minimizing the damage to itself, rather than minimizing damage to the whole system.

Is this an argument against articulation? One issue here is the extent to which stakeholders can understand and identify with the interests of the larger entity, whether this be identified by brand or consortium or community as a whole. This shared sense of identity is often absent.

Disowning problems.

One motive for outsourcing or franchising is to separate oneself from responsibility or blame for some unpopular or risky outcome. For example, a large organization that handed its branch network over to local staff on a franchise basis might then try to disown responsibility for any subsequent branch closures.

This is the kind of move that can be seen as intelligent but possibly lacking in character.

The use of building blocks from different sources, or of different styles, can promote biodiversity.

Biodiversity means: the multiplicity of available solutions to a given problem or requirement. For example, an office may run some of its computers using Windows NT and some using Linux. Such software biodiversity is often regarded as a cause of dissatisfaction in its own right, and IT directors may dream of imposing a software monoculture across their organizations.

Q Can you think of other examples of software or technological biodiversity?

Q Can you think of any examples of biodiversity in business processes or practices?

There are many costs associated with biodiversity, but there are also some potential benefits:

> evolution

> requisite variety

> robustness (especially in the face of software viruses targeted at a particular platform).

Biodiversity reduces single-point-of-failure in the larger system. It also promotes creativity and evolution.

Vulnerability of monoculture.

A dominant environment may provide considerable benefits, not merely to the suppliers, but also to users. This is evident in the case of the PC world, currently dominated by Microsoft software and Intel chips. A high degree of compatibility between users seems to make communication and interconnection much easier.

However, there are risks associated with a dominant environment, similar to the risks faced by farmers who plant their fields with a single crop. Recent worms and viruses have swept across the Internet, prompting comparison with the ease with which disease organisms sweep through human populations, and their herds and crops.

One form of insurance against this vulnerability is the software equivalent of biodiversity: software diversity. Art Amolsch, editor of *FTC Watch*, a Washington policy newsletter, is quoted as proposing that no government agency be allowed to run more than 34 percent of its personal computers on one proprietary operating system.

> Do you regard Amolsch's proposal as a solemn technical fix or as a sarcastic technical challenge? What are the chances of his proposal being implemented?

Innovation from the fringes.

Not only is a homogeneous culture vulnerable to external attack from predators and parasites, it can also be slower to adapt and evolve. In his book **Guns, Germs and Steel**, Jared Diamond uses this fact to explain why China, once way ahead of Europe in agriculture and technology, slipped behind over the past 500 years.

Recap.

In this chapter, we've introduced two system properties: intelligence and character. These are system properties that seem to deliver some value to the owners of systems, as well as other interested parties, and this leads to the possibility of intervention (on behalf of these parties) to increase these properties. We have seen how the construction of a system from building blocks, or the deconstruction of a system into building blocks, may have an important impact on the intelligence and character of the system.

In the next two chapters, we shall look in more detail at the building blocks themselves (Chapter 3) and at the interfaces between them (Chapter 4).

3. Components with Character: Principles Governing the Design and Use of Building Blocks

If you want to design, deliver, deploy or depend on building blocks, you need to make judgements about them. Traditional engineering approaches have a fairly small number of ways of making tactical judgements about components – either in terms of their technical "quality" or in terms of their commercial "value". But these notions do not support strategic thinking about components: the potential value of a given component, or the viability of a component in a competitive and dynamic market.

This chapter describes components (or the business services they deliver) as competing in several different ecosystems. This perspective allows us to pay attention to some of the aspects of components that your competitors may be overlooking at their peril, and to think more broadly about the components that are likely to be successful. It also allows us to identify ways to share in this success – whether as developers, users or other interested parties.

A component may both exploit a niche and adapt to change in the niche. However, the adaptability of a system may not derive from the adaptability of the components of which it is composed, but from the substitutability of the components and the flexibility of the wiring. The degree to which a component fulfils a given requirement or can be replaced by another equivalent one depends on both the system and the component. Evaluating components from a local perspective is not enough.

In this chapter, we shall explore what makes a good building block. We shall derive some design principles from an ecological or evolutionary account of systems and their components, as well as from the notion of character introduced in Chapter 2, and explore some examples in order to illustrate the validity and limitations of these principles.

Because much of the recent activity in this area has been in the area of software components, I can't avoid talking about it a lot. However, as I shall try to demonstrate, the principles are much more widely applicable, and I have tried to find some relevant business examples as well.

How do we make judgements about components?

Components – human and artificial.

In this chapter, we're going to look at components, the building blocks from which business systems are constructed or emerge. These components provide services, and these services may be delivered by people, machines (including software) or some combination of man and machine.

The logic of components implies that we can think of the services delivered by a component, without thinking of how these services are delivered. This means that we don't always know or care whether these services are delivered by people or by machines. Indeed, the principle of **encapsulation** (see Glossary) seems to suggest that we ought not to know.

For some purposes, a bank may regard a human teller as equivalent to an ATM or cashpoint machine. (For other purposes, of course, the bank is highly aware of the differences between a human being and a machine.) A bank may even have intentions of installing more machines and sacking some of the people. Business decisions are often justified by cost-benefit arguments comparing the costs of people with the costs of machines.

A business developing a new service or channel may initially install a human component to deliver a part of the business process manually. This might seem an attractive way for a traditional business organization to get a quick start into e-commerce, for example. At best, this could result in a process that is highly sensitive to the demands of the early customers, but is unable to handle large volumes of business. At some stage in the growth of the business, it might make sense to supplement or even replace the human workers with software artefacts.

Conversely, it may be possible to build a new business process using software artefacts, but with the ability for human beings to take over the controls, either for transactions going outside some predefined envelope, or simply at random. Perhaps the managing director herself might want to intercept a few of the transactions, in order to have some real contact with customers and check whether the automated service is working as smoothly as the software engineers claim.

Does this mean that it's okay to think about real people, and components involving real people, as if they were simply mechanical artefacts, fully interchangeable with such artefacts? Or is there an ethical imperative to remain continually alert to the differences between people and machines?

Unfortunately, we cannot live up to such high ethical principles all the time, even if we want to. In our everyday lives, we constantly use services without knowing or caring about the level of automation with which these services are delivered to us.

However, that's not to dismiss the ethical arguments altogether. When working with components, there are important human effects to consider, over and above the logic of components. And when business decisions are justified by comparing the costs of people with the costs of machines, there are a number of practical pitfalls as well as ethical concerns.

Doing things with components.

If large systems are too complex and organic to control, perhaps the best we can do is work at the level of the components. In this chapter, we're going to talk about the properties of components. Some of these properties appear to be under the control of a designer or manager or small team, especially if we talk as if the components are tangible things.

It turns out that even components are not entirely under the control of a human designer. This is certainly true of very large components, such as application software packages – certain ERP products spring to mind – where the control intentions of the designers are often diverted or subverted by the users. It is also true of small components, particularly where the component interacts with other components, or multiple copies/versions of itself, as well as software layers, platforms or frameworks.

However, if we are to engage meaningfully with complex systems, we seem to have no choice but to work with components – adding or removing them, changing them, changing their settings, rewiring and shuffling them – whether in a piecemeal or coordinated way. This calls for deliberation and design. Even if the designer isn't in total control, any intervention is based on the presumption that we can find things to do that are worth doing – at least better than randomly hitting the outside of the system with a hammer.

Furthermore, in any situation of incremental change, the change increment itself can be regarded as a designed component, with relatively clean or messy interaction with other such components. Changes can be combined serially or concurrently, and assembled into larger change programmes. The architecture of a change programme is an important topic in its own right, and we shall return to this topic in Chapter 5.

Reasoning about parts and wholes.

Design dilemma.

There is always a tension between thinking about wholes and thinking about parts.

On the one hand, the whole is usually too complex to think about altogether. So we have to spend some of the time thinking separately about the parts, as if they were independent of the whole.

On the other hand, the parts don't make sense without some context or environment into which they fit. So we have to spend some of the time thinking about the connections between parts, and about the connections with the whole.

A popular strategy for managing the complexity of the whole is to bury all the complexity inside the parts. This is a form of encapsulation. We may then be able to present the whole as a fairly simple assembly. However, if the encapsulation is incomplete or imperfect – and it usually is – then the apparent simplicity is merely an illusion.

Where are system properties located?

As we saw in Chapter 2, many of the desired properties of systems are emergent properties – in other words, they cannot be simply located in one or more components, but emerge from the complex interaction of many components. I argued that this applies in particular to the intelligence of the system.

There are some system properties that can sometimes be localized in a single component, but not always. For example, flexibility may be located:

> in an individual component – if we can reuse the same component in a new situation

> in a component kit – if we can substitute another component from the same kit for a new situation

> in a configuration – if we can plug the same components together in new ways

> in a system architecture – if we can plug together some new components for a new situation, without having to rebuild everything from scratch.

And there are some system properties that sometimes may be located, not in a single component, but in a group of components, or in some aspect of the process. For example, diversity may be located:

> in the component kit – if there are alternative components within same kit

> in the configuration – if there are alternative paths and connections

> in the nature of the connections

> in the management process.

Where are component properties located?

For that matter, we can ask where the component properties are located. Many of the things that appear to be properties of a component are dependent on the way the component is described, and the context in which it is used. For example, encapsulation can be regarded, not as an attribute of a component in isolation, but as a relationship between a component and a person or role.

What judgements do we want to make about building blocks?

Requirements.

To get at the requirements for components, we need to combine top-down analysis (what's wanted) with bottom-up analysis (what's available), including consideration of the second-order requirements of tolerance, flexibility and security.

There is an immensely difficult leap from the system or solution requirements to the requirements for individual components. At least, it's immensely difficult if you try to produce a rational design from first principles. Pragmatic designers, of course, don't do this. Consciously or unconsciously, they use heuristics – rules of thumb or design shortcuts – including patterns and frameworks. A good heuristic leads the designer towards reasonably good solutions using reasonably good components.

Heuristics themselves can be regarded as abstract components, and ought therefore to be subject to the same principles outlined in this chapter. However the forces for change appear to work much slower than for more concrete components, and it's sometimes extremely difficult to detect any learning mechanism. Thus it's not clear what if anything might lead the designer towards a reasonably good heuristic, or how good heuristics might propagate through the design community while the poor heuristics wither away.

Goals.

There are three basic positions for making judgements about building blocks: the supply side, the demand side, and an apparently neutral observer.

On the supply side, we have the people producing components or building blocks, and supplying services, including designers, developers, implementers, and vendors. Given that the production of a building block requires the investment of some energy, the producers want some value in return. Value may be realised in the form of payments from users, or third parties (such as advertisers), or some other benefits to the producers.

 Apart from financial reward or revenues, what other benefits might accrue to the producers or suppliers of building blocks?

On the demand side, we have people using these components, building blocks or services. This also uses up some of their energy, in addition to any financial payment or other exchanges of goods or services with the producers.

 Apart from the price charged by the supplier of a component or service, what other costs might be incurred by the user?

Of course, many users sometimes buy components, or negotiate business services, and then don't use them. This is usually regarded either as a procurement failure, or as a justifiable contingency.

 What are the possible reasons for a purchased component, or negotiated service not being used?

On both sides, therefore, a component generally realises its value by being used, or at least having the potential to be used. The more the better, presumably. And the longer it survives, the greater the likely use.

There are many stakeholders who care about the survival of components. People and firms on the supply side, including designers and developers, generally want their components to thrive and proliferate. Where there is competition between rival components, the winner usually gains commercially – and often in other respects as well.

Safety in numbers?

On the demand side, the situation is less clear-cut. Sometimes a user prefers to have exclusive use of a component – its rarity adds to the value. An arms race is often based on the belief that the other side lacks a given component, or the fear that the other side will acquire it first.

 Give some examples – actual or hypothetical – where a person or firm might want to have exclusive use of a business or software component.

But in most cases, the presence of other users alongside you gives you a sense of security. It seems to reduce the risk that you've made a poor decision, and it also seems to increase the likelihood that the suppliers will remain in the game.

Q To what extent do you think these probability/risk calculations are valid? Under what circumstances might this sense of security be misleading?

Q Think of a recent occasion where you were responsible for a procurement decision, or talk to someone who was involved in one. To what extent was this decision influenced by the weight of other users/customers?

Value in use?

In the preceding discussion, I talked as if a component realised its value by being used. But this may often be a simplification.

For example, what is the "value" of a nuclear bomb or landmine? From a NATO perspective, we might try and reckon its contribution to "peace", perhaps in terms of the cost of an equivalent contribution made by "traditional" forces. The calculation is simpler if we assume that the device will never be used – but this assumption invalidates the supposed effectiveness of the device. If the device is used, it has an enormous negative value, at least for the victims, and possibly for humanity as a whole. Opponents of these technologies will argue that they always have a negative value, and should therefore never be used.

But what does "used" mean for this kind of device? Is a bomb "used" when it is flown over a conflict zone as a deterrent, or only when it's dropped? Or to take an apparently more benign example, is a first aid kit used whenever it's taken to a football match, or only when someone scrapes his knee and needs a bandage? Is a supplier only used when I place a purchase order with him, or also when I look something up in his catalogue?

This discussion has enormous implications for the pricing of components, and the commercial status of business relationships. If I bookmark a software component for possible use in disaster recovery, this software component is effectively providing me with some level of insurance. Should the software supplier get something in return for this? Or does the software supplier only get paid when I actually need the component? Similar considerations apply when I negotiate a backup supply contract, to be activated in the event that my primary supplier lets me down.

There is potentially a structural flaw in such arrangements. Whether the backup component is an item of software sitting on a server, or an entire factory on standby, it needs to get enough energy from somewhere (probably in the form of funding) to ensure its survival. There is often a dilemma: either you pay for something when you're not actually "using" it, or you pay an extremely high premium for something when you actually do "use" it. In some cases there may be a role for some joint action (industry consortium) or central planning (market regulation, corporate infrastructure) to fund such components.

What judgements can we reliably make about building blocks?

In the previous section, I discussed the judgements that people typically want to make about building blocks. But we are usually not in a position to make these judgements with any degree of confidence.

Some people have seen the material in this chapter and said: "Oh, so you're insisting that a component must have all these properties". But that's not what I'm saying at all.

I'm saying that a component with these properties is likely to be more successful than a component without them. And even if its not always possible to detect these properties in advance, and to predict with perfect accuracy which components are going to be successful, it is often possible to explain success after the event in terms of these properties.

Even such retrospective judgements are open to question, to the extent that success and failure, or the very existence and identity of the component itself, are subject to multiple perspectives.

Quality.

In this chapter, we shall explore a number of different perspectives on what is a component. Each perspective leads to a different notion of the quality of a component. In an open distributed world, there is no single value system or global intentions against which the goodness of a component – or anything else for that matter – can be evaluated. Any fixed position on component quality is going to be arbitrary.

In this book, therefore, we're taking an ecological view instead. Given a global soup of firms, people, markets, machines, components and other devices, components follow a Darwinian logic: the survival of the fittest.

In fact, as Bateson pointed out, this should really be called the survival of the fit – or perhaps the unsurvival of the unfit. In practice, the second fittest and third fittest often survive indefinitely. The fittest may have an advantage over the second fittest in the current environment, but this doesn't always lead to the immediate extinction of the second fittest. And if the environment changes, it will sometimes be the entity that is best fitted to the old environment that has the greatest difficulty adapting to the new environment.

> Q   Can you think of any business examples of this?

In this chapter, we're exploring the "fitness" factors for business and software components. What are the ecological principles that determine which components are more likely to be widely used and referenced within a large complex ecosystem?

Negative quality.

Sometimes it appears that negative judgements can be made more reliably than positive judgements. It seems easier to determine that a building block is completely unfit, than to determine that it is fit. This is clearly noticeable in the work of the pattern guru Christopher Alexander, who is far more precise and eloquent on the patterns he dislikes and disapproves of, than on the patterns he recommends.

A biological view of components.

There are several different ways of viewing systems and components. In this chapter, we're going to view systems and components from a biological or ecological perspective.

If a business or software system can be regarded as an organism, then the components may be separate organs or cells – depending what level of granularity we want our metaphor to have. Like a cell, a component takes energy from its environment and yet maintains its own little enclosed world, with no reference to the outside except through a carefully controlled interface.

Instead of looking at the transformation of inputs into outputs, in this chapter we're going to focus on the transformation of energy into value. This leads to a concept of component **vitality**. As soon as a component ceases to provide some value to the larger system into which it has been configured, it is functionally dead.

How does a component use energy? Components cost something to build, procure and maintain. Each component uses human energy every time it needs to be maintained, reconfigured or tested. In so far as its very presence in the larger system adds complexity (or at least mass) to the larger system, it potentially adds to the human effort to perform any task on the larger system. It may be a source of faults in the larger system, or feature interactions, which are often difficult to diagnose, and complex to fix. Furthermore, a component may draw on the energy of other components.

In addition, business components absorb energy in the form of resources and spare capacity; while business relationships require management, and an investment in TLC ("tender loving care"). And of course software components use hardware energy – disk space, memory space, network bandwidth, processing time.

Power source.

Components can also draw energy from a local source of power. For example, a company may mandate the use of a particular building block. This mandate may give the designers of the building block some protection against the ecological forces described in this chapter – or so it may seem. However, from the designer's perspective, there are several risks associated with a single source of power. Some of these are shown in Table 3.1.

- ○ **Arbitrary** – power source may be switched off without notice or reason.

- ○ **Cautionary** – power may granted grudgingly, after a long and tedious verification and validation exercise.

- ○ **Unwise** – immature or unlucky component may drain power from the source, thus weakening it.

Table 3.1 Risks associated with single source of power

What other risks can you identify, from the designer's perspective? What are the risks from other perspectives?

Requirements for components and services – four contexts.

We're going to look at four contexts for making judgements about components.

Solution context.

The popular engineering approach to determining the requirements for software components is in three stages. This approach has been carried forward from so-called structured methods to Object Oriented Analysis and Design (OOAD).

➤ First you identify a group of users who need a software solution for an identified business problem.

➤ Then you define the requirements on the software system. In OOAD this is usually specified as a set of use cases. These requirements may be based on a model of the business process, and are negotiated with the users.

➤ Then you design the software system as a set of interacting components.

Of course, if you are trying to build generic components for multiple use, there may not be a specific business process to analyse, or even a specific software system to design. Furthermore, there may not be any specific users to negotiate requirements with. Undaunted by this, software engineers typically adopt the same approach but at a different level of abstraction. A **domain** is defined, which is a generic business process or generic area of automation.

➤ First you identify a group of domain experts, who are supposed to stand proxy for a class of potential users.

➤ Then you define the requirements for the domain, in collaboration with the domain experts.

➤ Then you design a generic kit of interacting components, which will be usable for any system or business process that satisfies the generic domain description.

➤ Then you assemble systems from these components that satisfy the specific needs of particular users within the target area.

➤ Real business components need to be provided with staff, resources and infrastructure.

In both of these approaches, the context for the design of a component is some **solution** – either specific or generic. I shall refer to both of these approaches as **solution-driven**. Many software artefacts are designed as generic solutions, including frameworks and platforms.

The solution-driven approach seems to imply a division of labour: in the software industry, some engineers shall specialize in the creation of small lumps of functionality (called software components); while other engineers shall specialize in assembling these components to produce large lumps of functionality (known as software applications or systems).

Technical context.

An interface is both transparent and opaque at the same time. This probably seems paradoxical, so let me explain what I mean. A television or computer screen apparently provides a transparent window onto the world, but it can only do this because the glass is essentially opaque. In other words, you cannot see what is physically the other side of the glass – the electronics of the display.

Similarly, a software interface provides an apparently transparent window onto the pure logical functionality of the software, and a business interface provides a window onto some pure business service, but this apparent transparency hides more than it reveals. For many purposes, it is the opacity of the interface that is of greater significance. That's what enables you to use the component as a component.

The opacity of an interface is called encapsulation. This is often taken to mean that the user is not supposed to be able to see inside. (As we shall see, some care is needed with this notion; it turns out that there are different degrees of opacity, from different perspectives.) It is also taken to mean the converse: that the person responsible for the insides of the component shouldn't know anything about how the component is going to be used, lest this knowledge corrupt the technical purity and perfection of the component.

In business, the key equivalent concepts are delegation and autonomy. This leads to use of such terms as "apparent simplicity" and "open book".

In practice, of course, this works out as a difference between informal knowledge and formal knowledge. The designer may in fact have a lot of informal knowledge, but is not permitted to use this as a formal basis for any design decision. Not so much a Chinese wall, more of a paper screen.

The history of design is littered with design judgements that turned out wrong, because of limitations in the designer's view of the world. Informal knowledge is always incomplete, and usually slanted towards the recent and familiar. Ruling out the use of informal knowledge is intended to avoid these mistakes.

Here are some examples, taken at random. Expecting all customers to be able to use the telephone. The use of two-digit dates in software. Designing buildings as if everyone can use stairs. Designing products as if everyone has 20-20 vision. Designing tools as if everyone spoke English, or at least used the standard American character set.

What examples can you add, in which the designer's informal knowledge corrupted the design? Can you offer any examples in which the designer's informal knowledge enhanced the design? On balance, do you think the prohibition of informal knowledge is justified?

But this raises a serious conceptual challenge for the designer of a component. If you don't know how your component is going to be used, how can you know if it's any good? It therefore seems as if we're going to have to fall back on a purely technical notion of quality, with no connection to the solution-context or use-context.

 In your view, does it make sense to talk about quality in this way?

Conformity matters. Obviously part of the technical judgement about a component is whether it conforms to its specification. The specification, the whole specification and nothing but the specification. What you see is what you get. No hidden extras. No side effects.

 Do we have a way of recognizing side effects, without reference to a specific solution or usage environment?

Standards matter. Another aspect of conformity is the adherence to various technical standards, as put about by various vendors and industry bodies.

Size matters. If you don't have much experience of using your component, then at least you can discuss its size. One of the most commonly discussed questions about software componentry concerns the "right" level of granularity for software components. Within product marketing, there are some discussions about the "right" level of product bundling.

Quality matters. Encapsulation also interferes with quality assurance from the user side, at least as traditionally practised. Pure delegation should leave total design autonomy and control to the supplier. The user should be satisfied with the WHAT, and should not meddle with the HOW – neither the designed mechanisms, nor the design process itself, should be visible to the user.

Ecological context.

But the solution-driven approach assumes that it is meaningful to think about requirements in terms of a fixed lump of functionality or capability, delivered to a fixed community of users. In business, this is known as **the** business; in software, this is known as **the** software system or application.

This also assumes that one person or team has design control over this lump. In business this is supposed to be the CEO and her direct reports; as for software, there are several possible job titles, including system architect.

The limitations of this approach emerge when we are faced with large open distributed dynamic networks of business and software. It is both a business imperative and a technological imperative for business organizations to connect their business processes into these networks. These networks lack central design authority or architectural control, and evolve organically. Overall functionality and structure may change unpredictably from one day to the next. Connecting to these networks raises a number of difficult management dilemmas, including control, security and stability.

Taking our cue from Kevin Kelly, these networks are "Out of Control". Traditional engineering approaches are inadequate for operating effectively in this environment. As Kelly has shown, biological and ecological metaphors seem to have more relevance than engineering metaphors.

The biological approach to creating business and software components is radically different to the traditional engineering approach, and is based on biological and ecological metaphors.

> First we identify an **ecosystem**, which may contain both human users and existing artefacts.

> Then we identify **services** that would be meaningful and viable in this ecosystem.

> Then we procure **devices** that enable the release and delivery of these services into the ecosystem.

Design context.

We'll return to the ecological context later in the chapter, but first I just want to mention a fourth context we can construct for making judgements about components. This is based on the work of Christopher Alexander, whose work has been widely referenced by software engineering gurus, usually after a time-lag of around 10-15 years.

Alexander's first book *Notes on the Synthesis of Form* was published in 1964. This was referenced by Ed Yourdon, Tom De Marco and other software engineering gurus during the 1970s, and provided a degree of intellectual underpinning for a number of related software methods, commonly known as structured methods, which were widely practised from the late 1970s onwards.

Alexander's next major contribution was his work on patterns. His book *A Pattern Language* was published in 1977, and this started to get serious attention within the software engineering community from about 1989 onwards.

More recently, Alexander has developed an approach to the organic evolution of complex artefacts, contained in his 1987 book *A New Theory of Urban Design*. This has not yet received much attention in the software engineering community.

Central to Alexander's view of design is a notion of wholeness. (He sometimes refers to this as the Quality without a Name.) This relates to the notion of character we introduced in Chapter 2. Alexander argues eloquently for the importance of this quality. This establishes an ethical or aesthetical context, in which wholeness or character are seen as good healthy properties in their own right, not requiring separate or individual justification.

There are some deep and important questions about the relationship between this context and the three previously mentioned contexts. Is character something more than mere technical elegance? Can we sometimes see character as a means to an end (e.g. satisfaction of some solution properties or ecological goals), and sometimes as an end in itself? Are these two sides of the same coin, or two entirely distinct notions? We'll need to come back to these questions later.

An ecological view of the world of components.

Context.

In this section, we aim to understand the component environment in more detail. We define a series of what we call **ecosystems**. We use this word, rather than **markets** or **industries** or **networks**, because it is more general. An ecosystem may contain human agents or organizations, or it may contain intelligent software agents, or it may be a hybrid.

The natural world can be regarded as a single global ecosystem, because there are some connections between all the parts. (Birds may visit even a remote island, carrying new species of plant or insect.) However, for many purposes it is simpler to regard a semi-isolated part as a separate ecosystem.

Separation.

To analyse the environment for business and software components, we separate the whole into four ecosystems, by making two orthogonal cuts.

First we make a cut between the demand/use side and the supply side of the software industry. This separation will be familiar to many readers. It can be found in many procurement and quality models, including the ISO 9000 quality standard and its derivatives. Component-based development enables a further separation, between the external service (accessed through a component interface), and the internal component assets or devices that deliver the service. This second separation applies equally on the demand/use side and on the supply side, yielding four ecosystems altogether, as in Figure 3.1.

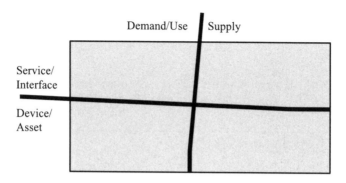

Figure 3.1 Two separations, four ecosystems.

Service Use Ecosystem	**Service Supply Ecosystem**
○ using services ○ demanding services ○ architecting and configuring the use of services ○ subscribing to service publications	○ providing or delivering services through stable interfaces ○ architecting services ○ publishing available services
Ecological principles: *pleasure, connectivity (critical mass)*	*Ecological principle:* *commodity (or availability)*

Device Use Ecosystem	**Device Supply Ecosystem**
○ configuring devices ○ installing, connecting or calling devices ○ predicting device behaviour ○ predicting system behaviour	○ architecting devices ○ providing devices to deliver services (build, buy, assemble, reuse) ○ managing devices as assets
Ecological principles: *firmness (quality), flexibility,* *biodiversity*	*Ecological principle:* *conservation of energy (also known* *as economies of scale or reuse)*

Figure 3.2 Four "ecosystems".

Each of the four ecosystems involves a different set of activities and collaborations, and each has its own vocabulary and logic. In each of the four ecosystems, we can identify one or more ecological principles or economic imperatives.

Now let's look at each of the four ecosystems in turn.

Service Use Ecosystem.

The Service Use Ecosystem considers services as commodities – it is concerned with WHAT and not HOW. The primary activities of the Service Use Ecosystem are shown in Table 3.2.

°   Using services
°   Demanding services
°   Architecting and configuring use of services
°   Subscribing to service publications

Table 3.2 Activities of the Service Use Ecosystem.

There are two important factors influencing these activities.

An important element of strategic thinking around a business process is to decide: which bits are to be routine and mechanical, consuming as little management time and attention as possible; and which bits are to be strategically interesting, on which management time and attention is to be focused. Thus some business services need to be as boring as possible, while others need to be as exciting as possible. And it's important to get the balance right – too much excitement is painful or stressful, while too little excitement is death. This balance is a critical survival factor for the Service Use ecosystem as a whole; we call this the **pleasure principle**.

Furthermore, some services give value to their users by being unique, while others give value to their users by being common. The best-known example of the latter is communication services: how much value you get from your email or fax service depends on how many of your friends and associates are also using email or fax. Thus your decision to use a given service sometimes depends on your estimate of the number of other users. We call this the **connectivity principle**. (It is sometimes known as the **critical mass principle**.)

Service Supply Ecosystem.

Like the Service Use Ecosystem, the Service Supply Ecosystem considers services as commodities – it is also concerned with WHAT and not HOW – but this time from the supply side instead of the demand side. The primary activities of the Service Supply Ecosystem are shown in Table 3.3.

°   Providing or delivering services through stable interfaces
°   Architecting services
°   Publishing available services

Table 3.3 Activities of the Service Supply Ecosystem.

In the Service Supply Ecosystem, services are competing for survival. Between two otherwise equivalent services, the more available service will usually win over the less available. Some aspects of availability are as follows (depending on the nature of the service):

➢ Global 24-hour access. Instant response.

➢ Any hardware and software platform. Available in Arabic, Chinese, English, Hindi, Russian and Spanish.

➢ Easy to use. Low entry cost. Good support. Minimum learning curve.

➢ High reliability. Safe and secure. Low risk.

Hence there is a strong technological and commercial pressure for services to increase their availability; we call this the **availability principle**. (Or following a well-known advertisement for a popular brand of alcohol, it is known as the **Martini principle**: *Any time, any place, anywhere.*)

Device Supply Ecosystem.

In contrast to the Service Supply Ecosystem, the Device Supply Ecosystem focuses on the devices and mechanisms and resources used to deliver a given set of services. In other words, it is concerned with HOW as well as WHAT. The primary activities of the Device Supply Ecosystem are shown in Table 3.4.

°   Architecting devices
°   Providing devices to deliver services (build, buy, assemble, reuse)
°   Managing devices as assets

Table 3.4 Activities of the Device Supply Ecosystem.

In the Device Supply Ecosystem, competitive survival depends on delivering the greatest quantity of service with the smallest amount of work. This is often called **reuse**; software reuse should be focused on achieving **economies of scale** in software, based on effective asset management and knowledge management. We call this the **energy conservation principle**.

Device Use Ecosystem.

Finally, the Device Use Ecosystem focuses on the devices and mechanisms and resources used to deliver a given set of services, but this time from the demand side. The primary activities of the Device Use Ecosystem are shown in Table 3.5.

°   Configuring devices
°   Installing, connecting or calling devices
°   Predicting device behaviour
°   Predicting system behaviour

Table 3.5 Activities of the Device Use Ecosystem

In the Device Use Ecosystem, competitive survival depends on getting the expected services (and their associated benefits) from a given configuration of devices. This in turn relies on an ability to predict and control the behaviour of components-in-use, including the emergent properties of large distributed systems. We call this the **consistency principle**.

Also relevant in this ecosystem is the ability to easily substitute devices and reconfigure systems. We call this the **flexibility principle**.

Within the Device Use Ecosystem, there is also an interest in the technical efficiency or performance of a component, within the context of a given system. This is another aspect of the **energy conservation principle**, but now focused on the demand/use side, rather than the supply side.

Finally, the robustness, flexibility and evolution of the ecosystem depends on a reasonable heterogeneity of software and services. We call this the **biodiversity principle**.

Seven ecological principles – and a hypothesis.

The Roman architect Vitruvius, who lived at the time of Jesus Christ, defined quality as commodity, firmness and delight. Bill Gates has quoted this definition, and explained it as shown in Table 3.6.

Vitruvius	**Gates Gloss**
Firmness	"Consistency"
Commodity	"Be worthy of the user's time and effort in understanding it"
Delight	"Engagement, fun"

Table 3.6 Quality from Vitruvius to Gates.

In your view, how do Microsoft products balance these three quality factors? How do you imagine these three factors map to Microsoft's corporate values?

Our discussion has extended the three principles of Vitruvius and Gates. We now have seven ecological principles, as shown in Table 3.7.

○ **Pleasure** (Delight, Engagement, Fun)

○ **Connectivity** (Critical Mass)

○ **Availability** (Commodity, Functionality)

○ **Conservation of Energy** (Economies of Scale, Reuse, Efficiency)

○ **Consistency** (Firmness, Reliability, Usability)

○ **Flexibility** (Maintainability, Portability)

○ **Biodiversity**

Table 3.7 Seven Ecological Principles.

Any reader interested in software quality standards and metrics may also wish to note that our set of principles covers and extends the quality characteristics of software products identified in ISO 9126: functionality, maintainability, efficiency, usability, reliability and portability.

If there are four ecosystems, where are the components? As a working hypothesis, I'm going to suggest the following answer. A successful component probably has a place in each ecosystem. Just as a frog must be viable both in the pond and on the shore, so a successful component probably needs to be viable and meaningful in all four ecosystems, and this in turn means that the component probably respects all seven ecological principles. Such a component is viable and meaningful, and is likely to survive and develop. I'm going to call this the **component viability hypothesis**. It leads to the following definition of component quality: **A good component is one that satisfies the ecological principles of all four ecosystems.**

The trend towards components is too recent to provide conclusive evidence for this hypothesis, but there are some early signs of its plausibility, as well as arguments from analogy. We'll look at some of this material in the remainder of the chapter.

Note that while some components may seem viable in isolation, other components may only be viable as a member of a kit or family or tribe of components. As in biology, the unit of viability may not be fixed. So sometimes we'll apply the ecological principles to individual components, and sometimes we'll apply them to groups of components. This may sound like an unnecessary complication, but it reflects what happens in real life – components are sometimes designed or evaluated in isolation, sometimes in groups.

Here's a well-known example. One of the factors that made Apple Macintosh successful was the common look and feel of Macintosh applications, although these applications were developed by independent teams in lots of different software companies. (We'll see how this was achieved later in the chapter.) This consistency is a property of the tribe, not just of a single application. Thus the viability of a single Macintosh application is bound up with the viability of the whole tribe. That's ecology for you.

Here's another example. In the early years of laptop computers, travellers with laptops faced enormous difficulties if they wanted to connect these computers into hotel telephone systems. (We'll return to the interfacing aspects of this example in Chapter 4.) Although many hotels have now greatly improved the services available to the business traveller, and the telephone systems themselves are much more reliable, an increasing number of businessmen now use their own mobile telephones rather than the hotel telephone for such purposes. A few hotels may invest huge amounts in making provision for business travellers, but this investment is wasted if the businessmen don't bother using these services. And now that they have found a satisfactory alternative, they might not start using these services again until the majority of hotels offer them, and perhaps not even then.

 What are the reasons why a business traveller doesn't bother using the hotel telephone? What would it take for an individual hotel to recapture the market for these services? And what would it take for the hotel industry to recapture this market?

An important implication of the component viability hypothesis is that if a component fails to respect one of the principles, this entails a risk for the viability of that component in the associated ecosystem. Therefore, the component viability hypothesis leads to the following design heuristic: **When designing a component, a designer should consider the viability of the component in all four ecosystems, and in terms of all seven ecological principles.** We'll explore this design heuristic in detail, in the course of the chapter.

The component viability hypothesis also has important implications for the players in the component marketplace. **The dominant players in the component marketplace will be those that can understand and engage with multiple perspectives, and can straddle multiple ecosystems.** We'll look at some aspects of this in the following section.

Articulation of ecosystems.

Instead of the biological/ecological metaphor of **ecosystem**, some readers may prefer to think in terms of a **political economy**. However, I think the ecosystem metaphor is more useful than the market metaphor in dealing with these multiple roles and the conflicts between them. A simple characterization of a market as a set of buyers confronting a set of sellers doesn't go far enough for my purposes.

A bird that wants to do well in the bird–worm ecosystem has to spend a lot of time pecking at the ground, but a bird that wants to do well in the cat–bird ecosystem has to spend a lot of time flying away. The features or defences that are useful in one ecosystem may be a handicap in another ecosystem. A successful bird is one that manages to find a good balance between the conflicting survival principles of the two ecosystems.

Note that I'm articulating the bird's environment in terms of two separate but connected ecosystems. (This conforms to the definition of articulation I gave in Chapter 2.) Some readers may prefer to describe the bird's environment as a single cat–bird–worm ecosystem.

 What are the conceptual advantages of separating the cat–bird system from the bird–worm system? What are the conceptual advantages of connecting the two systems?

Management dilemmas can often be characterized in a similar way – as an attempt to find a good balance between success and survival in two or more ecosystems.

Encapsulation reformulated.

Ecosystems can also be used as a mechanism for containing or hiding complexity. Earlier in this chapter, we introduced an informal notion of encapsulation. We can now characterize encapsulation more formally as a statement about the relationship between the Service Supply Ecosystem and the Device Supply Ecosystem. Certain aspects of a component are not accessible within the Service Supply Ecosystem, and are hidden behind the service interface. Encapsulation can also be expressed as an approximately equivalent statement about the relationship between the Service Use Ecosystem and the Device Use Ecosystem.

Component character – and another hypothesis.

In this chapter, I'm also going to explore the possible connection between component viability and the notion of character we introduced in the previous chapter. Let's call this the **component character hypothesis**.

Components for open distributed systems – five viewpoints.

For a component to be viable within a given ecosystem, it needs to be viable from five viewpoints.

➢ It needs to serve a useful **purpose**, relative to the **intentions** of some **community** of **agents**.

➢ It needs to be **semantically meaningful**. Its interface has to have an information model that is recognisable by other agents within the Service Use Ecosystem.

➢ Its **behaviour** needs to fit with the expectations of other agents. It must conform to standard or local interfaces and protocols.

➢ Its internal **design** must be compatible with the quality and performance demands of the Device Use Ecosystem.

➢ Its technical requirements must be compatible with the available **infrastructure** and **resources** within the Device Use Ecosystem.

Table 3.8 Component Viability from Five Viewpoints.

Articulation of supply chain.

Component triggers.

What then triggers the creation of a new component?

The initial stimulus may come from any of the four ecosystems.

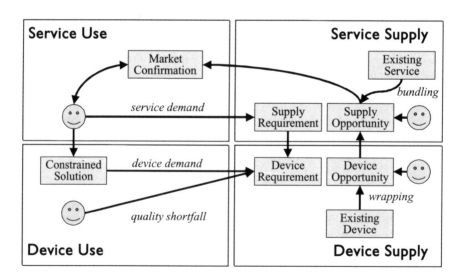

Figure 3.3 Requirements for components can originate in any of the four ecosystems.

Demand-driven. An agent may identify some service that he/she/it requires. This generates an unsatisfied service demand, which may be communicated to the Service Supply Ecosystem in hopes of a response. Alternatively, the service demand may be translated into a device demand, and communicated from the Device Use Ecosystem to the Device Supply Ecosystem.

Supply-driven. A supplier may identify an opportunity to extend an existing service to increase its availability, or to package a bundle of existing services and/or devices to provide a new service. An engineer may identify an opportunity to wrap or modify an existing device to provide new services. Prototype devices may be re-engineered to increase availability of services.

Regardless of the initial stimulus, a successful component needs to find sufficient acceptability on the demand side, and sufficient economies of scale on the supply side. This suggests a collaborative process of negotiating requirements, which needs to connect with both imperatives, but in no particular sequence.

Types of software supply.

Componentry increases the separation between demand-driven and supply-driven software organizations. (This applies to in-house software factories as well as to commercial software houses.)

Demand-driven	Supply-driven
Close relationship to customer base.	Close relationship to technology base.
Focus on the services that are wanted in the selected market.	Focus on exploiting existing assets.
	Competing on price/cost.
Competing on value.	

Table 3.9 Separation between demand-driven and supply-driven organizations.

In the past, the supply side could be divided into two modes of software supply.

Off the shelf. Some suppliers designed and marketed products for sale into an identified market (or ecosystem). These were standard products, with little or no variation, and were typically expensive to modify or integrate. If many users bought the same product, then the development and marketing costs could be shared between them, reducing the individual cost to each user.

Bespoke. Some suppliers designed and delivered one-off products to a particular customer's specification. These were typically much more expensive per user than standard off-the-shelf products, and took longer to deliver, but were (at least in theory) much closer to the customer's requirements.

Component-based development enables a third mode of software supply.

Mass customization. Suppliers who are able to respond to the needs of a single customer, while achieving economies of scale across multiple customers.

There are many ecosystems containing only off-the-shelf and bespoke suppliers, in which neither mode of supply can eliminate the other. However, as soon as mass customization becomes effective in a given supply ecosystem, then off-the-shelf and bespoke supply are ecologically doomed, and will eventually be eliminated from that ecosystem. These suppliers may survive in the short term by switching to other (perhaps smaller niche) ecosystems, but for how long?

 Do you think there are any software supply ecosystems in which a supplier can be safe from competition from software mass customization? How would you be sure?

According to this analysis, the growth of componentry creates challenges for both types of software supplier.

Challenges for software houses.

A software house that specializes in bespoke software development may detect increasing difficulties competing on price. If your competitors are achieving better economies of scale, without compromising quality and flexibility, then they will be able to undercut your prices.

Most software houses still bid for bespoke work on the basis of a simple formula: estimated cost plus contingency plus profit. There may be some opportunities for you to reduce costs or contingency, by improving your software process.

But if your competitors are doing this too, this won't be enough.

There are two possible strategies for survival. You can either move up the "food chain", concentrating on supply and packaging of services (while subcontracting the software engineering side to cheap suppliers in Bangalore). Or you can embrace the ecological imperative: conservation of energy.

Instead of bidding for bespoke work on a cost-plus basis, you must try to determine what the customer is willing to pay.

If this isn't enough to cover your costs, then you need to find a way of satisfying the customer that leaves you with some residual value. If you have developed some software components that you can sell to other customers as well, this might well make up the difference. (There are other forms of residual value, but this is the most likely one for a software house to exploit.)

Challenges for package vendors.

Meanwhile, a software product vendor with a standard fixed range of products may detect increasing difficulties maintaining market share, or entering new markets. If your competitors can offer more flexible products, with greater availability and lower total cost of ownership, then they can erode your customer base.

The challenge for such suppliers is to leverage the economies of scale, to get wider flexibility and availability from an equivalent device base, and to get much greater internal levels of reuse. This is basically an architectural issue: how to improve the internal configuration and layering of the product. (Some suppliers will choose to keep the benefits of this improved architecture to themselves, while others will choose to open up the architecture to customers and third parties.)

Solution-oriented judgements.

In this section, we're going to look at the desirable characteristics of a component from within the solution context. These characteristics include: correctness, flexibility, quality of service, and reuse.

Correctness of fit.

If we're following a solution-oriented design approach, the crucial question for a component is: does it correctly perform its allotted function within the overall solution, or within a defined class of solutions.

The functionality of a component or service is typically specified in terms of defined behaviour under defined preconditions – often without constraints on the quality of service. This leads directly to a series of test cases, to confirm the correctness in this sense.

 To what extent can the correctness of a component be guaranteed by testing? What are the limits of testing? How effective is testing in practice? Why do you think testing often falls short of the ideal?

In conventional procurement, attention is given to the gap between a statement of requirements and a contract or artefact. The bigger the gap, the greater the failure of the artefact to fit your requirements.

In practice, the fit may never be perfect – there is always some gap, however small. Usage of a particular artefact usually involves some compromise. Perhaps you have to do without something, or accept some complication elsewhere. Perhaps it's more expensive than you'd hoped, either in the acquisition cost or in the cost of ownership.

In practice, there is a tolerance of slight (or even substantial) misfit. This tolerance varies according to several factors, and can be regarded as a requirement in its own right. (We can call it a second-order requirement, because it specifies the relationship between the **requirements** and the solution, whereas the first-order requirements specify the relationship between the **users** and the solution. Flexibility is another example of a second-order requirement.)

Note that accepting a misfit doesn't necessarily mean changing your requirements. Suppose I advertise for a personal assistant who speaks fluent French, German, Spanish and Russian. I may decide to give the job to someone who speaks French, German, Dutch, Russian and Italian – perhaps an excellent choice, but still a slight misfit relative to my requirements. This doesn't mean that my requirement for Spanish has gone away – merely that this requirement has not been satisfied by this particular recruitment. Perhaps I have to hire in an extra translator on those occasions where Spanish is spoken, or even pay for Spanish lessons.

Both with conventional outsourcing and with software application packages there was an expectation that a given partner or package would satisfy a long list of requirements. Package evaluation methods make judgements based on such lists. With components, the expectation is likely to be quite different – that a single component would contribute to satisfying one aspect of one requirement.

It therefore doesn't make sense to say that a component (evaluated in isolation) fits the requirements (understood as a whole), because we're not comparing like with like. All we can really say is that a given component fits **with a number of other components** to produce a satisfactory solution. This is much to do with the interfaces and connections between the components, as to do with the components themselves. We shall consider these aspects of fit in Chapter 4.

Flexibility.

Within the solution-oriented context, flexibility for a component means one of two things. It either refers to the range of solutions in which the component can be used, or to the contribution this component makes to the flexibility of the whole solution.

If we're trying to build systems with a particular property, the components may themselves need to possess the desired quality (e.g. flexibility or intelligence) to an appropriate degree.

Small throwaway building blocks may not need much intelligence or flexibility at all. However, larger building blocks may need higher degrees of intelligence or flexibility, if you don't want to have to throw them away.

We need to balance the costs of replacement against the costs of non-replacement (preservation through flexibility).

Reconfiguration.

Can I change the overall functionality or performance of my system by rewiring the same components? Can the components be plugged together in many different ways, without interfering with their functionality or performance?

Substitution.

On the user side, clarity has an effect on flexibility. The user often wants to change the overall functionality or performance of a system by replacing one component with a similar component, without changing any other component.

(Note: this probably means that the new component has the same interface as the old one, but a different specification. Beware of gurus who tell you that interfaces and specifications are the same thing.)

 Q Under what circumstances (if ever) can components be substituted without having to retest the whole system?

Quality of service.

In some cases, some technical requirements of a component can be explicitly derived from the overall solution requirements. In other cases, they are left implicit, or delegated to "technical" personnel. These requirements may include such factors as availability, reliability and performance.

These requirements are often regarded as second-class ones, deserving less respect and attention. Much time and energy is typically devoted to getting them right, but this is often grudging and carries less status and reward. Businessmen sometimes call these "hygiene factors", as if to say that they're about the same level as cleaning the office toilets. And software engineers convey a similar attitude when they refer to requirements as "non-functional" – they might as well call them dysfunctional and be done with it.

(If non-functional requirements are second-class, then maintenance ranks even lower. We'll look at maintenance in Chapter 5.)

Reuse.

Since the early days of computing, programmers have saved energy by putting commonly used pieces of software into special libraries, so that they could be used again and again.

If we're looking at components from the point of view of a single solution, or class of solutions, reuse has two main impacts.

The first consequence of reuse is on the delivered solution itself. Use of the same component to perform the same function throughout a large system gives a degree of homogeneity to the system. This has three potential benefits: it may make development more efficient, it ought to make current operations more consistent, and might make future maintenance more straightforward. If you're designing a component with these benefits in mind, for a specific solution, then you're going to care about the extent to which the same component or service can be slotted into the same solution in several different places.

> Q Does the use of a common component throughout a system always make
>   operations more consistent, and maintenance more straightforward? If
>   not, why not? Are there any other benefits? What are the risks
>   associated with common components?
>
> Q Does the use of a common platform or framework carry the same benefits
>   and risks?

In traditional organizations, some capabilities are provided in the form of central services, while others are provided locally. Central services are thought to enable economies of scale – for example, in procurement, the ability to negotiate larger discounts on larger purchase orders – but the centre is often seen as unresponsive to local needs. This sets up a management dilemma – centralize or decentralize – which often manifests itself in an oscillation between central and local services.

Some writers have suggested that Information Technology is capable of resolving this dilemma, yielding the best of both worlds, by encapsulating some part of the service in software, which can then be distributed to local operations and embedded in local practices.

> Q Do you believe this? What would it take to make it true?

A second consequence of reuse is as follows. If you can use components that already exist, this can greatly reduce the development costs, and shorten the lead times. In

Chapter 1, we saw how some firms, such as Tesco in the UK, are able to construct a new business very quickly, by plugging existing components together.

In many cases, this means that the solutions hadn't been thought of at the time the components themselves were built. Thus we can only assess the reusability of the component in retrospect. What designers would like is to estimate the future reusability of a component in advance. What I'm arguing here is that this cannot be done by focusing on a solution, or even a class of solutions, but requires an entirely different context – what I'm calling the ecological context. We'll come back to this later.

Technically-oriented judgements.

Cohesion and coupling.

Cohesion.

From the supply side, the design of building blocks is usually focused on achieving some form of integrity. In the software industry, this is commonly characterized in terms of **cohesion**.

Software components may possess cohesion in various ways. The cohesion may be based on the data structure, on the perceived function of the component, or on some other factors. These forms of cohesion may be visible to the developers, but not mean much from the user's side of the fence. In any case, if you're wrapping some software up as a component, perhaps the internal cohesion is not supposed to be visible to the users.

Business components also need to possess cohesion. This is typically based on a common set of skills, knowledge or resources. These are the factors that are often used when dividing a business organization into separate departments.

It's worth noting here that many business organizations devote considerable time and energy to frequent structural changes.

Let me give an example from my own experience of working in several software and service companies. Typically, one year the company would be organized in divisions according to some technical criteria – perhaps an IBM mainframe division and a DEC minicomputer division. The following year, this structure would be discarded, and replaced with a geographically-based organization – a Northern Division and a Southern Division, say. Then this structure too would be discarded, and the company would be organized by industry sector – a Finance Division and an Oil–Gas–Utility Division. Every service company I've ever worked for has undergone this kind of repetitive cycle.

At the time, I generally interpreted this repetitive cycle as a sign of management weakness and confusion – in short, a lack of character. It seemed obvious to me that any organization structure would be inadequate to reflect fully the complexity of the task facing the organization; but instead of acknowledging this, management presented each reorganization to staff as if it were the final solution to the problems experienced in the previous structure. (Of course, if management didn't actually believe this, but were cynically putting up a rational façade for the staff, this would also count as a lack of Character.)

On the positive side, periodic reshuffling creates development opportunities for individual managers, and may create more linkages than it destroys.

> Q   What are the possible pay-offs from a repetitive cycle of reorganization? For whom?
>
> Q   What are the likely costs and risks of regular reorganization? What are the possible risks of sticking with the same organization structure for a long time?

Note that when I attribute a lack of character to management, I'm referring to the management as a system. As we have already seen in Chapter 2, this may not reflect the character of the individual managers.

Given a complex set of requirements, designers use techniques of clustering, to decompose a complex set of requirements into separate chunks, which are supposed to have maximum cohesion and minimum coupling. There are several different clustering techniques, with significantly different outcomes.

From the supply side, what are the perceived benefits of cohesion or integrity? This question can perhaps be better asked in reverse: what are the costs and risks of poor cohesion and inadequate integration, or excessive coupling?

These benefits can largely be expressed in terms of productivity and control. Cohesion reduces wastage, resulting in better utilization of scarce resources, and simplifies management controls.

In terms of the ecological principles listed earlier in this chapter, this can be reduced to a question of the **conservation of energy**.

Hidden coupling – feature interaction.

From a technical point of view, it would be good to be able to eliminate hidden coupling between components, or illegitimate side effects. Interference between the intended features of two or more components or services is known as **feature interaction**. Many complex distributed systems manifest unwanted and destructive interactions between components, and these are surprisingly difficult to predict or screen, especially when the components or services are from different sources. Many of these interactions are only found when the systems are in active use.

Simple example: you are in a hotel room, trying to access a voicemail service back in your office, while charging the call to your telecom billing card. The voicemail system wants you to hit *** to get next message, but the billing card interprets this as a signal to disconnect.

The telecoms industry is plagued with problems of feature interaction, and these problems are expected to have a growing significance within the software industry, especially with moves towards component-based development.

 Can you identify any business examples of feature interaction?

Economies of scale.

Let us now return to the supplier challenge of **economies of scale**. We can now articulate a supply strategy for achieving economies of scale in terms of the five viewpoints shown in Table 3.8 on page 98.

A supplier of software components achieves effective reuse by combining maximum variation in one viewpoint (i.e. **customization**) with minimum variation in another viewpoint (i.e. **standardization**).

For example, a supplier may define a standard information model, and then seek to deliver this on as many platforms as possible.

Or a supplier may make a strategic commitment to a single platform (e.g. Enterprise Java Beans), and then attempt to deliver a highly flexible information model from a common code-base.

 How do service businesses achieve a balance between customization and standardization?

Generalization and specialization

Generalization

One strategy for achieving adaptability is generalization. The more that the engineer can abstract away from a particular set of detailed requirements, the larger the class of situations that the solution can handle.

In component-based solutions, this may be achieved **either** by using more generalized components **or** by using components that are easy to replace and reconfigure.

> Take a look at the range of prams and buggies for new-born babies. You can spend a lot of money on an elaborate system of components, that can be configured in various ways as the baby grows – as a pram, as a car seat, as a moses basket, as a pushchair for an older toddler. That's what we "invested" in when our son was born. It was a mistake. None of the configurations was perfectly adapted to our requirements, and we would have spent less money buying two or three better adapted but less adaptable items.

Component producers usually aim to build components that have as large a potential user base as possible, increasing reuse and yielding scale economies. Generalized components may have advantages for users as well:

- increasing the flexibility of solutions using these components – perhaps;

- reducing the cost – if the producer chooses to share the benefits of the economies of scale with the purchaser;

- allowing the consumer to belong to a community of co-users, which may support communication and sharing of information and resources – if this is appropriate.

However, these advantages must be weighed against the higher usage costs of many generalized components:

- increased transaction costs for acquisition

- increased testing costs – including increased concerns about feature interaction between multiple components

- increased configuration costs – you may have lots of parameters to set, and you may have to talk to the component in XML rather than simple input/output

- increased operational cost – you may be paying for functionality that you aren't using

- generalized components may actually reduce the flexibility of the overall solution in some respects, because they make the solution too complicated or expensive to change.

And from the component producer's or broker's perspective, a component that is excessively generalized may be hard to sell:

- it doesn't fit into a neat category within the product catalogue

- potential purchasers may never find the component

- or they require much more collateral information when they do.

This is where the concept of Character comes in. Among other things, Character means clear identity and functionality, which is lost when a component is overgeneralized. If a component is so generalized that only advanced mathematicians and object-oriented software engineers can appreciate its elegance, then it's lost it as far as the general population is concerned. (Some of us with long memories might remember data models that possessed a similar quality.)

Specialization

Sometimes a component producer can get the economies of scale from a highly generalized component, but this doesn't have sufficient character to sell in this form. Instead, the producer uses this component to generate a series of specialized components. Each specialized component can be given a clear brand identity, and a separate entry in the product catalogue. It can be tuned to a price and performance that a particular section of the market can stand.

As an example of this specialization strategy, many software houses nowadays possess inhouse class libraries that are used to deliver cheaper and faster solutions to their customers.

Cheaper and faster, but what about flexibility? The software house may well claim that, even though the generalized components are not directly available to the customer, the flexibility benefits can be made indirectly available through an ongoing maintenance service provided by the integrator. The customer then has a normal procurement decision, whether to avail himself of this form of flexibility, on these terms.

If the generalization is made available to the user in the form of a maintenance service rather than already embedded in the purchased component, this changes the way the generalization is funded and billed – who owns the reuse. The provider should start by planning a family of services, and consider multiple commercial mechanisms for delivering and billing these services. These management issues may then dominate the technical choices of generalization/specialization mechanism.

Reliability.

Design for quality and reliability.

From an engineering perspective, all systems should be robust and fault-tolerant. In practice, only a few systems achieve high standards in this respect. Examples include military systems and the Internet itself.

Does a system work robustly? Is it safeguarded against rogue or poor quality components? And is it dependent on hero components?

A hero component is one that is extra-strong, fault-tolerant, compensating for the weaknesses and errors of other components. Many engineers are ambivalent about hero components. An extra-strong component may be capable of reinforcing an otherwise weak system, or may be a "fail-safe" mechanism to prevent local failures causing wider system collapse. But this reinforcement may create hidden weaknesses elsewhere. And a hero component can be a single point of failure, so when it fails the system crash is louder than ever.

The trouble with apparently fail-safe devices is that they may not be fail-safe under all circumstances. And yet the presence of a fail-safe device has a distorting effect on the visible behaviour of neighbouring components. People get distracted, software errors remain undetected.

In the short term, hero components may be needed to compensate for obvious and widespread weaknesses in a legacy system, and to enable transition and evolution. But long-term reliance on these components may perpetuate subtler weaknesses.

This comment applies both to software devices and to human workers. In the world of software process improvement, immaturity is often associated with excessive dependence on individual acts of heroism.

> "Pity the land that has no heroes."
> "Pity the land that has need of heroes."
>
> Bertold Brecht, Galileo

Invulnerability.

In many cases, people want a component to be robust – steadfast against the fluctuations of the environment, and proof against mischievous or malicious attack or invasion, whether by human agents, remote devices or random noise. Components should tolerate erratic system behaviour. This is an aspect of the **integrity** of the component.

 Q   What mechanisms can be built into a business operation or service to make it proof against fraud?

> **Q** What mechanisms can be built into a software artefact to make it proof against hackers or alien agents?

Testing.

Given our ecosystem model of the component world, two distinct forms of testing are needed. (Similar remarks apply to verification and validation.)

Intra-ecosystem testing.

Testing components and component interactions within one ecosystem.

➢ For example, within the service supply ecosystem, we may test that services satisfy their specifications. We can also test interactions between a bundle of services.

➢ For example, within the device supply ecosystem, we may test conformance of components to various specifications or standards.

Most of the available tools and techniques for testing belong to a single ecosystem.

Inter-ecosystem testing.

Testing components and component interactions across two or more ecosystems.

➢ For example, testing that a device satisfactorily implements an interface.

➢ For example, end-user acceptance testing.

Testing across two or more ecosystems needs a collaboration between multiple roles, where each role represents a given perspective within a given ecosystem.

Components respecting ecological principles.

Availability.

"Goods that are available to us enrich our lives and, if they are technologically available, they do so without imposing burdens on us. Something is available in this sense if it has been rendered instantaneous, ubiquitous, safe, and easy." [Borgmann]

Availability means accessibility, power and choice for the user.

Availability is defined as making things more widely accessible, eliminating the barriers to use. Wherever you want it, whenever you want it. Minimum delay, downtime or difficulty. Safe and cheap. Easy to install and easy to use.

According to the relentless logic of technological development, components should be as available as possible, in order to offer the greatest possible value (utility) to the greatest number of potential users/uses.

The apparent trend of technology is towards a fantasy of "infinite" availability. Table 3.10 compares this fantasy with more realistic goals.

Fantasy goal		Realistic goal
Total satisfaction	*Instant gratification*	More rapid
		Faster response
	Wherever I want it	More widely available
		Distributed, global
		New markets, new customers, new technical platforms
	Whenever I want it	More often available
		24 hours, 7 days, minimum downtime
Total quality	*Zero difficulty*	Easier to use
	Zero defects	Reduced skill barriers, faster to get started
	Zero risk	Improved quality
		Greater reliability, predictability, security, …

Table 3.10 Increasing availability: from fantasy to reality.

Recent technological trends significantly increase the availability of computing power, although they do not (and perhaps never can) live up to the infinite expectations of some of their adherents.

Availability as accessibility and convenience – retail consolidation and "whole product".

One way of making things more available is bringing them under one roof. A department store or superstore is more convenient for shoppers. An e-commerce website takes this principle of convenience further, and should make as many choices available as possible.

How easy is it to find, evaluate and acquire a component? Anything that makes it easier and safer – documentation, demonstration versions, case studies, user or analyst recommendations, quality accreditation, clear price-list – increases the availability of the component. These are aspects of the "whole product".

The concept of "whole product" refers to the integrity of the whole package as bought by the purchaser. The whole product may include training, documentation, and a range of support services. The availability of these ancillary products and services boosts the availability of the main product.

Availability implies certainty.

We looked earlier at the business traveller in a strange hotel. All hotels seem to provide a somewhat different range of services; and even if you've stayed in the hotel before, you may not be certain exactly what you will find in the room, or what you can get from the housekeeper or concierge. Will there be a proper connector for the laptop computer? Will there be a hairdryer or iron? Will there be a decent radio? What do I need to pack, and what can I safely leave at home?

Once I've packed something, then I'm no longer interested in the fact that the hotel could have provided it for me. I may not even discover that it could. Thus if a service is not visible or certain to me in advance (i.e. when I'm packing), it is effectively unavailable to me.

Lots of business travellers have had bad experience with hotel telephones – perhaps technical problems or overcharging or both. When an alternative solution is available – mobile phones with international roaming, direct mobile connection for the laptop – they may just stop using the hotel telephones altogether. Even if the hotel telephone service now becomes much cheaper and more reliable, it may take a long time before these travellers find this out.

 In practice, how would a traveller learn about a hotel service she wasn't using?

Thus the use of a service may be foreclosed by a prior commitment or expectation, which may be based on the information available at some previous point of time. Availability depends on history, not just on the characteristics of a service at the time it might be used.

Availability as power – functionality.

Availability is partly a question of functionality – but only partly.

In support of the functionality argument, Figure 3.4 shows how, in a typical situation, a traditional application package only covers some of the user requirements, whereas a number of fine-grained components may be able to come much closer to covering the whole set of requirements, as represented by the cloud shape.

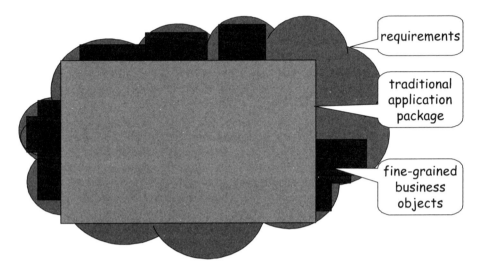

Figure 3.4 How components improve functionality.

Some components try to make themselves useful to everyone by piling on surplus functionality. The trouble with this approach is that the added functionality merely makes the component baroque and complicated.

> Q Can you identify any business services that are baroque and complicated, as a result of trying to please too many people?
>
> Q Can you perhaps think of any well-known software artefacts of which the same is true?

Availability as choice – diversity.

This is related to the concept of **requisite variety**. A component that runs on many different platforms, a component that offers a choice of operating protocols, a component that can handle multiple data formats – these are components whose variety makes them available to a wide range of users/uses.

Identity.

It should be easy to understand what the component actually does. It should perform a clearly identified service.

And where there is a choice of components, these should be easy to compare. Obviously, it makes things simpler if you can compare rival components for the same slot, independently of your choice of components in other slots. (This of course depends on the clarity and integrity of the interfaces, among other things.)

Granularity.

It doesn't matter what the granularity of the component or service is, as long as it makes sense to the user. However, ease of installation and use depends on the granularity of the components you're using.

A healthy component market may be one that offers a good mix of granularities, from small-grained to large-grained. Obviously there may be producers and traders who specialize in a particular level of granularity.

Although perhaps most of the early transactions in the software component market have been in fine-grained components, there will be a trend towards a greater choice of granularity. For some, the transaction costs of buying lots of small components may be greater than the transaction cost of buying a few large components. For others, the reverse will be true. Thus the transaction cost argument works both ways. And in any case, the same user's preference for a given level of granularity may vary according to context. Sometimes you may want to acquire complete subassemblies; sometimes you may want to acquire small units separately.

As consumers, we are often presented with a choice between separate components or integrated solutions.

For example, when buying a home computer, hifi or video or camera equipment. Or when making decisions about personal finance and investment. Some people prefer to buy whole packages of products and services from the same supplier, while others prefer to combine things from different suppliers.

> Q   When else have you been faced with this kind of decision? Do you have a
>   recent example?

How do you choose between separate components and an integrated solution? You might take some of the following factors into consideration:

➢ greater control
➢ reliance on other people's expertise

> ➢ convenience
> ➢ ease of repair and upgrade
> ➢ cost of purchase and repair.

Q Are there any other factors you would consider?

Q Under what circumstances do you prefer separate components? Under what circumstances do you prefer an integrated solution?

Q Now apply this thinking specifically to software. Under what circumstances would you choose an integrated software solution? Under what circumstances would you prefer to procure components separately?

Availability from producer's perspective.

If a component is available to large numbers of consumers, this results in a larger potential market, with fairly obvious advantages for the producers. A producer should aim to make a component useful and usable within (and accessible from) as many use-contexts as possible.

Biodiversity.

To what extent can a single component possess biodiversity? A component may differ significantly from the mainstream, and this often entails additional costs and risks for users, as well as reduced benefits (especially the benefits of connectivity). Why would any user choose to use a non-standard product or service?

For example, in a world where the software mainstream is Microsoft, any non-Microsoft component may be seen as non-standard.

In some cases, the choice is forced by so-called legacy. Perhaps this is the only component that connects to the stuff you've already got. Biodiversity often seems to be backward-looking, the consequence of past decisions and investments; IT managers in particular often see the diversity in their hardware and software inventory as a major problem in its own right.

Where companies have grown by acquisition, the separate parts usually start with diverse components. There is usually a considerable battle after any merger, between the people who want to go on using the components and services they understand and trust, and the people who want to impose common standards across the newly merged company.

In your experience, how long does it take before the last remnants of difference are erased?

Many procurement procedures institutionalize the desire for mainstream, middle-of-the-road products, as a way of achieving a safe, consistent and homogeneous set of systems. Purchase of any non-mainstream component is regarded as a failure of these procedures, attributed either to a misjudgement by the purchaser or a misrepresentation by the vendor.

In 1989, at a conference in East Berlin, I talked with a Russian representative who stated proudly that he had obtained authority to implement a standard operating system across the whole of the Soviet Union – MS-DOS. At this time, users around the world were already abandoning MS-DOS in favour of newer operating systems, such as OS/2 and Microsoft Windows. From a Western perspective, it was difficult to see standardization onto MS-DOS as a step forward.

How does a component benefit ecologically from this? In many cases, the non-standard component will be exposed to extreme pressures from a hostile environment, and will perish. But in some cases, a non-standard component will create an opening for innovation and change, and will find itself taken forward into an entirely new environment. As Kevin Kelly points out, it is often at the margins and fringes that innovation occurs.

Connectivity.

In a connected world, connectivity is clearly an important property. It means that a building block connects with other building blocks, or for that matter with many other copies of itself. The more things it's compatible with, the greater its value.

The fax machine provides a good example: my ancient fax machine can talk to any other fax machine in the world. Even when someone tries to send me a fax using a much faster machine, that machine will automatically reduce its transmission speed so that my slow machine can keep up.

The greater the tolerance to imperfect connections, the greater the connectivity. This is one aspect of a property we are calling character.

Network externalities.

Economists use the term **network externality** to refer to those costs and benefits that depend on the number of other users.

In many cases, the network externalities are negative. The utility of a car is reduced if there are too many other road users; the utility of a holiday may be reduced if there are too many other holiday-makers.

The most common examples of positive network externalities come from communications technology. A phone or fax has no value to you, if you are the only person that has one. The more people that share this technology, the more valuable it becomes.

Similar externalities apply in many other situations. My choice of word processor is influenced by the fact that I want to exchange word-processed documents with my friends and associates. An organization selecting a software development tool is influenced by the number of other organizations using the tool – among other things, they want to know that there will be lots of people in the job market (available as employees) familiar with the tool.

Success breeds success. To him that has, shall be given more. If you have a choice between using the largest e-bookshop in the world, and the second largest, which are you going to choose?

Design for connectivity.

If we are trying to increase the connectivity of a component, and to establish a critical mass (density) of use, the design focuses on the following:

➢ increase information content

➢ look for ways of making component more active, more intelligent

➢ expand connections with other components – networks enlarge small advantages.

Kelly uses the example of a nail. Even a dumb stick of iron can be connected with many different systems, in various ways.

➢ standard contractor size fits into standard air-powered hammers

➢ SKU designation fits into retail sales network

➢ bar code fits into laser-read checkout system

➢ embedded chip warns door of breakage – fits into smart house network.

Standards.

Markets, especially for intangible things like software components, need standards. Standards or standard notations for component description as well as standards for component execution (CORBA or COM).

Standards don't have to be universal. Often there are parallel or rival standards. CORBA and COM. PC and Macintosh and UNIX and UNIX and UNIX.

Within each market sector, if there are rival standards and competing notations, this adds complexity and reduces network externalities. But it doesn't follow that there should only be one standard, even within a single sector of the market, and certainly not across all market sectors. I certainly don't expect components for nuclear power stations to be documented in the same way as components for banking systems. (See also comments on biodiversity above.)

The practical value of a standard depends on one thing alone: the density of the population adhering to the standard. Technical purists may prefer Betamax to VHS, but it was VHS that achieved the critical mass. Microsoft understands this very clearly.

Critical mass.

With a barbecue on a windy day, there is a stage where the matches keep blowing out, and you have to fuss over the charcoal with lighter fluid. Then the barbecue reaches a stage where it is going to stay alight, and you can leave it burning and go get the sausages. The term critical mass refers to the point where a process (like a chemical or nuclear reaction) becomes self-sustaining, generating more energy than it absorbs. In other words, a defined threshold at which there is a qualitative change.

People often refer to critical mass when they are describing or planning the take-up of new technologies. This is particularly relevant with network technologies, such as fax or email, where the value of the technology to one user depends on the number of other users. When plotting the graph of such technologies, there seems to be a point where the usage suddenly goes up exponentially – and this is supposedly where a critical mass is achieved.

There is a danger of confusion here – an exponential curve doesn't have a single point where the growth changes gear, as it were, and if you change the scale of the graph it looks completely different. This is therefore a somewhat inaccurate but understandable use of the term.

Enough is as good as a feast – there may be enough sausages to go round – but that's not a critical mass. At some point in a commercial venture, the managers hope, there will be enough sales to enough customers to cover the fixed costs (the "break-even" point), but that's not a critical mass either. To use the term "critical mass" merely as a synonym for a load is a sign of sloppy thinking. Critical mass is where **quantity** becomes **quality**.

Strictly speaking, critical mass denotes a point where a given **density** of interaction is reached, causing an explosion to occur. Density implies **proximity** of interaction – either physically or via some network. This is a very good way of describing what happens with communication technologies such as phone, fax and email.

Size and survival.

In understanding this ecological principle of critical mass, it's important to distinguish the desirable (perfect) from the essential (good enough).

You may prefer to have a single universal standard. You may prefer to have a single universal platform. You may prefer to have a single search engine that will find every component in the universe, and present its description in a single universal notation.

But when you are operating in a given standard, on a given platform, using a given search engine or notation, what matters is how large and diverse a population this does give you access to. Perhaps there are lots of other components operating in a different standard, on a different platform. But if your search engine already gives you access to more components than you need, you must either decide to forget about the components it isn't giving you access to, or use a second search engine.

Ideally, I might want to be able to converse with everybody in the world. But I'd need to learn thousands of languages, which is impossible, even for the most gifted linguist (which I'm not). Most of us can only manage a few languages, and many people get by with only one. The major world languages have a large population of speakers, providing a critical mass of people, reading material, general opportunities. Minor languages, whatever their cultural importance or poetical wealth, lack this critical mass. This is why people who speak Basque or Finnish or Welsh are under greater pressure to learn other languages than those who speak Castillian or Russian or English.

In a real ecosystem (as opposed to Aesop's fables) the animals concentrate on eating the food that is available to them, and don't waste energy regretting the food that might be found in some other ecosystem. If there isn't enough food, they either migrate or die.

Design for availability.

If we are trying to increase the availability of a component, the design focuses on the following:

➢   Whole product – not just software, but also support, documentation, training and other services.
➢   Consider giving the key components away free – make your money elsewhere.

There are many examples where these tactics have achieved significant market share:

➢   browser wars
➢   search engines
➢   shareware
➢   Linux Apache.

Conservation of energy.

Economies of scale.

People talk a great deal about **software reuse**. The real benefits of software reuse lie in the **economies of scale** of software production and supply.

Lifetime costs.

Unlike simplistic notions of software reuse, the scope of conservation of energy is not just the one-time development of a software solution, but the lifetime costs of managing and evolving the solution. If a software solution goes through many different versions in its lifetime, each version should reuse much of the previous version – the more the better.

Recycling intellectual property.

The principle of **conservation of energy** is much broader than software reuse. We also want to reuse and recycle intellectual property, however it is bundled, as software or otherwise. This includes capitalizing on existing assets, including of course legacy systems.

Recycling, of course, implies movement and use. Conservation certainly doesn't mean hoarding. Competitive advantage doesn't come from possession and preservation of static intellectual property, but from the rapid development and exploitation of new intellectual property.

Supply consolidation.

Organizational economies of scale are also available through the software supply chain, from developers to retailers. Given the transaction costs in the supply chain, this is more likely to involve horizontal integration (for example, retailers offering a broader range of products, developers addressing a broader range of requirements) than vertical integration (one firm covering the whole supply chain).

Design to conserve energy (economies of scale).

If we are trying to exploit economies of scale, the design process focuses on the following:

➢ aggressively exploit and anticipate the learning curve

➢ align to the scale economies of your business / market

➢ repackage and reuse knowledge assets at all levels – working practices, design patterns, templates and software code.

In Chapter 1, we looked at the example of Fairchild Semiconductor, which showed us how an initial economic disadvantage could be converted into a strong economic advantage, thanks to the production economies of scale resulting from what economists call **learning by doing**.

Firmness.

Firmness means: reliability, performance, integrity and other technical aspects of the quality of service. This is also one aspect of a property we are calling Character.

Some components are easier to trust to maintain a service than others.

For users, the internal integrity of a component affects its **consistency** or firmness.

Consistency relates to a number of aspects of software product quality, including reliability and usability.

Assurance.

Who can tell me that the component will do what I want it to, in my own environment? What guarantees do I have? If other people have tested or inspected the component, how relevant is this to me?

Performance.

How can I get satisfactory performance from an assembly of components? If I buy your component, what performance will I get from the system as a whole?

Reliability.

When components fail, do they fail cleanly, or do they cause secondary problems?

Feature interaction.

Does each component continue to provide the specified service, regardless of unforeseen interactions with other components?

Apple Mac – common look and feel.

As noted earlier, one of the factors that led to the success of the Apple Macintosh was the common "look and feel" across all the applications.

This was achieved by a small group of Macintosh champions – people employed by Apple to put pressure on independent software developers, to conform to the Macintosh style.

Although Macintosh supporters may still claim that the usability of Apple remains superior to the usability of Windows, the usability gap has certainly narrowed significantly. Microsoft has now developed Windows to the point where any remaining technical advantage to Apple has become marginal, at least from a commercial point of view, although perhaps still emotionally and symbolically important to many people. Furthermore, many widely used applications are available in both Macintosh and Windows versions, with much the same look and feel, and this further erodes the technical differences.

Flexibility.

We've looked at flexibility from a solution point of view. And we've looked at connectivity from an ecological point of view. Connectivity also implies Disconnectivity. In other words, you should be able to unplug, perhaps as easily as you can plug.

From an ecological point of view, the important question now is: how do the flexibility characteristics of plug-and-play and substitution affect the survival chances of a component?

If a given component can be easily unplugged, this might be seen as an advantage, because users may be more willing to plug in components if they perceive that they can unplug them later.

Even if a substitute component doesn't exist today, if the component has clarity, this makes it easier for a future component to be developed with exactly the same interface.

> Q What are the factors that affect the development of substitute components?

This is certainly an advantage for a component kit or tribe, but is it an advantage to a single component?

Adaptation and adaptability..

Something survives if two conditions are met:

➢ it fits its environment, both in absolute terms and relative to any competitors (adaptation);

➤ and it continues to fit as the environment changes (adaptability).

There is an important trade-off here between these two conditions. Adaptation is focused on a secure and efficient position in a fixed ecological niche – in other words, an unchanging identity. But if the environment changes, it will sometimes be the entity that is best fitted to the old environment that has the greatest difficulty adapting to the new environment.

Disconnection and dismemberment.

The dismemberment of Microsoft is currently on the US Government agenda. It is highly debatable whether (and how quickly) a well-connected company can be prevented from coordinating its activities, even when formally divided into two or more legal entities.

With business relationships, it may be important to compare the cost of remaining in a non-ideal relationship with the cost of exit – for both sides.

Avoid integration.

If you want to be able to disconnect, maybe the answer is not to connect in the first place. Once upon a time, there was a large UK company with a French subsidiary. The IT department proposed a project to merge the French computer systems with the UK systems, which would yield economies of scale in IT provision. This proposal was resisted by management – the reason for this resistance became clear when the French subsidiary was sold.

 If the computer systems had been merged, how might this have complicated the sale of the French subsidiary?

Design for flexibility.

If we are trying to increase flexibility, the design focuses on the following:

➤ distribute intelligence
➤ don't just support the execution of transactions, support the design of transactions as well
➤ automate or animate change
➤ zero latency
➤ the weaker the interface specification, the more things will fit.

Pleasure.

The pleasure principle was first identified by Freud as a homeostatic principle: keeping tension and stress to a minimum. "The function of the pleasure principle is to make man always search for what he has to find again, but which he will never attain." [Lacan, Seminar VII]

Satisfaction, delight, excitement.

Without some degree of excitement and novelty, a solution is dull and boring. But too much excitement and novelty is experienced as pain or risk. Obviously different users in different contexts have different thresholds of pleasure and pain.

Design for pleasure.

If we are trying to increase the potential for pleasure, the design focuses on the following:

➢ reduce tension and stress (where this may be a result of excess choice or excess attention)
➢ support self-preservation
➢ engage users.

Successful design involves a balance of contradictory forces:

➢ change against nochange
➢ evolutionary (small change) against revolutionary (large change)
➢ attention against inattention
➢ risk against reward.

There are several examples of small changes that turned out to have revolutionary potential:

➢ email as substitute for office memos
➢ Amazon.com as substitute for traditional bookshop.

Components possessing character.

Clarity.

Clarity means that a component is easily identifiable. This is an aspect of **availability** that we've already looked at. Clarity also contributes to substitutability, which we've looked at as an aspect of flexibility. It should also be honest about its **bearing limit** – its ability to contain problems, regardless whether these are generated by itself or by other components or by interaction between components.

Correctness.

A correct component does what it's supposed to do. From a technical point of view, this means conforming to its specification – we've already looked at this within the technical context.

But correctness means a lot more than technical correctness. It includes conforming to social and business norms. It includes compliance with legal and regulatory constraints, and to customer expectations. (Exceeding customer expectations is an entirely different matter – we've already looked at this under the heading of Pleasure.)

Some business services steer fairly close to the wire in terms of conforming to regulations. For example, a marketing service may abuse a list of customers, come close to prosecution under data protection legislation, and only escape through a legal technicality or loophole. If there are components or services that regularly abuse the spirit of regulations, then we might expect the regulations to be changed to remove the loophole. This may kill the component in that form, although it may survive by mutating into something else.

Engagement.

A building block has engagement to the extent that it responds to the context or situation. On the supply side, there is considerable ambivalence about engagement, because it is often perceived to interfere with the conservation of energy.

Domain specificity.

Even in software, whose professionals claim to be comfortable with high levels of abstraction and generalization, there is some evidence that domain-specific software components achieve higher levels of reuse than over-generalized ones. (This has been explored by Biggerstaff.)

With business components, this phenomenon is much more evident.

Customization.

Engagement relates to customization. What does this component have to offer me in particular?

Engagement includes the ability to satisfy unexpected requirements.

It is a rainy night. Jan is driving home, turns a corner, and finds the road flooded. The car has been designed and tested for a range of driving conditions, but can it drive through shallow water? There is no reference in the driver's manual to floodwater.

Jan actually has two requirements:

i.   For a vehicle that can get them safely through the water hazard;

ii. For information as to whether (and with what modifications) the actual car is capable of satisfying the first requirement.

Note the following points:

Jan does not want to be stranded in the middle of the floodwater, and will not attempt to drive through it unless confident of getting through safely. Therefore, requirement (i) is not satisfied unless requirement (ii) is also satisfied.

Would an inability to drive through floodwater count as poor quality? Jan's requirements were not stated when buying the car.

Jan's two requirements are interdependent. As we have indicated in Chapter 2, quality evaluation applies properly to whole systems, not to subsystems. In this instance, it must apply to the car and the driver's manual together, not one independently of the other.

 Think of some situations where this notion of quality would be relevant to software components.

Standing out.

A building block stands out to the extent that it demands attention.

Attention.

The only factor becoming scarce in a world of abundance is attention. (Kelly attributes this thought to Herbert Simon.)

Some suppliers may interpret this as a need for promotion and publicity: brand image management, advertising, public relations. On the supply side, attention would seem to be a good thing.

On the demand side, there is considerable ambivalence about components that demand attention. After all, attention is a scarce resource.

We've probably all seen the **intel inside** stickers on the outside of computers. Some analysts even question the commercial value of this campaign to Intel. But just imagine if all the other suppliers of all the other components – hardware and software – wanted to put a sticker on the outside of your computer. You wouldn't be able to see the screen!

Some people think that the whole point of a component is that it should be invisible most of the time. You probably don't have a sticker on your car, telling you what is the brand of spark plugs in the engine. Indeed, the spark plug manufacturer may not care whether you've even heard of him. The only attention he wants is that of the engine designer, and possibly the engine repairer.

Visibility.

As users, there are some services that we use so frequently we hardly notice unless they're not there. There are other services that we might only need once in a lifetime – for example, medical treatment that we hope we'll never need, and prefer not to think about in the meantime.

But visibility is deeper than merely awareness of the existence of the component. Visibility means that the user can see beyond the component-as-device or faceless service, and can engage in turn with the whole system of which this component is merely a representative.

Wholeness and integrity.

Component as system – system as component.

Each building block can be regarded as a whole system. Conversely, each system may be regarded as a building block of something larger.

 Q   Of what systems can a car be regarded as a component?

Christopher Alexander has proposed an evolutionary process for creating wholesome systems, based on the development of integrity at all levels. He says "wholeness" instead of "integrity", but it's the same property. So he says that each project should create wholeness at one level, and contribute to wholeness at a higher level.

We'll return to the management of this process in Chapter 5.

Recap.

If we're going to work with building blocks, we need some basis for making judgements about them: what makes a good component?

° The designer's judgement is separate from, but should be connected to, the user's judgement.

° We can identify four different contexts (which we call ecosystems) which components occupy.

° Different ecological principles reign in each ecosystem.

° A good component is one that satisfies the ecological principles of all four ecosystems.

° When designing a component, a designer should consider the viability of the component in all four ecosystems, and in terms of all seven ecological principles.

° The dominant players in the component marketplace will be those that can straddle multiple ecosystems.

In this chapter, we've gone through four ways of thinking about components and their design. We've discussed components according to the conventional manner of speaking, as if they were objects. We've mentioned in passing some alternative notions of components: component as declaration or speech act, component as bundle of associations.

The traditional ways of thinking focus either on the role of the component within a specific solution or class of solutions, or on the technical elegance of the component. We have looked at two alternative ways of thinking, in terms of ecological success and character, and shown how these add to our understanding of the quality of a component. This enriches and enhances the judgements about components made by designers and others.

We've argued that components may possess something called character, and that this property often appears to be relevant to the success and survival of the component, as well as to the character of the larger systems in which the component plays.

This thinking can be applied to various types of object. Software engineers will want to apply the principles of this chapter to the design and evaluation of software components, business managers will apply it to the definition and construction of business services.

One of the most important domains of component thinking is change itself. When a manager, consultant or other change agent tries to engage with complex systems, each intervention needs to be designed and evaluated according to similar principles to the ones outlined in this chapter: does it contribute usefully to a solution, is it technically elegant, is it likely to be successful within the larger ecosystem, does it possess clarity and integrity? We shall return to this in Chapter 5.

4. Interfaces with Intelligence: Managing the Connections Between Building Blocks

To the extent that the components of business are off-the-shelf services, then the business attention switches to the configuration of the business process. If we are going to talk about components, whatever they are, we've also got to talk about the relationships and interactions and collaborations and connections between components, the "glue" or "wiring". In plugging together a component-based business, we need to pay attention to the interfaces between the business components – in other words, the business relationships.

Interfaces are not just a matter of technical fit, they may be where most of the crucial action is. Business interfaces are where competitive advantage lies, where deals are made, where aggression or authenticity may be mobilized. Brand management, customer relationship management – these are the battlefields where competition is won and lost.

Componentry exposes some of the key strategic issues: where is business attention and innovation focused, how can we promote flexibility and trust, what relationships or collaborations with whom?

As we indicated in Chapter 2, intelligence and character of systems depends at least as much on the wiring and configuration of the components, the spaces between the components, as on the components themselves. In this chapter, we turn our attention to the properties of the interfaces between components.

A simple perspective on interfaces considers it as something located between two components or subsystems – or perhaps between two classes. As such, there are several properties of the interface that may be meaningful or relevant for various purposes. For example, interfaces may be loosely coupled or "uptight". Both styles of interface contribute to whole-system phenomena. It's therefore tempting to regard the interface as a subsystem in its own right, and to attribute whole-system properties to specific interfaces. For example, trust is an essential lubricant of business relationships, and exists metaphorically in relationships between technical artefacts as well.

But trust is itself an emergent property of the whole system, and we can be serious misled if we try to locate trust (or mistrust) in one place. It is often useful therefore to take a broader perspective on the interface, viewing it instead as a whole collaboration, perhaps with several other participants or interested parties.

How do we make judgements about the connections between components?

In the previous chapter, we established a context for making judgements about separate components. In this chapter, we're going to look at judgements about the connections and interfaces between components.

Interfaces connect and separate components or subsystems.

Before looking at interfaces in detail, let's start with some motivational stuff – what's important and interesting about interfaces, therefore what types of interfaces and aspects of interfaces do we need to understand and manage?

In Chapter 2, we defined articulation as connection and separation. The things that connect and separate components are called **interfaces**. If we are going to engage in "joined-up thinking" about component-based business, we obviously need to pay attention to the interfaces between the components. Where the systems span organizational boundaries, these interfaces imply the existence of formal or informal business relationships, which may be governed by a legal contract and/or by some external regulatory process.

Where systems span different human cultures or technological platforms, or when the English language crosses the Atlantic Ocean, some form of translation may be required. Often the translation that is required within a single organization – for example between Marketing and Production, or between IT and everybody else – is just as tricky as that required for communications between separate companies, or between companies and individuals.

 What misunderstandings and communication slips have you experienced in business organizations? Do you think that external communications are more or less prone to error than internal communications?

Interfaces are where things fit together – or fail to fit.

If we're interested in the notion of plug-and-play, then the interfaces are the plug points. Let's look at some extreme examples of this.

If you're in a hotel room with a laptop computer and modem, what's the likelihood that you can plug your modem into the hotel telephone? Firstly, there's the challenge of making the physical connection. Perhaps the hotel provides a simple and clearly labelled socket, or perhaps you have to crawl under the bed to unplug the telephone. If you're in a foreign country, the sockets might be a different shape to those at home – experienced travellers often carry a large collection of adapters. In extreme cases, people have been known to take a screwdriver to the telephone set itself. But that only gets you to first base. Then you have to align your computer's settings with the expectations of the hotel network, and of the public telephone system beyond. Having done that, there might be so much noise on the line that you cannot maintain a connection more than a minute or so.

So the initial question – whether my computer will plug into the hotel telephone system – doesn't have a simple yes/no answer. Instead, we can identify a spectrum of difficulty, with a potentially large set of additional devices and actions that might be required to effect the connection. And the quality of service obtained over this connection may also be variable.

The initial question is apparently a technical one, but of course there's a human context. Can I personally tolerate the difficulty of making the connection, or the unreliability of the connection itself? That may depend on the amount of time I have to fiddle with the settings, the importance and urgency of making the connection, and how I intend to use the connection once I've made it.

This shifts the analysis onto an entirely different interface: between me and my intentions on the one side, and the computer–telephone connection on the other side. If I have a pressing need to transmit a large file over the Internet, then I cannot bear a complicated and unreliable connection. The more time and energy I have to spend on the technical connection, the less time and energy remains for me to check the content of the file. On one occasion, I might be willing to fiddle with it for hours; on another occasion, I might abandon the attempt altogether and plug myself into the hotel bar system instead.

 What other interfaces might be relevant here?

(Ironically, as we saw in Chapter 3, just as business hotels were getting to the point where they recognized such requirements and started to provide seriously for them, businessmen were increasingly recognizing that it was simpler and cheaper to use their own mobile telephone for such purposes.)

We might suppose that, given enough time and effort, and with access to appropriate bridging technologies (including adaptation techniques and devices), any two systems or organizations can be force-fitted together, not just to achieve a physical connection at the lowest level, but to achieve a fully operational working-together. However, there are many situations where such bridging is painful, impractical or otherwise inappropriate. Some years ago, a highly publicized merger between two financial institutions was called off, apparently because it would have proved too difficult to merge their computer systems – and this has undoubtedly happened in many other situations. Of course, computer system incompatibility may simply be an excuse for (and symptom of) some deeper cultural or political incompatibility. If in doubt, blame the technology.

Engineers sometimes refer to the difficulty of bridging as **impedance mismatch**. This difficulty is an emergent property of the attempted whole system, and cannot always be foreseen.

> Q Do you agree that any two systems or organizations could in principle be connected at the required level? If not, give examples of two systems or organizations that could never be connected.

> Q Under what circumstances would it be inadvisable to attempt to connect two systems or organizations? Have you experienced any situations where such an attempt failed or was abandoned? Do you know of any situations where such an attempt succeeded against a background of pessimistic or sceptical voices?

Like an unhappy marriage, a forced interface is likely to be unstable or brittle, and to drain resources from the system as a whole. But there are often other factors in play; beware quick judgements.

> Q One large software development project deployed more people to build the "interfaces" to corporate legacy systems than to build the "new" system. What's going on here?

What judgements do we want to make?

There are a number of different types of judgement that may be required, as shown in Table 4.1.

Where	Where do we want to draw interfaces? What is the division of roles and responsibilities?
With whom	Selection of partners.
What	Specification of services to be provided.
How	Maintaining healthy interfaces: ○ negotiation and trust ○ monitoring and control ○ flexibility and substitution
When	When to make each judgement, in what sequence? ○ Commitment ("Much Binding") versus Openness ("Late Binding")

Table 4.1: Types of judgement about interfaces.

There is also an question of ownership: who is in a position to make these judgements, for whom?

What is the basis for making such judgements?

There are several techniques available to support such judgements.

Responsibility Modelling	This represents the responsibilities associated with each agent or agency within a complex network structure. This technique is used in a number of methods, including Ordit and Scipio.
Collaboration Modelling	A form of collaboration modelling emerged from the Object Oriented Software community, and a technically oriented version was included in the so-called Universal Modelling Language (UML). A more abstract form of collaboration modelling can be found in the Catalysis method.
Interaction Stamps	An interaction stamp is a form of **business pattern**, which represents the structure of an interaction.

Table 4.2: Techniques to support judgements about interfaces.

How do we understand interfaces?

What is an interface? (From what stuff is an interface composed?)

So far in this chapter, I've been talking about interfaces as if we all knew what they were. Perhaps the time has come to define the notion (or notions) of interface more carefully.

There are three basic notions of interface.

It is a common pattern of technical materials, to provide a definition of a notion taken from a well-known dictionary, as if a technically adequate definition could be produced by refinement from the everyday usage of the word. If you go to the dictionary expecting to find a clear and simple definition of a complex notion, you will usually be disappointed. But if you go prepared to find several diverse definitions, you will usually be rewarded.

The *Oxford English Dictionary* offers three different notions of interface. It is not obvious at first reading whether these three notions can be combined into a single complex notion, or whether it would even make sense to try.

➢ An interface may be a surface or boundary between two portions of matter – a spatial separation.

➢ An interface may be a meeting point between two systems – a bundle of interactions, liaison or dialogue.

➢ An interface may be a device connecting two or more other devices.

These three definitions represent three different perspectives on interfaces. Each of these perspectives is useful; during this chapter, I shall deploy all three as appropriate.

Interfaces have various properties.

To illustrate the usefulness of the three perspectives, let's look briefly at the different properties we might want to ascribe to an interface.

For example, when we talk about the **alignment** across an interface, this seems to make sense if we're thinking of an interface as some kind of boundary. Two pieces of a jigsaw puzzle fit together if their shapes and markings are aligned.

 In easy puzzles, the markings continue from one piece to the next. Difficult puzzles are designed with discontinuous or misleading markings, so there is less redundant information. What lessons can we draw from this analogy for business or software components?

On the other hand, when we talk about the **flexibility** or **bandwidth** of an interface, this seems to make more sense if we think of an interface as a bundle of interactions, or as a device.

At some times we want to talk about the structural properties of interfaces, while at other times we want to talk about their dynamic properties. A traditional jigsaw puzzle has a fixed structure, and so the alignment between the pieces is a fixed structural relationship. But elsewhere, as for example in the relationship between business and IT, alignment is not fixed at all. Instead, we need to regard alignment as an ongoing process, maintaining some relationship between two separately evolving systems.

There is some danger of confusion here. Feedback is often proposed or assumed, as a mechanism for maintaining alignment between two separately evolving systems. But it's important to separate the alignment itself (whether regarded as a state, or as an ongoing co-evolution process) from the mechanisms that achieve this state, or support this process.

 When you see two systems that are well aligned, can you always infer that there is a direct feedback loop connecting these two systems?

Q When you see two systems that are not well aligned, can you always infer that the information flows connecting these two systems are inadequate?

When I'm working as a consultant to large organizations, I am often faced with strong evidence of misalignment between two parts or aspects of the client organization. But I have to be careful not to jump to conclusions about the underlying causes of this misalignment, or to the appropriate intervention. For a start, the two misaligned systems are always part of at least one larger system, and the misalignment may be a symptom of something much wider or deeper. Furthermore, my perception of misalignment is my own judgement, from my own view of a wider system, and this view may or may not be shared by other stakeholders. What I see as severe misalignment may be perfectly acceptable, or even desirable, from some other points of view.

 What examples can you think of?

There are many different metaphors for interfaces.

Let's see if we can extend and enrich the three simple notions of interface by looking at some common metaphors:

➢ skin, wall or membrane

➢ surface of pond

➢ doorway or gateway

➢ keyboard or screen.

When we think about interfaces, or try to describe their properties, we usually prefer to think in terms of something simple, tangible and visible. We then hope that we can apply the same thinking to more abstract or complicated interfaces.

One way of thinking about interfaces is as a boundary, as a **skin** protecting and containing a body, or as a cell **wall** protecting and containing a cell. There is something slightly paradoxical (or at least ambiguous) about this concept of boundary. The boundary is itself part of the system being bounded, and is continuous with it. The skin is part of the body, and is itself composed of cells. The cell wall both encloses the cell and mediates between the cell and its environment. Although the cell takes energy from its environment, it is in some senses closed, and maintains the closure of the body.

One of the prime concerns of any living body is to control the flow of fluids in and out. In a commercial enterprise, the first level of control is a financial one. So let us think of benefits, costs and risks as being fluid. Unless properly contained, revenues may leak out of an enterprise, and excess costs and risks may leak in.

So what is the business equivalent of the cell membranes that prevent the body from drying up or bursting? The structure and viability of the enterprise are maintained by its interfaces: the commercial contracts and intra-organizational agreements that regulate the inward and outward flow of benefits, costs and risks.

Classical organization theory defines the boundary of an organization in terms of import and export. The organization is a sociotechnical system, taking in resources of various kinds (including information) and producing goods and services. The boundary is the "interface" between the organization and its environment.

One of the functions of such a boundary is that it acts as a kind of semi-permeable membrane, protecting the organization from much of the uncertainty in the environment. Managers coordinate and control what goes on inside the boundary, without responding to every little fluctuation outside. Without such a boundary, activities inside the organization would be wholly unpredictable and unorganized – in other words, there would be no organization.

If we think of an interface as a semi-permeable membrane, there are other possible examples. Whereas the skin serves a biological function for the animal, the surface of a pond serves an ecological function for the pondlife. Here, the interface is a barrier, separating two ecologies. Some things can cross the boundary, other things cannot.

Note that whereas the skin "belongs" to the animal, it doesn't seem so easy to say that the surface of the pond "belongs" to the pond. (From within the pond, it might make equal sense to say that the surface "belongs" to the air above.)

Even those animals (such as frogs) that are equally happy on either side of the pond surface must change their configuration or their behaviour when they are under water. (Among other things, they have to hold their breath. They use different ways of moving around. There are different things to eat, different dangers.)

For these animals, therefore, the pond surface represents a point of transition between two worlds, a kind of **doorway** or **gateway**. An interface is a set of transition or meeting points. In management theory, the control of gateways is seen both as an important management role (the gatekeeper), and an important source of power.

 In your organization, or in organizations you have known, who is the "gatekeeper" for the business–IT interface? How is this gateway controlled, and what are the consequences (for good or ill)?

There are some important design rules or patterns for doorways, which may apply to the design of a wide variety of interfaces.

1 The entrance of a building should be clearly visible as you approach the building. The access to (or egress from) an organization or a system should be equally clear: there shouldn't be any difficulty finding the gate (and the gatekeeper).

(Note: some idealists believe that there should be no gates and gatekeepers at all. In the real world, people often take advantage of the lack of formal gatekeepers, and seize informal control of these transition points themselves. These self-appointed gatekeepers can sometimes be more difficult to deal with than official ones would be. To design genuinely gateless organizations requires radical and complex intervention; if you simply dis-appoint the existing gatekeepers and hope for the best, this is unlikely to be enough.)

2 There should be a symbolic transition to match the physical transition. This allows (or reminds) people to shift their behaviour patterns or expectations as they cross the boundary.

(Note: there are many software designers who appear to believe that, because an interface ought to be seamless, therefore there should be no visible sign that you are crossing a boundary, and no clue about where you are. They are like the office designers who think that all corridors should look the same.)

Table 4.3: Design guidelines for interfaces.

Q Can you think of information systems that conform to this pattern? Have you experience of information systems where the transitions from one subsystem to another are abrupt?

Q What are the implications for website design, particularly for e-commerce?

Technically oriented readers may be impatient for some technological interfaces.

A computer **keyboard** translates key presses into binary characters. This may be a good way of starting to think about interfaces as devices that translate messages from one "language" into another "language".

Similarly, a piano keyboard translates key presses into notes. If you take the front panel off a piano, you will see that there are several intermediate (mechanical or electronic) translations between the pianist's fingers and the sounding of the note.

When we characterize the interface in terms of the keyboard alone, we are using a form of metaphor (or, more precisely, metonymy) known as synecdoche: the part represents the whole.

Is keyboard an input device or an output device? It is tempting to regard it as an input device – because the device paradigm focuses one's attention on the machine that is receiving the messages rather than on the human system that is generating them.

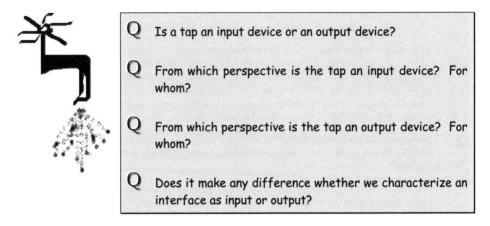

Q   Is a tap an input device or an output device?

Q   From which perspective is the tap an input device? For whom?

Q   From which perspective is the tap an output device? For whom?

Q   Does it make any difference whether we characterize an interface as input or output?

From a keyboard, we might go on to think about a **screen**, onto which messages are projected. A screen filters and distorts as well as displays. When the word "screen" is used as a verb, it usually implies hiding information, or displaying carefully selected portions. This is as true of computer screens as of television screens.

The computer offers information as services through a screen. The screen is both literal and metaphorical. It is a surface on which the data are presented, and also a filter that controls what the user sees.

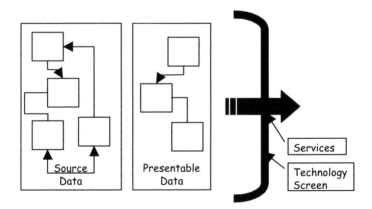

Figure 4.1: The Screen.

As with any technology, a computerized information system alters what is visible (which objects attract your attention) and what is invisible (which objects are taken for granted).

The first (obvious) level at which this is apparent is in the distinction between source data and presentable data. (If the source data are known as raw data, then it seems logical to refer to the presentable data as "cooked" data.) Lots of MIS processing is devoted to converting source data into a form that MIS professionals deem more meaningful (and therefore presentable) to "users". Among other things, this typically involves:

➢ filtering out bad (i.e. erroneous or incomplete) data

➢ use of simple statistics to reduce the volume of data (especially subtotals, averages and ratios)

➢ conversion of data to a single homogeneous format, supposedly to aid comparison between data.

But this distinction is relatively open. MIS professionals appeal to the concept of **drill-down**, whereby users are able to retrieve the raw data on demand. This apparent openness further obscures more subtle invisibilities.

Finally, let's think about the "skin" around components. This is sometimes called **encapsulation** and is usually assumed to represent a hard and opaque boundary, rendering the internal structure invisible and inaccessible from the outside. But it may be more accurate to characterize the skin of a component as offering varying levels of visibility and access to different people in different roles. The same is true of human skin, which provides some degree of protection from airborne germs, but is no match for an insect's bite, or a hypodermic needle.

In a given situation, there may be multiple interfaces, of different types.

Let's explore the human skin analogy further. Imagine a cosmetic product, such as soap or deodorant, that causes skin problems – or worse. (Some cosmetic products have been speculatively linked to breast cancer and Alzheimer's Disease.)

How do you protect yourself against the possible dangers of a cosmetic product? You might monitor the reaction of your skin to different products. You might want to inform yourself about potentially dangerous chemicals, and avoid products containing these chemicals. We can regard this set of protective measures as a kind of information system. This system provides a virtual membrane around your body, providing you with a secondary protection. It is therefore another interface.

> What does this information system need, in order to protect you effectively against dangerous products? What public services does it draw upon?

In order for you to be able to protect yourself in this way, you need some assurance that product labelling is adequate and accurate. You might expect Government agencies to collect relevant information, to demand reassurance from suppliers, to commission independent tests where necessary, and to ban the manufacture, import and sale of dangerous products. This public information system provides yet another protective membrane around your body – another interface again.

Some consumers will be content with the assurances of retailers, suppliers and Government agencies, while other consumers will want the additional protection of a personal information system.

> Q How does a personal information system provide additional protection? Does it reduce risk? At what cost?
>
> Q In what circumstances are you content with standard public protection mechanisms, and in what circumstances do you try to supplement these mechanisms by obtaining (and processing) extra information? What prompts you to do the latter?

The important point here is that there are other important interfaces besides the obvious one. And there are important choices to be made, which affect cost and risk for each stakeholder.

Let's retrace our steps further. How did we get into this complication, where we seem to need multiple layers of protection against the potentially evil effects of deodorant? After all, the purpose of deodorant is to interfere with the normal functioning of the skin, and to enhance one's social relationships. The deodorant is therefore itself yet another interface.

This illustrates another important point: interfaces proliferate. Every time you install an interface, you find you need several more. This is something like a marriage: you may enter into a relationship with one person, and find you've acquired a series of relationships with a set of in-laws. Some of these relationships will be visible from the start (like mothers-in-law), some of them will become visible later (like brothers-in-law), and some of them may remain concealed until you make special efforts to reveal them.

Some people might draw the conclusion that the simple life means as few interfaces as possible: the life of a hermit. This may indeed be true, but needs to be balanced against the principle of connectivity discussed in Chapter 3. Hermits don't always live longer.

What form (shape) does an interface take?

An interface may be binary or n-ary.

Most simple examples of interfaces involve two sides or parties. These are called **two-way** or **binary** interfaces. Interfaces involving more than two sides are called **multiple** or **n-ary**.

Binary interfaces are considered easier to design and manage than n-ary. Many experts claim that all three-way or four-way interfaces can (and should) be decomposed into a set of binary interfaces. However, there are many cases where such decomposition seems impossible, inappropriate or premature.

Let's look at an example: direct debit payment. This is a fairly standard pattern of payment for consumption of services such as electricity, gas and telecoms. Among other things, this pattern allows for regular payments (monthly or quarterly, say), with a variable payment amount depending on the quantity of service consumed.

The consumer signs a direct debit mandate or agreement, which authorizes these transactions. Who are the parties to this direct debit agreement? At first sight, this appears to be an instruction by the consumer to his/her bank. In practice, the direct debit is administered by the utility company, in collaboration with its bank. Interactions between banks are mediated via a clearing system – in the UK the clearing system is known as BACS. Thus there are at least five parties to the direct debit. This is shown in Figure 4.2.

Although this picture apparently shows several binary interfaces, such as that between the utility company and its bank, these may not be visible from, say, the perspective of the consumer. And even though the consumer apparently has a separate relationship with his own bank and with the utility company, these relationships are closely related for many purposes.

From the perspective of the consumer, then, a single direct debit mandate can be regarded as a three-way relationship, involving three roles: payer, payee and bank. The consumer plays the payer role, while the utility company plays the payee role. This perspective is shown in Figure 4.3. I instruct my bank to pay my gas bill on direct debit. I send this instruction, not directly to the bank, but to the gas supply company. I don't actually know what happens to this piece of paper, or the information it contains. Perhaps the gas company passes it onto the bank straightaway; perhaps it is kept until there is a dispute. (Even on occasions that I have disputed direct debit charges, this detail has not been visible to me.)

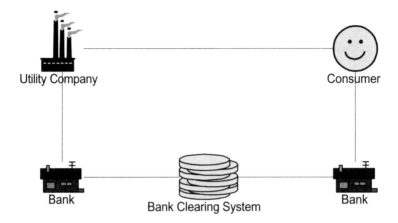

Figure 4.2: Direct Debit – Bank's Perspective.

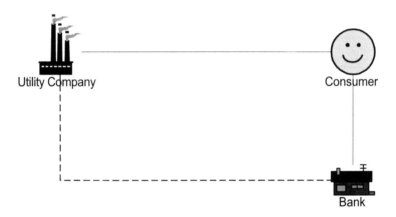

Figure 4.3: Direct Debit – Consumer's Perspective.

Let us suppose I wish to write a computer system to handle my domestic accounts. One of my requirements is to check the consistency between the gas bill and my bank statement. I specify this requirement by reference to the rules governing the three-way interaction known as direct debit.

The reason I cannot decompose this into two-way interactions is because I do not know or care the nature of the (indirect) interaction between the gas supply company and my bank. I'm not interested in knowing which bank the gas supply company holds its accounts with. I'm not interested in the details of the clearing system. All of this is irrelevant to me. As I consumer, all I need to know is the aggregate outcome of this collaboration as it affects me – for example, the time to clear payments.

> What would I need to know about the (indirect) interaction between the utility company and my bank, before I could accurately decompose this three-way interaction into two-way interactions?

Although an omniscient requirements engineer might be in a position to work out the full interaction between all the parties, this is not necessary or relevant to solving my problem. In more complex cases, it may be impossible for anyone to have the complete picture. Of course, two-way interactions are easier to implement than three-way interactions, for a variety of reasons. But that isn't a good enough reason to force all interactions to be expressed as two-way interactions at the requirements stage.

My position here is based on three key methodological principles:

➤ I want to be able to express requirements based on partial information, or based on a particular user viewpoint. And I want to be able to test particular solutions against such requirements. I don't want a method that assumes I've got a complete picture of a closed system.

➤ I want a notation that is as permissive as possible. I may then want to provide design guidelines warning designers that the full complexity and power of the notation is not currently supported by available tools and techniques. I don't want a notation that is unduly limited by current tools and techniques.

➤ There are often several different ways of decomposing a three-way interaction into a set of two-way interactions. I see this as a design choice – several solutions to the same business requirement. Although I recognize that I cannot eliminate all design choices from the statement of requirements, I don't want to have more than I can help.

Thus my answer to the experts who urge me to decompose three-way interactions into two-way interactions is that I don't want a requirements or design method that forces me to do this. What I might be willing to accept is a design method that helps me to implement such structures by converting them into more manageable structures, at the appropriate stage of the design process.

An interface or collaboration may be actively managed by one party or all.

Different stakeholders may have different degrees of power, proximity and interest over the interface itself. The interface may be invisible to some stakeholders, and differently perceived by others.

We can describe or compare interfaces in various ways. Some of these qualities could be expressed in the form of metrics.

In 1967, in an early use of the word "interface", the **Economist** indicated a way to measure the size of interfaces. . "The North Sea and Channel ports form the biggest frontiers in world trade–or the biggest interface, in the language of the modern transport man, meaning the place where the greatest quantity of international cargo changes its mode of transport."

An interface may be strongly or loosely coupled. People talk about the bandwidth of an interface, or the interaction distance. Interfaces may be broad or strong.

There is a set of related concepts describing interfaces, including: alignment, matching, fit and tolerance. We commonly talk as if we could at least recognize greater and lesser degrees of these qualities. It is also possible to talk about good-enough degrees of these qualities. Any notion of adequacy or satisficing must, of course, be linked to a firm notion of stakeholder and intentions: adequate for whom, adequate for what purpose.

These qualities typically change over time. Things get out of alignment, sometimes by spontaneous mutation, or as an unintended side effect of some other action.

An interface represents a step function in proximity and interest.

We can usually identify a different set of concerns, operating principles and other factors on each side of the boundary. We can sometimes identify a different way of looking at the world on each side of the boundary. This is sometimes reflected in a different language (or use of language).

Interfaces can be found or perceived in all types of sociotechnical systems.

Use of the term "interface" emerged simultaneously for describing social systems and technical systems. The first modern usage of the word in the *Oxford English Dictionary* is taken from McLuhan's *Gutenberg Galaxy*, where he describes the Renaissance as the interface between mediaeval and modern. (This interface is also crucially important in Umberto Eco's novel *Name of the Rose*.)

We often describe sociotechnical systems as if they had clearly articulated interfaces. Perhaps sometimes they really do. An interface may reflect a logical separation of concerns that is projected onto an organization or tribal split, or vice versa. Interfaces are therefore constructed entities, with a complex relationship to "reality". Just like the systems themselves, in fact.

Systems change at interfaces.

Changes in systems usually involve the interfaces between the systems. If the interfaces are flexible, it may be possible for some kinds of change to take place simply by flexing the interfaces, without any changes to the components themselves. (This applies to all sorts of change, from explicitly managed change to undirected drift.) On the other hand, some kinds of change may be impossible without re-engineering the interfaces – the resistance or inertia in the system appears to be located in the interfaces, rather than in the components themselves.

Managers and engineers usually want to build systems that are reasonably stable, resilient against certain forms of unwanted change or drift. At the same time, managers and engineers want to build systems that are flexible in certain respects, and will accommodate future demands, whatever they might be. Of course, there is some conflict between these design aims, but that's nothing new: all design is about finding a good trade-off between conflicting requirements and objectives. The important point here is that these people are unlikely to achieve any of their design intentions in regard to stability and flexibility without paying attention to the structure and dynamics of the interfaces.

Interfaces can sometimes last longer than the components or systems or processes that use them.

Let's start by looking at biological systems. When discussing evolution, Bateson said we should not talk about the survival of the fittest, but the **survival of the fit**. This phrase has two meanings. Firstly, it highlights the fact that an individual or species may be fit enough to survive, without being the most fit. We discussed this meaning in Chapter 3. Secondly, it focuses our attention on the fit itself, as a relationship between an entity and its environment, or as a relationship between two or more entities. This is the meaning that we shall consider in this chapter.

For example, two species may be locked together in a symbiotic relationship or a predator–prey relationship. These two species evolve together; the relationship is preserved, even though the species themselves may be altered beyond recognition. In other words, the fit survives.

Similar observations can often be made when studying the evolution of an urban environment over time, as has been done by Stewart Brand. A curved street remains curved, even though none of the original buildings remain. A new building inherits the site boundaries of its predecessor. Even when cities are rebuilt after widespread devastation, such as war or fire, they often stick fairly closely to the original ground plan, because this allows rebuilding to take place more quickly, without lengthy negotiations. Although some cities have been re-engineered with straight streets – Paris is a good example – this requires extremely forceful planning. We shall return to these issues in Chapter 5.

The same is often true of information systems. A new bespoke information system inherits the footprint of its predecessor. It may add functionality within this footprint, or it may extend into previously uncharted territory, but beware of invading the space of some other system, unless you're willing to replace it completely.

Q Where an information system replaces two or more previous systems, is it always a good idea to allow the former interface(s) to disappear? Under what circumstances would you want to preserve internal interfaces?

Q If you have experience installing an application package, such as ERP, did the package fit into an existing 'footprint', or did the interfaces have to be re-engineered? How much of the installation effort was devoted to fixing the interfaces?

Some of this effect is the perpetuation of people's thinking about how the problem works. Component-based business may provide an opportunity to challenge this old thinking – but this opportunity is rarely taken.

Let's now look at a business example. In Chapter 1, we looked at how a grocery company can create a banking operation, by taking banking services from an existing bank. There are many business relationships between major groceries and banks, following the example pioneered by Tesco and the Royal Bank of Scotland in the UK. In many cases, as these relationships have grown over time, the bandwidth of the interfaces has increased. Typically, there are now several different products and services on which the companies collaborate, and several different business processes crossing the organizational boundary between the grocery and the bank.

It is perfectly conceivable that such a relationship might outlast all of the products and services on which the two companies are currently collaborating. In five years time, there may still be a strong relationship between them, but the products and services and business processes may be transformed beyond recognition.

Another possible scenario is that the relationship between the two companies may be terminated altogether. In general, why do commercial relationships fall apart? Sometimes there are internal flaws (or irreconcilable differences) in the relationship itself. Sometimes the parties grow apart, in size or strategy. Sometimes one party has a better offer elsewhere. And sometimes industry consolidation triggers a complex ripple of shifting alliances.

Q Which of these do you think is the most common reason for the break-up of commercial relationships? Can you think of any recent examples?

But, even if the relationship between a supermarket and a bank broke up, what is the likely action for the supermarket? They would quickly establish a relationship with another bank, to provide the same set of services, as near as possible on the same basis, although they might welcome the opportunity to negotiate lower cost and higher quality. In other words, the interface itself remains broadly the same, they've simply plugged a different component (i.e. a different bank) into the same interface.

That's not to say that the interface can never be re-engineered. But if the supermarket is swapping banks, and trying to preserve levels of customer service and satisfaction, the management priority is likely to be on operating the interface with as little change as possible. This is probably not a good time for a radical restructuring job.

Q   Under what circumstances would you take the relationship as primary, and when would you take the interface as primary?

Q   In your experience, do interfaces only change significantly at time of crisis? Are interface changes typically catastrophic?

Interfaces are perceived as potential intervention points.

To change a system, it seems, there are three basic strategies: change the subsystems, change the properties of the subsystems, or change the connections between subsystems. We shall look at these strategies in more detail in Chapter 5, where we review the management of evolution and change.

Interfaces are perceived as the major source of system problems.

Junior engineers typically look for problems within components. Given the structure of most engineering organizations, senior engineers are mostly confronted with the problems that are not found and fixed by the junior engineers.

Interfaces typically involve more stakeholders than single components do. This itself often causes problems, or makes problems worse. And it may make it more difficult to solve problems. *Many cooks spoil the broth.* But also *many hands make light work.* Sometimes more stakeholders can be a help, rather than a hindrance, in getting a perceived problem fixed.

Q   Do you think both propositions are plausible? Find examples of each.

Managed change sometimes requires the creation of (temporary) interfaces.

If you want to change a large system, you may need to divide the change up into separate areas.

A recent example of this in IT was the conversion of computer systems and data stores from two digit dates to four digit dates, required to enable smooth operation into the year 2000 and beyond. Given that it was usually impossible or impractical to switch all the systems at the same time, it was necessary that systems using the old date be able to communicate correctly with systems using the new date. In some cases, this meant dividing very large systems into subsystems, with internal interfaces, and converting (and testing) one subsystem at a time.

Having created an interface for transition purposes, some engineers would be inclined to eliminate the interface after the transition was complete, while other engineers would prefer to leave the interface as a permanent part of the structure.

(In practice, these interfaces are rarely removed, even when there is an overwhelming technical argument for doing so. This is because, like most preventative maintenance, such a task is not regarded as a business critical one. Restructuring incurs cost and risk, and the benefits are difficult to prove. We'll discuss maintenance in Chapter 5.)

The main argument for removing the interface when it is no longer required may be that it complicates the structure, thus inhibiting future change. The main argument for retaining the interface is that it may increase the articulation of the overall structure, thus enabling future change. In order to determine which of these arguments is stronger in a particular situation, we need a good understanding of the complexity and flexibility of the structure, as well as a good appreciation of the likely demands to be placed on this structure. This is a good example of the type of problem where the intelligence of the system appears to be located in the interfaces, and we can affect system intelligence by our interfacing decisions.

In business situations, interfaces have traditionally been regarded as a major source of cost and risk. It is therefore common practice for managers to attempt to remove organizational interfaces as soon as the immediate need for them has passed. This practice may take many forms, from cutting out the middleman – for which we now have the word disintermediation – to smoothing out a recently merged organization.

 In any structure you are familiar with – whether a business organization or a software architecture – can you identify an interface that could be eliminated? What were the original reasons for creating this interface? What is the present effect of this interface on the "intelligence" of the structure as a whole?

One way of managing a temporary or transient interface is to bury the wiring (and the transience) in a specially constituted interfacing or bridging component. There is a wide range of available software components, collectively known as middleware, which are intended to provide flexible bridging services.

The concept of **broker** has been transferred from the business domain to the software domain – in both domains, it refers to a component that provides interfacing services. It is commonly argued that the presence of brokers increases the intelligence of the system as a whole – although this argument makes some strong assumptions about the intelligence and character of the broker. Poor or untrustworthy brokers may have a disastrous effect on the whole system.

Boundaries are problematic.

The business–IT interface is perceived as particularly problematic.

A recent book of popular psychology characterizes the difficulties experienced in communications between men and women in terms of astrological or planetary stereotypes: **Men are from Mars, Women are from Venus.**

Similar stereotypes could easily be used to provide a reasonably accurate and plausible account of the perceived problems of the interface in many organizations between the IT department and the rest of the organization. These are typically a diverse set of people, although IT folk typically lump them all together as "users", as if IT were some kind of controlled drug.

 If businessmen are from Mars, what planet are IT people are from?

Distributed design activity is also problematic.

Several obstacles have to be overcome specifically when software components and information about them are passed across organizational boundaries. The problems are partly technical, partly human, and partly a consequence of the way software is procured.

Organization boundaries are increasingly fluid.

In the past, an organization could expect to keep its form more or less unaltered for decades. Nowadays, there is no organization safe from either take-over or sell-off, or that can afford to turn its back on opportunities of merger, joint venture or partnership. Activities and relationships are outsourced, disintermediated, reintermediated, or radically re-engineered. The boundaries of the organization are fought over, move in apparently uncontrolled jumps, and seem more unstable than ever.

This of course poses problems for traditional methods of central planning, especially IT planning. The assumption behind these methods was that you could produce a high-level map of all the information system requirements of an enterprise, which would remain valid for many years. This map (often known, rather optimistically, as an "architecture") would be used to define an ambitious (and usually lengthy) development programme.

These methods have now been largely abandoned in most organizations, largely because the planners seemed even further removed from the real and immediate business requirements than the ordinary IT folk, and because these ambitious development programmes rarely came to anything. We can now see that even if the basic assumption underlying this central planning was ever true, it is now almost everywhere false. In general, there is no stable model of business processes or business knowledge, on which a comprehensive long-term plan can be reliably based.

In Chapter 5, we shall look at alternatives to this central planning.

Organizations that maintain a double boundary.

A mediaeval castle usually had an outer wall and an inner stronghold (known as the "keep"). When the community was under attack, the local peasants and livestock could gather inside the wall for protection. The noble family and a few privileged associates withdrew into the stronghold, so that they could be safe even if the outer wall was breached.

By giving some level of protection to the peasantry, the nobles appear to increase the protection to themselves. In order for any attackers to reach the keep, they have to hack their way through a mass of other people first.

The modern corporation has a "lean and mean" core (equivalent to the noble family), plus a loose feudal community of contract workers, fools, freelance consultants and other outsorcerers (sic), which it will defend only if it feels like it. This community serves as a buffer, providing the "lean and mean" core with additional protection against the risks and anxieties of the outside world.

Who benefits from this structure? At first sight, the structure seems to provide strong benefits for the nobles, and lesser but still significant benefits for the peasantry. But let's consider this more closely.

 Under what circumstances are the peasants safer outside the castle wall than inside? Under what circumstances are the peasants safer if there was no castle wall at all – or even no castle?

Any argument that the peasants are safer inside the castle wall depends on a set of assumptions about the nature and intentions of a possible attack, and the development of a possible siege. If the attackers intend to wrest control of the region from the nobles, they may want a thriving peasantry to survive.

It's also important to distinguish between benefits for the peasantry as a group, and benefits for an individual peasant. In some cases, a single peasant may be able to find a safe hiding place outside the castle – but this might be more successful if most of the other peasants are inside.

If we follow this line of argument, we could reach the conclusion that the peasants would sometimes be better off outside the castle. Even if they feel safer inside the castle wall, this could simply indicate that they've been conned by the nobles, in order to persuade them to contribute to the nobles' safety.

But we can go further, and ask whether this structure is even in the interests of the nobles themselves.   Does it really provide the level of protection that we have imagined?

Again, in order to answer this question, we'd need to consider the nature and intentions of a possible attack, and any alternative protection or defence strategies.   And what represents the greater risk for the nobility: attack from other members of their own class, or rebellion from their own peasants?

If the mediaeval castle is seen primarily as a device to protect both the nobility and the peasantry from external attack, then this draws attention away from the interface between the nobility and the peasantry, towards the geographical rivalries within the nobility.

 How does this historical analogy compare with the situation facing the management elite within an organization you are familiar with?

Is the castle self-sufficient?   Does it have what modern management consultants would call a "complete end-to-end process"?   In normal times, the castle depends on an extended set of services from the surrounding countryside and nearby towns.   But at times of crisis, it can operate without these services.   The double boundary corresponds to a tiered defence strategy, which corresponds in turn to a reduced operational process.

Here's another example of a double boundary.   A very large IT services company has a habit of taking over IT departments from its customers.   The acquired IT staff go onto the company's payroll, but are not regarded as equivalent to "home-grown" staff.   There is a permanent "them and us" boundary, which the acquired employees almost never manage to cross.

One enterpreneur devised a boundary as a mechanism for getting rid of poorly motivated staff.   He engineered a glamorous new venture, carefully packaged to attract managers who were both dissatisfied with their current position and eager to be presented with an apparent career opportunity without having taken any personal initiative – and then sold the division quickly before its poor performance had become evident.

These examples illustrate the importance of considering the human and cultural factors in the design of boundaries.   In the days before component-based business, organization design seemed primarily an internal matter: structures could be changed and changed back, individuals and teams could be relocated and reallocated, mistakes could be costly but rarely irreversible.   But when an enterprise spans multiple separate organizations, the human and cultural implications are much more difficult to predict, and mistakes may be impossible to reverse.

Societies that sustain multiple divisions.

In some domains, institutional interfaces proliferate, fold upon fold. For example, health provision in many countries is performed by complicated and brittle institutions, with large numbers of internal interfaces, both formal and informal. The National Health Service in the UK is composed of many separate organizations containing many cultures and subcultures.

Just as with organizations, so with societies and states. Effective administration demands some degree of decomposition. Furthermore, local autonomy, diversity and subsidiarity are popularly regarded as Good Things In Principle (although often strongly resisted in practice). Otherwise perhaps we'd just have World Government and be done with it.

A small number of these interfaces will be selected for institutionalization. For example, it is common practice in many countries to institutionalize the interface between a city and the countryside by putting the two regions under different local administrations. In the UK, the interfaces between England, Scotland and Wales have recently been strengthened, by creating new political bodies within Scotland and Wales. This is an important element of institutionalization.

When there are so many possible ways of carving up a society, deciding which interfaces to embed into institutions is itself an important political question.

 Whose interests are served by dividing Yugoslavia on ethnic or religious lines, rather than on some other basis?

Some US states have growing Hispanic populations, with the real possibility of a Hispanic majority in the near future. There is a growing political awareness among Anglos of the importance of the Anglo-Hispanic interface. Should California or Texas be formally partitioned into an Anglo half and a Hispanic half? But perhaps it has already been partitioned. The rich Anglos are already cordoned off into secure suburbs, with separate access to different services. There are more ways of institutionalizing an interface than taking a ruler to a map. And it is possible to institutionalize Apartheid without any overt racism at all.

Similar considerations apply within business organizations, where differences in style and attitude between different professions or job functions will often be represented as cultural divisions, and institutionalized into organizational divisions.

Retreating from boundaries.

In his classic study of organizational behaviour, *The Workplace Within*, Larry Hirschhorn developed the analytic model shown in Table 4.4.

1	Organizations can function only when its managers draw and maintain appropriate boundaries between the organization and its environment, and between its different divisions and units. These boundaries determine where particular responsibilities and authorities begin and end. They represent a particular articulation of the organization's division of labour.
2	A boundary creates anxiety by signifying where the risk of working and deciding is located, and where aggression must be mobilized.
3	In responding to anxiety, people retreat from the boundary. The root of this anxiety is typically a compound of an estimate of the genuine risks being faced, the links connecting these risks and the inner fantasies of being rejected or destroyed, and a fear of mobilizing aggression lest it destroy others.
4	Much of an organization's process is directed toward managing the anxiety of working by systematically organizing the retreat from the boundary.
5	When people retreat from boundaries, they psychologically injure their co-workers.
6	By occupying task-appropriate roles and mastering task-appropriate skills, people may be able to stay at the boundary, because the inherent value in the work they do contains their fear of hurting others or being hurt in turn.

Table 4.4: Boundary principles.
[Source: Hirschhorn].

Boundaries are therefore crucial for an understanding of such organizational phenomena as stress and anxiety. Good managers will be aware of the effect of these phenomena on human productivity and effectiveness. Software engineers may be particularly concerned about these issues as they affect the design and effectiveness of the Human–Computer Interface. If we want to consider these issues, we need to pay attention to the behaviour around the interface, and not just its formal structure.

The boundaries between business components may be internal or external. Interfaces between components typically create anxiety. So the locus of value generation by the workers is a crucial aspect of architecture and component design.

What are interfaces good for?

What are the desirable properties of interfaces and boundaries?

Boundaries should be well drawn, both logical and clear.

Boundaries between organizations or organization units should be well drawn. Interfaces between building blocks should be well defined.

Boundaries allow movement.

In loosely coupled systems, boundaries allow slippage and adjustment. Following a geological metaphor, they allow the tectonic plates to be rigid in an otherwise dynamic environment. We expect rich conversations and movement in healthy interfaces.

Behaviour on both sides of the boundary should be respectful of the boundary.

Respect for a boundary entails neither overstepping the boundary, nor retreating from it. Software components should not break encapsulation. In business relationships, business partners should be **authentic** in relation to one another. Interface costs can be reduced if there is a degree of mutual **trust**.

The boundary should itself be contained.

Interfaces between building blocks should be tolerant. Building blocks should not unduly disrupt their neighbours. It is sometimes tempting to see all problems in systems terms, necessarily involving multiple parties. At the extreme, every problem becomes a boundary problem. This is intellectually satisfying, but wholly impractical. The outcome of this is that you end up with nothing except boundary. And you cannot change anything without consulting everyone.

What are typical problems with interfaces and boundaries?

Environment inhibits conversations.

The physical environment can inhibit conversations. An office, factory or laboratory provides space in which some conversations (interactions) are made physically easier and/or given symbolic importance. Good architects are conscious of these implications of physical design. However, we don't transform an organization merely by moving it into open-plan offices, or rearranging physical status tokens.

The information environment can inhibit conversations. Formal information management systems (including bureaucratic measurement and reporting systems, computerized data processing systems, and library and archive systems) provide a data platform for conversations. This means that strategic judgements are based on evidence provided by these systems, and are formulated in terms of the vocabulary of these systems. In most organizations, the information environment relies on an inadequate, simplistic and outdated enterprise model. Underlying the design of these formal systems is a model of the enterprise from the IT perspective – or more often, a series of mutually inconsistent models.

Symptoms

Dependency	Mismatch of power, proximity and interest. Typically an individual or group has responsibility for achieving something, or has a requirement for something else, but lacks the authority or influence to make it happen.
Alienation	Mismatch between objective interest and subjective interest. An individual or group behaves as though something were not important.
Blame	The "outside" is scapegoated or devalued in some way to preserve the "inside".
Leakage	Inappropriate transmission of knowledge or information. The boundary is too porous.
Secrecy	Inappropriate retention of knowledge or information. The boundary is too impermeable.
Hesitation	An individual or group possesses authority or influence or knowledge, but is reluctant to use it.
Abdication	An individual or group renounces authority or influence or knowledge. Typically, this leads to a false culture of pseudo-democracy.

Table 4.5: Symptoms of flawed boundaries.

Boundaries and space

Coping with scoping

Boundaries enclose and delineate space. So one way of thinking about boundaries is how they create space.

One aspect of this is scoping – the separation between what is included and what is excluded. This is undoubtedly an important aspect, particularly for honest project managers who want to control costs and timescales of engineering activities, by eliminating a common devil known as Scope-Creep. Meanwhile, some dishonest project managers welcome Scope-Creep as an ally.

Scope-Creep has many other names. When he fiddles with the problem, he is called Requirements-Creep; when he fiddles with the solution he is called Feature-Creep;

when he tries to engage extra stakeholders he is called Log-Roller; and when he tries to seduce stakeholders by promising extra benefits he is called Benefits-Scrounger.

 What tactics do honest project managers traditionally use to ban Scope-Creep from their projects? How does Scope-Creep provide comfort and aid to dishonest project managers?

But hold on, you might say. By condemning Scope-Creep as a devil, are we not being unfair to the poor old chap. Of course, there may always be some tediously narrow-minded project managers who are incapable of seeing him in a positive light, but he has a heart of pure gold. He has many close friends, who help him at all times, and I'm sure they will be happy to speak up for him.

 Is Scope-Creep always a bad influence on a project? Apart from dishonest project managers, who would welcome Scope-Creep? What happens when project managers devote all their energies to resisting Scope-Creep?

As a consultant, I have frequently been faced with project managers who have strongly resisted my suggestions for improving their projects, because they regarded any change as a sign of Scope-Creep. Dear reader, you may imagine that I am eager to construct arguments why I was right and they were wrong. But this is not a chapter about me, but a chapter about interfaces.

The project manager sits on the boundary of a project, protecting the activity inside the boundary, making demands from people outside the boundary, managing communications across the boundary, and resisting all attempts to move the boundary. From the project manager's perspective, the boundary is an interface of a particular kind, which she perceives in a particular way.

As a consultant, I may want to support the project manager, but I don't do this by accepting without question the project manager's view of the world. And this includes the project manager's focus on scope. There are other important aspects of the project boundary besides scope, and it is often useful for the consultant to focus on these aspects instead, to provide a view that is complementary to the project manager's view.

As the project manager perceives it, what the consultant has proposed is usually to add something to the project, in order to make the whole thing smaller and/or more effective. To the cynical project manager, this seems implausible if not paradoxical. Meanwhile, the consultant may not perceive the suggestion as adding anything at all. How can we account for this difference in perception?

What the consultant sometimes hears is: *We're too busy to get things right first time.* And the consultant then responds: *So when are you going to have time to repeat it until it's right?* But of course, that's not necessarily what the project manager thought she said. This is a fairly common pattern of misunderstanding between consultant and project manager. One way of viewing this misunderstanding is to hypothesize that the consultant simply doesn't see the boundary of the project in the same way as the project manager does. (This hypothesis, of course, takes a perspective outside both project manager and consultant. Whose perspective is this?)

After all, we consultants have an agenda too: we usually want to add value in some way to a project, preferably in a way that is visible to all concerned. And it isn't always only the project manager that we're trying to please or impress.

Maintaining healthy business relationships demands attention to several factors.

Boundary Negotiation	Agreeing an allocation of power, proximity and interest between negotiating parties.
Boundary Transactions	Managing exchanges of knowledge/information and other resources across the boundary.
Shared Process	Managing joint activities, with fair shares of benefit, cost and risk.
Maintaining Alignment	Coordinating strategies, requirements and models.
Repair	Engaging authentically with business partners across boundaries, to repair any actual or perceived insult or injury.
Role for trusted third parties	In some business situations, there is a role for trusted third parties, including independent facilitators, conflict arbiters, guarantors and regulators.
Role of software components	Where these relationships are supported by software components, these factors must be considered in the design and implementation of the components.

By what processes does an interface take shape, establish itself, evolve?

Interfaces emerge over time.

The insurance industry combines a number of very different capabilities. Underwriting demands calculation and flair; risk management demands prudence and discipline; retailing demands the ability to develop customer relationships. Retailing insurance is not very different from retailing other financial services – or for that matter any form of retail operation.

Over time, these capabilities have been distributed between different organizations, even different financial centres. Different styles of underwriting can be found in the large German and Swiss reinsurers, as against the smaller and more flexible Lloyd's syndicates. The Lloyd's insurance market has always been articulated between various functions. Now this degree of articulation – although not in the same form as found in the Lloyd's market – is spreading through the insurance industry.

What's interesting here is not only the nature of the emerging interfaces between retail and "manufacturing", but the processes by which they emerge. The commercial advantage is shifting towards the specialists, and the generalists are being forced to divide or be conquered.

If you're going to outsource some insurance function, it makes sense if possible to draw an interface that is common with other players, to get the commodity benefits discussed in Chapter 3. Sometimes this is done institutionally, via formal or informal standards committees, but sometimes such commonality merely emerges without any explicit or deliberate process.

> Q Which process is quicker: standards committees or haphazard convergence? Which process produces better quality interfaces?

Earlier in this chapter, we discussed organizations with a double boundary, based on the analogy with a mediaeval castle. How did this structure evolve? Starting with the mediaeval case, one can imagine several different scenarios (with no particular historical validity).

1 First the nobles built themselves a keep. The envious peasants perceive the benefits of the keep, and demand similar protection for themselves. The nobles agree, either because they perceive that this provides additional protection for themselves from external attack, or because they feel the need to conciliate the peasants to avoid a rebellion.

2 First the nobles build themselves a castle wall. As the community grows, the inside of the castle fills up with peasantry. The nobles build themselves an inner keep in order to withdraw from the peasantry – to protect themselves from the peasantry as much as from external attack.

3 Both castle wall and keep were built at the same time, copying a pre-existing pattern of social division.

Table 4.6: Scenarios resulting in double boundaries.

In all of these scenarios, the conscious motives of the stakeholders may be irrelevant to the actual outcome. The design pattern would have received some evolutionary reinforcement if such castles turned out to have better survival chances against a range of attacks – from Nature as well as from rival barons. But it is perfectly possible that such a design pattern might have survived (and been replicated and reused) for centuries without any real benefit to the inhabitants.

Which of these scenarios is closest to the way the modern "lean and mean" organization has evolved?

Sometimes (but not always) the interface can be traced back to a specific design decision.

Many design projects include the conscious and deliberate design of interfaces. This may include internal interfaces, between two or more artefacts being designed by the same team at the same time. It may include interfaces to allow for communication with existing artefacts or services. And it may include interfaces intended for future communication with artefacts and services that don't yet exist.

Where several artefacts or services are being designed at the same time, by separate teams, the design of the interface between them may be imposed unilaterally, or it may be subject to negotiation. In the latter case, we can regard this as a collaborative design activity.

Standards emerge from a similar process, although this process is often much broader, with many more people involved, with much longer timescales, and with excruciatingly bureaucratic procedures, at least for formal international standards. There is often a collective sigh of relief when a powerful player (such as IBM or Microsoft) produces a de facto standard interface – then we can complain about it in public, while getting on with some real work.

Sometimes the interface derives from a shared model of the world.

Standardization committees sometimes acknowledge that they are involved in a negotiation exercise, an agreed solution. But sometimes, they talk as if they are trying to achieve a consensus, which is not the same thing at all.

If everybody involved in a collaborative design activity has the same underlying view of the domain, then the solution may seem obvious to them, and they may not be aware that they are making any design choices at all.

 What are the advantages of a shared view of the world? What are the dangers? Do you have any examples, from your own experience?

There are processes that refine an interface, making it clearer and simpler over time.

For example, there is a polarization process that can take place along an organizational boundary. Sometimes each side forms a simplified image of the other side, and interacts on the basis of this image.

Sometimes a formerly cohesive unit can become fragmented, progressively more hetereogeous over time, until new internal interfaces emerge. Something like this is what Bateson called **schismogenesis**.

There are welding and melding and folding processes, which tend to blur or complicate, and can even eliminate the interface altogether. For example, there is a reverse polarization process that can take place along an organizational boundary.

Sometimes the people on the boundary identify more with the people on the other side of the boundary than with their nominal colleagues. This is a known phenomenon in many environments, including consulting, and is known as "going native".

And think of lasagne.

Much of the history of a legacy system (technical or organizational) can be read in the interfaces.

The identity and memory of an organization (including an IT architecture) is contained in the structure of relationships.

In Chapter 1, we looked at "Back Office". We noted that this term is commonly used as if it had the same meaning everywhere, in all financial organizations, equally for paper-based and electronically mediated processing. Back Office is apparently the name of a universal service, and we discussed a hypothetical finance company sharing a single Back Office between several Front Offices, outsourcing Back Office to a generic Back Office service provider, or becoming a Back Office provider to other companies.

Let's take a look at the history of the split between Front Office and Back Office. Many organizations, particularly in the finance sector, maintain an interface between "front office" and "back office", which dates back to a time before widespread computing. The back office was established to manage vast quantities of paper-based transactions and information that could not be processed "in real time". This front/back interface was then replicated in the design of computer systems: front offices were provided with fast information displays to support trading and suchlike functions, while back offices were provided with efficient information capture and control suites to support administrative functions such as billing. This interface is strongly embedded, not only in the IT architectures, but also in the organizational structures and cultures of these companies, and is extremely difficult to change.

But as soon as you look at the detail, the interface between Front Office and Back Office turns out to vary significantly from place to place. This has the consequence that although it may be possible to share a single Back Office between two Front Offices, or conversely to distribute the support for a single Front Office between two Back Offices, it's by no means a trivial exercise.

Looking at the detail means looking at the history – explicitly or implicitly. The current structure of relationships reveals the history of interaction and collaboration. Among other things, this has implications for change agents, who need to respect and respond to the **culture** and its **resistance**.

Interaction follows recognizable patterns, rather than fixed rules.

Hebb's rule says that joint activity between two entities will increase the connection between these entities. This rule was originally formulated for the connections between neurones in the brain, but seems to have a much wider applicability.

The rule sets up an important linkage between memory and structure. Memory involves a structural change. This linkage is particularly manifest in social and cultural systems.

Joint activity is not necessarily friendly. Two competitors – or for that matter two communities – may be caught in a trap like two foxes, directing all their aggression at each other. We can view hostile interaction as a form of interaction or collaborative system, especially if it is ongoing.

Where the entities are neurones in the brain, Hebb's rule is the basis for a theory about learning and memory, known as Connectionism. Where the entities are people, we can expect an increase in either affection or hostility, but we cannot predict which. In the case of the business–IT interface, any joint activity has an important effect aside from the actual deliverables.

Sometimes the memory of past activities may be unhelpful. The relationship may be stuck in a rut. Some people prefer to find a new partner, rather than to repair the relationship with the current partner. This is a very common preference, and tells us something about the way people commonly perceive the relative difficulties of different change strategies. Most people are aware of the flaws in this strategy – except when it applies to themselves.

Interfaces and systems

The quality of the interfaces affects the quality of the larger system.

A number of system properties can be perceived as located in its interfaces, including intelligence and trust.

Intelligence can be located in the communication and coordination between components.

An intelligent component doesn't make an intelligent system. Unevenly distributed intelligence can have an unbalancing effect on the whole system. System intelligence often cannot be located in any particular component, but in the effectiveness with which the components are wired and coordinated.

The trust within a system is located in the interfaces.

Trust is an emergent property of a system of relationships. Where such a system manifests some form of bad faith or betrayal, it may seem obvious which of the players in the system is "guilty". The rest of the players, together with informed observers, now mistrust this player, and perhaps avoid doing business with him. But the phenomenon may be more complex than that, and the ostracized player is merely a scapegoat. Mistrust by symptom, mistrust by association.

Recap.

Interface as crux.

Interfaces are crucially important in a component-based structure, because they enable or disable, promote or pre-empt change. Good interfaces increase the articulation of the structure; poor interfaces merely add complexity.

Interface as whole system.

In this chapter, there have been several examples where I've started by looking at one interface, and then found myself wanting to fold other interfaces into the analysis. Interfaces proliferate.

In Chapter 1, we saw that componentry may be used both to understand things and to build things. The same is true of interfaces. Interfaces are constructed things, and appear differently according to your perspective. Different people draw boundaries in different places, or may not perceive a boundary at all. If the boundary is invisible from some points of view, then the components themselves may also be invisible.

There is a temptation to focus on the interface as if it were merely a component of the whole system, albeit a special kind of component. Interface as plugware, connector or adaptor, interface as translation engine, interface as bridge.

We need to complement this view of interface with a holistic view of interface: interface as the whole system, with all the tucks and pleats to be found throughout the fabric of the system.

5.   Evolutionary Change

A component-based business can be regarded as a loosely coupled system.   We therefore need to look at the management of change in loosely coupled systems

Large complex systems aren't planned, they emerge from many separate actions. Systems develop and manifest complex properties over time.   Among other things, intelligence and character manifest themselves over time. (Snapshots at a single point of time may give a misleading picture of these properties.)

Businessmen and systems engineers "develop" solutions.   However large and apparently greenfield these solutions are, they can always be regarded as incremental changes within a larger system. All "development" can be regarded as maintenance (preservation or self-preservation) of something larger.   Even a forest fire can be seen as maintenance in these terms – the cycle of revitalization starts before the smouldering stops.

A "successful" solution fits the larger system(s) into which it is embedded.   An "unsuccessful" solution is rejected, or may even trigger a deterioration in the larger system.   Judgements of success or failure are provisional, subject to revision after further evolution cycles.

From this perspective, changes are often neither fully planned, nor fully emergent, but somewhere in between. If the emergent properties of larger systems are key to business success, then we must select for them when working at a local level.   Alexander's organic approach to planning appears to fit this situation.   Opportunism but with wisdom and insight.

Influence and control goes in concentric circles. If you think you're out of control, look for a smaller scope that is within your control. If you think you're in control, look for a larger scope that is beyond your control.

Evolution cannot be engineered.   But revolutions cannot be engineered either.   What does this mean for action? You are always both a passenger and a helmsman, and the effects of your actions may be surprising.   Therefore eschew meddling or tamperingrenounce mastery, adopt a light touch.

Evolution.

Large systems are constantly changing. New components and connections are appearing, existing configurations are being shuffled and shaken, interesting and often surprising things emerge. Over time, a system may become more complex in some respects, yet more simple in other respects.

And the components and connections also evolve. New mutations appear – these are sometimes called Versions. The old versions may become extinct, or they may survive in parallel with the new versions, according to the ecological principles outlined in Chapter 3.

In popular use, there is a contrast between two types of change: Evolution and Revolution. One refers to slow, continuous change, while the other refers to sudden, dramatic and discontinuous change. The explosion of Internet, the explosion of E-Business, are these evolutionary or revolutionary?

Many discussions of system evolution – whether in the context of business development or software maintenance – imply the goal of managing and controlling evolution.

How far this goal can be realised remains debatable. There are certainly some useful pragmatic steps that can be taken, but we need to start with a clear understanding of what evolution is, or could be, in the context of managed systems.

Any kind of progressive change over time may be described as evolution. But is this a fair description?

A sudden change is often described as a revolution. A progressive change over time is often described as an evolution.

Even in biology, the distinction between sudden change and slow change is problematic. If you had been sitting on the seashore many millions of years ago, you might have seen the first sea creatures crawl onto land, and this might seem a sudden and dramatic event, from a human perspective. However, a squid might see this event as relatively unimportant, merely as one of many tentative explorations by a few creatures at the margins of the oceans, or as a fairly routine extension to previous innovations within a large and diverse community of sea creatures.

Many present-day commentators characterize the emergence of computing, or the Internet, or E-Business, as revolutionary. From one perspective, these appear to be previously unseen phenomena, emerging suddenly into public awareness from the obscurity of some other domain. From another perspective, the same phenomena appear to be a natural consequence of a large number of independently planned and executed moves by a large number of engineers, businessmen and others, whose origins can be traced back to innovations made years ago, decades ago, perhaps even centuries ago.

Thus the same phenomenon can be described as revolutionary AND evolutionary at the same time, depending on where you're standing, and the amount of history you're prepared to absorb.

If I describe a change as revolutionary, I'm inviting you to concentrate your attention on certain aspects of the change. I want you to see it as a dramatic break with the past, with sweeping implications across a fairly wide domain.

If I describe a change as evolutionary, I'm inviting you to take a different perspective. I want you to be aware of the links between the past and the future, and the extent to which previous patterns and innovations are being adapted and reused.

Some people feel safer with evolutionary descriptions of change, while others feel happier with revolutionary descriptions. As a manager or consultant, I might feel the need to motivate some people, while reassuring others. Sometimes I want to emphasize continuity; at other times, I want to emphasize novelty. At least from a logical point of view, I'm not necessarily contradicting myself if I describe things differently for different stakeholders – although there may be ethical or practical difficulties if the descriptions diverge too greatly.

Q   What do you think are the ethical implications of deploying contrasting descriptions with different stakeholders? What are the practical implications?

Q   Have you ever done this yourself, or detected someone else doing it? Was it justified in this particular case, or did it merely complicate things further?

For some people, the labels "evolutionary" and "revolutionary" don't just mean "slow" and "quick", but carry a lot of other dogmatic associations. For example, revolutions are supposed to be violent while evolution is supposed to be peaceful. Or there are particular mechanisms associated with revolution and evolution.

In this chapter, I'm going to try and be as undogmatic as I can about the nature of evolution. I shall make some weak generalizations, but these are to be understood as typical patterns rather than universal truths.

For the purposes of this chapter, my definition of evolution is simply this: **Something interesting emerges (develops, unfolds) from a large number of small changes and interactions.** Let's take a new section to explore this definition.

Something interesting emerges (develops, unfolds) from a large number of small changes and interactions.

This is my own definition of evolution, and I want to make some points about it, which some readers might regard as controversial.

Very interesting ...

Firstly, my insistence that evolution results in the emergence of something **interesting**. Can't uninteresting things evolve? Or must everything that we describe as evolution be interesting, by definition?

Interesting to whom? Firstly, we may presume, interesting to the person who goes to the trouble to observe it, record it, and communicate it to other people.

But I think I'm saying more than this. Evolution produces things that are interesting. Not only are they interesting to the observer, who has a particular reason for taking an interest in some phenomena rather than others, but they are also supposed to be interesting within the system, in that they produce some value and fulfil some purpose. Even the apparently random arrangement of leaves on a tree may serve both the biological interests of the tree and the aesthetic interests of an amateur painter.

If I claim that a system is capable of containing or displaying evolution, I need to perceive this system as complex enough to contain or display interests, and interested entities. A large organization is most evidently the result of an evolutionary process – even the most directive leader cannot control all the elements. These elements serve a complex range of overlapping and conflicting, visible and invisible interests.

Of course, I don't have to claim that any of the entities within the system are conscious or rational, but I have to perceive the interactions within the system as driven by some interests. In a market system, the interests may be described in commercial terms; in a biological system, the interests may be described in biological terms. And so on.

This prompts an obvious challenge. What about artefacts, such as buildings or software systems? Can they be said to evolve? And if so, where are the interests within the artefact itself?

I answer this challenge as follows. If I want to talk about such artefacts evolving, I must refuse to see them as pure lumps of matter or material. Instead, I must understand them as inextricably linked to the social systems that drive them, and to the interests of the people that use and abuse them.

This seems the right place to introduce one of the books that has influenced this chapter, *How Buildings Learn*, by Stewart Brand. The author has assembled many sequences of photographs of the same building, or the same streetscape, over many decades, to show

how the structure and appearance of a building or site are transformed. A reader who merely skimmed through the photographs, and who interpreted the title of the book literally, might imagine that this was telling a story about buildings as independent artefacts, separately from the social systems in which they are embedded. However, Brand's text tells a much more **interesting** story. Interesting to me, among other things, because it exposes and analyses the commercial and professional and political **interests** of developers, architects and other people. (He is strongly critical of the architectural establishment; some cuts were made in the British edition after a legal dispute involving a well-known British architect.) With these interests visible, talking about a building as something that can learn is to identify it as a social artefact within a social system, and not just as a material artefact within a narrow engineering paradigm.

Genetic articulation.

In biology, there are some features whose evolution is difficult or impossible to explain in isolation – these features represent a significant cost or burden while initially conveying little apparent benefit. These features are sometimes presented as challenges or counter-examples to the theory of evolution: as if the existence of these features proved that evolution was wrong.

Defenders of the theory of evolution often try to explain the development of these features by a form of genetic coupling or feature interaction. One feature piggy-backed on another feature, until it reached a point where it was providing some selective benefit in its own right. In other words, features do not evolve in isolation, but may evolve in clusters. This mechanism may apply to whole components as well as other system features.

A similar process is visible in the history of pop music and other popular entertainment. Some relatively untalented musicians have become world-famous stars, by playing alongside much more talented musicians. Many solo artists have started their performing career as members of groups. There may be a strong link between talent and success, but that doesn't mean that every star is individually talented or that every talented individual will become a star, because talent is often expressed in groups and star-clusters rather than individually.

Q Imagine yourself as the manager of a pop group. How would you respond if the most talented member of the group wanted to go solo? How would you respond if the least talented member of the group wanted to go solo?

Q Have you experienced similar things happening in business organizations or markets? What practical conclusions can you draw from this experience?

When a previously buried business function is exposed to direct competition, outsourced or hived off, this is akin to going solo. Such a move may be forced by regulators or grasped by senior managers; or it may merely result from a series of smaller moves whose overall effect had not been fully understood or planned.

At this point, we can formulate one of the central questions of the book in evolutionary terms. Since we are interested in the grouping and clustering of business functions into separate components, how does this grouping and clustering change over time, and how can these changes be managed?

The question of clustering has important management and engineering implications. How is genetic or any other material articulated, to provide appropriate connections and separations? How are developments bundled, so that interesting opportunities are not prematurely selected out? When should developments be unbundled, so that non-contributing parts can be duly selected out?

Strategic management and change management often require that some necessary changes and developments are kept invisible, bundled with other stuff, and are not subjected to the harsh demands of the marketplace or to board-level supervision. (This is sometimes known as **skunk works**.) In other words, protected against premature **interest**. The critical skill is in timing the gradual exposure of these developments to proper competition and challenge.

Evolution as emergence.

The other important point to highlight in my definition of evolution is the notion of **emergence**. This means, among other things, that the complex properties of the whole system are often capable of surprising even the most capable observer. They are often reasonably predictable at one level, while being unpredictable at another level. Trends and patterns can be perceived, advantages and success factors can be postulated, but the exact course of events is usually too complex to chart in advance, and often ambiguous even in retrospect.

This is true of many sciences, in which there is apparent chaos at one level, yet reliable prediction at another level. Meteorology is one such science; there are many aspects of the weather that can be predicted fairly accurately, but it's often the things we're most interested in – is it going to rain at a precise location on a particular afternoon? – that seem most difficult to predict. Economics is another such science. There is a whole branch of mathematics, called chaos theory, designed to support these kinds of sciences.

Dogmatic philosophers often regard evolution with suspicion, because of its apparent inability to make accurate and testable predictions at any level. It is even sometimes lumped together with Marxism and psychoanalysis, as a pseudo-science that can supposedly explain everything and predict nothing. Genetic engineering seems to bring the forces of evolution into the laboratory, and subject them to repeatable experiment and control. For some people, this makes it respectable science, and they may therefore be tempted to equate evolution and engineering.

But even if the most optimistic technological claims for genetic engineering are valid, the equation with evolution is not valid. What I'm focusing on in my definition of evolution is precisely that which cannot be replicated under laboratory conditions, nor controlled by engineers – the emergent properties of large and complex systems. There are many excellent examples documented in Kevin Kelly's book *Out of Control*.

Evolution and biodiversity.

Biodiversity is self-generating. A rich and diverse ecosystem is likely to manifest greater and more divergent evolution, resulting in further biodiversity.

Of course, it doesn't follow from this argument that biodiversity is a Good Thing. Indeed, we haven't even established that evolution is always a Good Thing, everywhere it occurs. Indeed, as evolution has winners and losers, it obviously isn't a good thing for the losers.

However, we don't usually evaluate these matters impartially. If the evaluation is done retrospectively, from the perspective of the survivors, then evolution is likely to seem like a good thing. And yet, from the perspective of the survivors, the persistence of biodiversity will often make it seem as if their success is incomplete.

The argument points at an essential contradiction, between success for an individual or species within an evolutionary system, and the continued evolutionary capability of the system itself. This means that there is considerable ambivalence about biodiversity. Actively engaged stakeholders may pay lip service to biodiversity, but many of their actions may be intended to reduce biodiversity in their favour. Economic giants pay lip service to healthy competition, but they don't always act consistently with this doctrine.

 In your opinion, how effective is Government intervention at restoring and maintaining healthy competition and economic evolution? What do you think are the real motives of Governments when they intervene (or refuse to intervene) in these matters?

In biology, biodiverse ecosystems are typically highly complex and robustly stable (at some level and timescale) Stressed ecosystems contain a much lower number of species, with the tendency of populations to crash. This analogy seems to fit commercial markets as well.

Evolution may either be seen as moving towards an envisioned goal, or moving away from a mess.

Evolution is often discussed in the same terms as progress and enlightenment – or in the same terms as problem-solving and innovation. Some people emphasize the desire to

move towards an envisioned goal, while others emphasize the desire to **move away** from a mess. Moving towards has a sense of **convergence**, while moving away has a sense of **divergence**. Necessity as the mother of invention.

Of course, just as we saw with evolution and revolution, two apparently opposing descriptions can sometimes turn out to be complementary – descriptions of the same situation from different perspectives.

When engineers talk about the evolution of engineered systems, they may mean several different things.

➢ Progressive steps towards an envisioned goal. The engineer has a vision of the ultimate solution, and is implementing this vision in stages.

➢ A series of changes to a system, usually involving local adjustments, sometimes revealing global patterns.

➢ Competition and feature-exchange between rival solutions, resulting in general improvement in the state-of-the-art.

These differences reveal different notions of what exactly is supposed to be evolving, and the role of the engineer in the evolution process. This is an important difference, which needs further attention.

Meanwhile, a businessman may talk about the evolution of an organization in response to changes in its environment, or the evolution of a system in response to changes in the business.

Software and business are two different life forms, often found yoked together in a quasi-symbiotic relationship. In this context, it seems to make sense to talk about co-evolution – both software and business are changing (evolving) over time, and these changes are somehow linked. Causal influences and information may flow in both directions, or there may be common influences from third parties.

The emphasis on software and business leaves out some other important life forms with relevance to the evolution of both software and business, including military, academic and Government. The evolution of the Internet, for example, cannot be understood merely in terms of a co-evolution of software and business alone.

The alignment or coupling between two or more life forms may sometimes help and sometimes hinder change. Often the IT world needs to develop something that has no direct relevance to business, but is intended to enhance future IT capability. Excessively tight coupling, or strictly enforced business/IT alignment, may inhibit investment in IT infrastructure.

In talking about co-evolution of software and business, we should try to be clear about the granularity and the logical level of the entities involved. Are we talking about an evolving but permanent relationship between an individual of one species and an individual of another species: **this** software solution in **this** company? Or are we talking about a relationship between two species, in which individuals of one species may have temporary or transient interactions with individuals of the other species: **this** collection of software components and services used within **this** market?

Evolution sometimes involves feedback, but this is neither necessary nor sufficient.

Where two or more systems are evolving in parallel, there may be causal influences between the systems. These influences will sometimes be obvious, sometimes only imputed. Some people refer to these causal influences as feedback (positive or negative) or feedforward. However, these terms imply some communication between the systems, and it's not always appropriate to describe systems as if they were connected by information flows. (Although some people deploy a watered-down notion of feedback that doesn't involve communication, this seems to lack any content.)

For example, there are many situations in Nature that involve the co-evolution of two species, one predator and one prey. As the predator learns to run faster, then the prey learns to run faster. Today's cheetahs and antelopes are much faster than their ancestors were.

 Draw a model of the evolution of antelopes and cheetahs, showing a feedback loop joining the two species. What information flows from antelopes to cheetahs in your model? What information flows from cheetahs to antelopes? Does this seem a natural way of modelling the situation? Can the information flows be observed?

It's perfectly possible to explain the co-evolution of the two species without postulating any information flow between the two species. Reliance on feedback as a general explanatory mechanism is therefore a metaphysical preference, rather than a scientifically grounded fact.

From a practical engineering viewpoint, feedback may be a useful mechanism in many situations. But in some situations, feedback may merely reinforce the problem. We can think of the feedback mechanism as a component of a larger system, which may contribute to the properties of the larger system in complex ways.

In any case, feedback is based on the immediate past, is often poor at reflecting the influence of the distant past, and has no way of referencing the future. In the particular case of the co-evolution of software and business, the desired alignment between the two worlds needs to be focused on a shared view of the future. Although this almost certainly depends on strong communication between the two worlds, it is misleading to describe this communication as feedback.

Natural selection requires the unsurvival of the unfit.

Darwinian evolution is often expressed as the survival of the fittest. As we saw in a previous chapter, following Bateson, it is more accurate to speak of the survival of the fit. This phrase is deliberately ambiguous: it could mean either the survival of fit individuals and species, or the survival of the fitness relationship between multiple individuals and species, or between the entity and its environment. In other words, it may be the fitness relationship itself that is preserved, while the species itself may change almost beyond recognition.

There is an important trade-off here between evolution and efficiency. Efficiency assumes a secure position in a fixed ecological niche – in other words, an unchanging identity. Evolution involves a dynamic engagement with the Fit – in other words, a constant challenging of *who* and *what* and *why* as well as *how*.

Evolution implies that something may evolve. But what is this thing? In biology, are we talking about the individual, the species, the gene, the genome, or something else? In business, are we talking about firms or markets, specific products or whole technologies? In software, are we talking about lumps of program code, assemblies of software components, or something more abstract? **What are we trying to manage, and why?**

Evolution entails death – the non-survival of the unfit.

Survival of the fit is only meaningful in relation to the non-survival of the unfit. In other words, evolution entails death.

Sometimes this means the death of unfit individuals within a species. If the slowest or weakest antelopes get eaten by cheetahs, this improves the average speed and strength of the remaining antelopes. Over time, evolution "encourages" those attributes within a species that are linked to survival and reproduction, but this only works if there is a selection mechanism. (This was Nietzsche's principle: what doesn't kill you makes you stronger.)

Sometimes evolution involves the extinction of an entire species or genetic line, as incapable of surviving within a given ecological niche. Many recent examples involve native species unable to compete with or escape from imported species – red squirrels driven out by grey squirrels, water voles driven out by mink, earthworm versus earthworm.

How effective is biological evolution as a mechanism for eliminating unfit individuals, recessive genes, or unfit species? It's a mechanism that operates at different speeds for different logical levels; and can often appear painfully slow and even wasteful. The same is of course true of change within large hierarchical organizations, where similar differences in timescale and efficiency are also manifest. Higher levels of management are believed to operate at much longer timescales than their juniors, with far slower learning and improvement cycles, thus supposedly demanding greater feats of strategic intelligence, and so claiming much higher financial rewards. And yet, paradoxically, top managers are subject to perhaps the shortest time horizon of all: the fickle preferences of the stock market.

Business failure is commonly seen as a form of tragedy. Clearly the collapse of any enterprise, whether a small project or a large business organization, has unwelcome consequences for many people. And when any artefact is consigned to the rubbish heap, this often represents a real loss for those who have invested their energies in building it, or who have long associations with it. This is evidently true of well-loved institutions and buildings, but is often true of technical products as well. Software gurus traditionally deplore the fact that many projects fail, and that many software artefacts are unused.

And yet failure may be healthy. Cells die, so that the body survives. (Cancer involves cells that don't die when they're supposed to.) And in many situations, failure may be essential to preserve the legitimacy of the system. An exam or audit is only worth passing if some people fail it – a 100% pass rate is rightly regarded with suspicion.

 Do you think it is possible to protect business organizations from failure? Do you think it is desirable? What are the consequences of such protection?

If we look through history, from the ancient Chinese to the Soviet Union, there have been many economic systems that have attempted to control and protect existing organizations. These systems have had varying degrees of success and longevity. But each of these systems seems to have suppressed evolution, to a greater or lesser extent, and this can surely be reckoned as a factor in the eventual collapse of the whole system.

Some commentators regard this, especially the collapse of the Soviet Union, as a moral victory for unfettered competition.

For the purposes of this book, all we need to observe is that competition and evolution are powerful forces, and there are practical limits to the ability of any person or institution to control or suppress these forces. For most of us, we have no choice but to live in a world that is dominated by these forces.

Misfits can be protected – for a while.

Technological misfits and business misfits may be preserved – but at a cost. Sometimes innovation and diversity, as well as contingency against environmental change, can be advanced by the temporary protection of things that are not currently self-supporting. But if this policy is taken to excess, it can threaten the survival of the larger system.

Natural selection performs a testing function.

Similar principles apply to technical artefacts. If we are serious about evolution in this domain, we have to have an effective mechanism for killing "bad" technology – not just tweaking it for Year–2000 compliance.

One of the concerns provoked by component-based business is caused by the encapsulation of the bought-in services, which often seems to represent a serious business risk. Encapsulation means that the internals of the service are hidden from the purchaser. This simplifies things for the purchaser, but may leave a residue of anxiety or guilt: am I failing due diligence, am I exposed to risk, is someone ripping me off without my knowledge?

These questions have always been important ones. Componentry hasn't created a wholly new problem here, although it certainly exposes and sometimes multiplies existing issues.

Suppose I represent an insurance company, and I use a component-based service from another company to help me perform the underwriting. Don't I need to know the algorithm that the other company is using? Suppose that the algorithm is based on factors that I don't believe in, such as astrology? Suppose that the algorithm neglects factors that I believe to be important, such as genetics or genomics? Am I not accepting a huge risk by allowing another company to define an algorithm that is central to my business?

There are three main attitudes to this risk. One attitude, commonly found among civil servants, lawyers and software engineers, is to break encapsulation, crawl all over the algorithm in advance, and spend months testing the algorithm across a large database of test cases. If and when the algorithm is finally accepted and installed, such people will insist on proper authorization (with extensive retesting) before the smallest detail of the algorithm can be changed. Another attitude is denial: impatient businessmen and politicians simply ignore the warnings and delays of the first group.

There is a third approach, which is to use the forces of competition as a quality control mechanism. Instead of insisting that we find and maintain a single perfect algorithm, or kidding ourselves that we've already achieved this, we deliberately build a system that sets up several algorithms for competitive field-testing, a system that is sufficiently robust to withstand failure of any one algorithm.

An algorithm has a finite amount of "energy", represented by the funding or other resources of the company that operates it. If the algorithm frequently gets the "wrong" answer, it will lose energy and eventually die. Death in this context may mean that the algorithm is withdrawn or replaced, or may even mean that the operating company goes under. So what is the mechanism by which the algorithm loses energy?

The most direct mechanism is a straight commercial one. If the company operating the underwriting algorithm also bears all or some of the underwriting risk, then its commercial success should be directly linked to the "correctness" of the algorithm.

Where this kind of direct mechanism is not available, then we're looking for feedback mechanisms that simulate this, as closely as possible. Just as the survival of the company using these underwriting services may depend on having access to several competing services, so the survival of the underwriting services themselves may depend on being used by several different insurance companies, with different customer profiles and success criteria. (This reduces the risk that all the customers for your service disappear at the same time, and gives you a better chance to fix problems.)

This leads to another important question: how can we be sure that the competition is genuine? Just as many apparently competing brands of computer may turn out to have the same chips and software inside, so several competing business services may turn out to have some common component or data source. For example, all the underwriting algorithms may be based on the same flawed database. If encapsulation goes all down the supply chain, the service providers themselves may not be aware that they are sharing critical resources with their competitors. So can we (or anybody else) ever discover this without getting inside the service, thus breaking encapsulation?

Change.

The reasonably fit survive by changing themselves. Survival usually implies maintaining one's identity, and perhaps also autonomy.

Recall Bateson's characterization of evolution: not the survival of the fittest, but the survival of the fit. This could mean fit individuals, fit species, or the fitness relationship. Any of these could be the subject of an evolutionary process.

In business evolution, what exactly is evolving? The products, the organization, the business, the marketplace? Does an organization change slightly every time a person joins or leaves?

Sometimes an organization suffers a clear death. The Soviet Union failed to survive. Some politicians and historians attribute this to long-term environmental hostility: the Cold War. Others attribute this to internal contradictions: the inability of central planning systems to satisfy expectations fairly. Note that these explanations are not mutually exclusive: external hostility and internal injustice may each have reinforced the other. Note also that both explanations rely on the notion of long-term attrition: another theory of what actually finished the Soviet Union off was that it was not the contradictions themselves, whether internal or external, but the brave attempt (by Gorbachev) to resolve them.

Sometimes, however, the survival or death of an organization is itself problematic. Does a corporation survive (in some sense) even when it is chopped into pieces (Standard Oil, British Rail, Microsoft)? Does a company survive (in some sense) even through a history of insolvency (Rolls Royce)? Does a company survive when it is taken over by a larger company, perhaps even based in another country (Chrysler, ICL, Rolls Royce)? What about an organization (such as the Third Reich) that only survives in the heads of its enemies or victims?

IBM is not the same as it used to be. It was once supremely powerful, confident, complacent. It went through a period of uncertainty and downsizing, when it lost its "identity". It is now finding a new identity. Has IBM survived? In one sense, it has not survived. But some of the characteristics of the old IBM may now be associated with Microsoft. What kind of survival is this?

If we extend this line of thought, we could argue that any sufficiently radical change to an organization makes it a different organization. An organization may change its mission, its entire management team, even its name. The organization may retain customers, staff, premises and legal obligations from before, or it may not. Or it may be that only the name remains the same – everything else has changed. In such cases, we have a notion that **something** has survived, but we find it difficult to say what that something is.

For change to be meaningful, something essential must be preserved.

Change requires stability and continuity.

In a large organization, every day sees many changes. Most of these changes seem fairly superficial and reversible; the challenge that is experienced by consultants and managers is to make deep and meaningful changes to the organization. However, the distinction between superficial change and deep change is not always clear-cut. What some people see as a minor reform, others may perceive as a major disruption. Indeed, as we have already seen in this chapter, the person championing the change may describe it differently for different audiences.

In the previous section, we looked at IBM, a business that survived by redefining itself. Xerox is another well-known example. There are countless examples of other organizations that have remained committed to a particular identity and have, as a consequence, not survived. There are many others in the IT industry alone whose long-term survival appears unlikely.

In understanding how change can coexist with continuity, we need to see both change and continuity as properties of **descriptions**. There are some descriptions of IBM and

Xerox that remain true, and there are other descriptions of these companies that were once true but are now false. Some examples are shown in Table 5.1. This notion of change has been well explored by Bateson, and more recently by K.K. Smith.

| For something to change, it must remain something. | IBM: "We are becoming a service company." | IBM: "We are still a major software vendor." |
| For something to survive, it must lose something. | Xerox: "We are pre-eminent in photocopiers." | Xerox: "We are pre-eminent in quality." |

Table 5.1 Change and continuity are properties of descriptions.

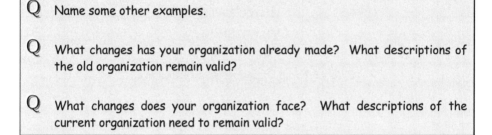

Q   Name some other examples.

Q   What changes has your organization already made? What descriptions of the old organization remain valid?

Q   What changes does your organization face? What descriptions of the current organization need to remain valid?

An organization is typically subject to several competing descriptions. (This insight can be traced to the industrialist Lord Brown.) The **effective organization** (what's "really" going on) will often differ in structure and culture both from the **formal organization** (as shown on organization charts and job descriptions) and from the **perceived organization** (as described informally by organization members in interviews and workshops). Lord Brown and his followers argued that organizational change was targeted at a fourth description – the **ideal organization** – and this would only succeed if you started from the right place. Chris Argyris has introduced a simpler distinction: between the **Espoused Theory** (what you say you do) and the **Theory in Use** (what you do). There is a large amount of work (by Argyris and others) promoting the idea that it is a good thing for these two to be aligned.

The formal organization is usually frozen. Formal responsibilities, authorities and reporting relationships are fixed. Changes are effected instantaneously, and the structure is immediately refrozen. Informally and covertly, the effective organization may nonetheless change. Formal reporting lines are bypassed, managers take more initiative than they are officially permitted, people find ways of evading the more bureaucratic controls. The level of awareness of these informal changes may be very variable. Politically naive participants may only gradually become aware of discrepancies in the formal account. Politically astute managers may be highly aware of them, may plan such changes consciously for their own benefit or what they believe to be in the interests of the larger organization, and may attempt to deliberately distort the way the organizational structure is perceived by others.

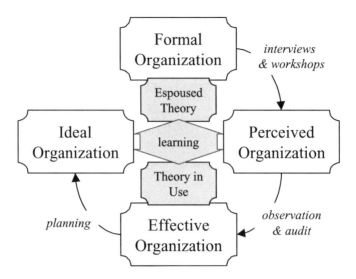

Figure 5.1 Four Organizations of Lord Brown.

Another way of putting this is that there is **loose coupling** between several different descriptions of what's going on. Changes to the formal organization may be reflected (perhaps with some delay and distortion) in the actual organization, or the formal organization may be realigned with actual practice. Changes to the espoused theory may influence the theory-in-use, or vice versa.

IT systems reflect this loose coupling. People frequently find ways of making computers do things that their designers had not intended them to do, or had even specifically intended that they should not do. Thus there may be several competing descriptions of an IT system. A similar consideration can be made at the engineering level where computer systems are constructed from heterogeneous components and principles, and are the work of many hands.

Change and Control.

System change usually involves subsystem changes.

To change a system, three strategies: change the subsystems, change the properties of the subsystems, or change the connections between subsystems. You cannot change the environment directly. But you can make changes to the system in the hope that this will trigger co-evolutionary changes within the environment.

Many business people treat the environment as if it were unintelligent. They seem to expect the environment to continue its behaviour – whether stationary, linear or random – regardless of their own actions. Or they expect the environment to respond automatically, in predictable ways. If we decrease our prices by X, then our market share will increase by Y.

In some situations, this may be a reasonable simplification. Even when the environment contains intelligent agents, such as customers and competitors, you may argue that there is little likelihood of a coordinated response, and therefore no significant level of collective intelligence. Indeed, in some markets, regulation may specifically prevent a coordinated response.

But it isn't as simple as that. If we decrease our prices by X, in an attempt to win market share, then the prevailing prices in the environment will change. Each of our competitors may reassess the prices it is charging. Each of our customers may review the quantity it is purchasing. The environment will change through the aggregation of a large number of intelligent responses by intelligent agents, working individually and independently to interpret the changes you have made, and to anticipate future changes you might make.

 Under what circumstances might a market environment seem to act intelligently? Could collective intelligence emerge without formal coordination or conspiracy?

There is a principle of Minimum Force. Other things being equal, the smaller the change (and the smaller the scope of the entity being changed) the better. There is a strong value system supporting this preference.

Small changes may have fewer inherent risks. This doesn't mean avoid radical change. It means avoid slashing wildly about at the roots. The smaller the change, the smaller the likely collateral damage – butterfly effect notwithstanding.

Of course, change isn't linear. Small changes can have chaotic or catastrophic effects. This is in accordance with the dialectic principle: quantity becomes quality.

To increase the degree of a given quality in the system, it is not necessary or sufficient to increase the degree of that quality in any one of the subsystems. In some cases, a lop-sided increase in the degree of a quality in one subsystem will impair the performance of the system as a whole. Inserting a highly intelligent person into a department doesn't always improve the performance of the department. Sometimes it destroys it.

 What kinds of companies can benefit from world-class specialists? What happens to a world-class specialist in a company that doesn't need this level of specialist expertise very often?

Q   Under what conditions is it worth putting a high-performance hardware component into a computer network? Under what conditions will a double-speed modem make any difference at all to the overall speed of data transmission?

Q   What are the constraints on upgrading software components to more "intelligent" versions?

We need to understand the group dynamics that allow individual intelligences (whether human or artificial) to collaborate positively.

Although we can sometimes predict and contain the interaction effects, there is no general rule for the management of interaction effects. (This is perhaps related to the phenomenon of feature interaction.)

However, in some cases, the best we can do is improve the subsystems, and try to manage or at least contain the second-order effects.

Given that the systems, subsystems and connections are, at least to some extent, mental constructions, it is sometimes possible to change outcomes by changing the way these entities are perceived and interpreted by participants.

Pruning.

If a tree is regularly pruned, it is likely to live longer, and the same is true of other things as well. Unless regularly pruned, complex artefacts usually evolve towards greater complication and reduced value. This applies to buildings, organizations, and software systems. The choice is sometimes between the death of the part (lopping off unwanted branches) or the death of the whole.

The evolution is typically a complication attempting to fit prevailing conditions. What needs to be cut away are the obsolete adaptations. However, even in gardening, the pieces pruned away may still take root elsewhere – in other words, it may still be viable, even when disconnected from its original source of energy. In business, this represents a form of demerger.

Limits to Control.

Let's start by talking about the control of cars and their drivers. We often talk about controlling a car in the context of a system description that excludes not only the driver but also the designer and the other people involved in its manufacture and distribution. Control of a car is also connected to infrastructure, such as road signs and road surface.

Although it's perfectly possible to talk about the driver controlling a car, this also implies a system model that hides lots of other people.

There is a theory of risk according to which the behaviour of the driver is "controlled" by his perception of the safety features. I think it's reasonable to refer to something that influences our behaviour in predictable ways as a control, especially if it's something we're not conscious of.

When there is a major transport accident, such as a rail crash, this often prompts discussion of some costly technological mechanism that might have averted the crash. The victims' relatives are often heard to insist that a safety control mechanism be installed before anything happens again. Any doubts about the value or effectiveness of this mechanism are dismissed with scorn: surely no price is too high for a human life. We seem forced to view the transport system as lacking some control; and to believe that this is a problem that can be solved by plugging in one or more components. What is usually overlooked in this debate is the overall architecture of the transport system, and the systemic nature of control across this system.

 Look at the media coverage of a recent transport disaster. What instant solutions were proposed to prevent a recurrence of this disaster? Do you think any of these solutions are likely to be implemented? Do you think the proponents of these solutions have thought enough about the effect on the whole system?

What often interests us more is the control of traffic.

There's an interesting phenomenon here. Drivers seem happier when traffic is controlled "automatically" (for example by a system that includes traffic lights). When a policeman or traffic warden takes over the direction of traffic, he or she becomes the target of a lot of criticism. The widespread perception is that the human being is less competent than the automatic system. Of course, the "reality" is often that the human being has taken over precisely because the automatic system has failed to cope with an abnormal traffic situation. The extra delay at a junction is not the consequence of human intervention, but the trigger for it. Cause not effect.

When faced with a person in uniform controlling traffic, we usually accept the authority – but we may criticize the exercise of the authority.

There are other "controls", including sleeping policemen and speed cameras, and these also provoke a range of emotional reactions in drivers.

The other main constraint on our use of the roads is the behaviour of other road users. When a dented pickup truck or white van carves me up, and forces me to slam on my brakes, I experience this as an unwanted interference in my driving. The other driver has a selfish agenda – more selfish than mine – to barge past other drivers at all costs –

or at least I imagine he has. Perhaps this is a good metaphor for the worst form of control in human interaction.

It may be worth noting that our emotional reaction to the behaviour of other drivers depends on a lot of quite small symbolic factors. Large vehicles may seem more threatening, expensive vehicles may seem more arrogant. We may defer to some vehicles – ambulances, buses – because we regard them as having a more important mission than a private car. If the driver of the other vehicle signals first, if we feel we have a choice to let him in or not, then we may feel much better about the encounter.

This thinking can be extended to other social situations.

It is an empirical social fact that there is a diversity of response to attempts by people to interfere with and control one another. Age, social class, ethnic background and gender are all relevant here, although many people believe they shouldn't be relevant, and would like them to become irrelevant.

There are particular modes of interpersonal influence and control that are particularly feared or disapproved of. A person of "good" character is supposed to be someone who gets what he wants without resorting to these mechanisms.

Character references are used to communicate the social standing of an accused person, although I suspect that by the time it gets to court, these character references are often counter-productive. (There are many cases where people use their social standing and connections to stay out of court, or to avoid proper investigation. That's the dark side of "good" character.)

We have come, by a roundabout route, to character. One of the attributes of a successful leader may be the charm, or other personal skills, which enables them to influence people, with their consent. There may be multiple layers of visibility and awareness here.

If people are to collaborate at all, some of this may always be required. But this slides over very easily into a form of domination, entering the world of the master–slave relationship. It is difficult to draw a line to say: "this exercise of influence is okay, while this is undue and unwarranted control".

I think it follows from this that the notion of Character is at least as problematic (epistemologically and ethically) as the notion of Control.

➢   A person (or other agent) may wish to control something. This wish for control is usually based on a set of intentions and beliefs – a particular value-laden view of the world.

➢   A person may see this as controlling something. The thing he imagines he is trying to control may be himself or a part of himself, an object, another person, or something else. In many cases, he may not have a clear picture of what it is he is trying to control. But we have a presumption that what he is trying to control has an existence in his world-view. (This means we can sometimes attempt to deduce his world-view from observing his attempts to control things.)

➢ A person may experience anxiety about the things in his world that he cannot control. Control often springs from anxiety. (But this is not a sufficient reason to dismiss all controls as irrational or unhealthy.)

➢ A person will typically legitimize and rationalize this wish for control, in terms of some public value system. For example, a man's desire to control his own emotions may be based on a shared set of cultural assumptions, among other things. (There may of course be considerable self-deception going on here.)

➢ By imagining that he has a right to control something, a person is positioning himself in a particular way in relation to that thing. For example, a driver may have the right to control a car because he owns the car. This right may of course be conferred by the owner onto other people – this rests on the relationship (whether direct or indirect) between the owner and the driver. Or think of a parent, trying to control some aspects of a child's life. (There are social mechanisms for overruling such rights.)

➢ Many of the mechanisms that people use to exert control over the things in their world follow some recognizable patterns. For example, feedback (whatever that is), or tit-for-tat (as a way of controlling a two-person game).

➢ Control is often projected onto technological devices (such as traffic lights, or a railway safety mechanism). This may be a defensive response to anxiety. An engineer may be asked to work on these devices, and is often not given the opportunity to work on the social system in which these devices are embedded.

➢ The same patterns can also emerge from complex interactions, and it is not always possible to detect a conscious design intention behind a given control mechanism. (In a particular situation, retaliation may be triggered by anger, rather than by deliberate game-theoretic calculation. But of course it may then be more effective, because it's more "authentic".)

➢ A person may resist some forms of control from what he perceives as other people, or outside forces. He is more likely to see controls that follow patterns with which he is familiar.

Based on this apparently value-neutral position, I can construct an ethic of helping people and judging their actions. There may be some modes of control that I regard as okay, some that I regard as definitely not okay, and many others that I'm dubious about.

An engineer may see ways of improving control mechanisms, or designing alternative mechanisms. He might even want to control the deployment of these mechanisms, to prevent them falling into the wrong hands. A consultant may want to help people clarify their intentions, and encourage them to relax "excessive" controls, or avoid "undue" interference with the legitimate autonomy of other people and systems. He may want to help people protect themselves against "unwarranted" control by other people and systems. He may even be willing to help people find ways of accommodating external controls, rather than waste energy and anxiety fighting them.

When I'm not writing books about systems, I sometimes act in an engineering role or in a consulting role. (That's why I used the male pronoun in the previous paragraph.) But as a systems thinker, I want to see control as a natural phenomenon within sociotechnical systems – but a phenomenon that is often displaced and distorted. However, given that my typical stance is that I want to expose these displacements and distortions, and then I need to find other stakeholders who will benefit from this exposure, in order to justify (and, if possible, fund) this work, this also influences the way I perceive these situations.

Flexibility.

One of the benefits claimed for certain technologies is that they enhance the flexibility of systems, and of the organizations using them. Such metaphors as "plug-and-play" are used to imply that systems and organizations can accommodate changed requirements simply by replacing and reconfiguring components. Even if the plug-and-play metaphor is an oversimplification, it certainly seems plausible to claim that increasing the flexibility of systems and organizations may be worth more to the business than increasing the speed and accuracy of a particular process.

But although it may be fairly easy to identify and eliminate specific or general patterns of inflexibility, it is much more difficult to define a positive notion of flexibility. If change is a property of descriptions, then flexibility is only meaningful relative to a given set of descriptions. Thus we can only make systems and organizations flexible, or even assess the degree of flexibility of a given design, within the context defined by a given business and technological agenda.

In the technical literature, change management is often formalized by specifying a class of changes that are to be considered, so that it becomes a formal mathematical puzzle. This work may be useful at the technical level, but raises questions about the extent to which these formal models represent the actual requirements for change and flexibility in the real world.

Some people think that flexibility is best achieved by being vague and non-committal.

➢ In business terms, this means keeping your options open. The "lean and mean" firm attempts to survive by exporting uncertainty to its customers, suppliers and contract workers.

➢ In technological terms, this means adopting highly generic systems and components, which will satisfy a wide range of descriptions.

An alternative view is that flexibility comes from cooperation and making commitments. This raises the question: what commitments should we be making, if we want to remain in business?

Many artefacts outlast or outgrow their builders.

Legacy systems.

Mention legacy systems, and your listeners will assume that you're talking about computer systems. Thanks to the so-called Year 2000 problem, many people became aware of legacy computer systems, and the efforts and anxieties associated with preparing them for an apparently trivial date change. Discussion of this "problem" and its imagined consequences spread from the specialist trade press to the business and popular press. Huge amounts of time and money were devoted to cleaning up large libraries of software. This effort was widely resented, or regarded as an unpleasant necessity, as most people could think of far "better" uses of the same resources. This is a common pattern of preventive and restorative maintenance.

 Which business assets require ongoing maintenance to preserve their value? Which business assets require no maintenance?

Legacy computer systems are commonly regarded as a liability rather than an asset.

IT managers commonly devote a large proportion of their energies and resources to managing so-called legacy systems. We may suppose that their general aim is to make maximum use (or reuse) of legacy assets, while minimizing the inheritance of legacy liabilities and constraints.

 Where is the value in reusing legacy systems? How can we quantify the value of a legacy asset?

If an application system is currently in use within an organization, there must be a reasonable degree of fit between the system and the organization. The fit may be imperfect, and the users may have to undergo various inconveniences and tribulations to make the system work, but at least it does work. Furthermore, the users are familiar with the system, warts and all.

To the extent that the system works, it must contain some knowledge about the business requirements. We might suppose that the system has a reasonably good internal model; this model may be implicit or explicit, depending on how the system was developed and documented, and how it has been maintained.

Of course, the value of a legacy system does not necessarily bear any relation to the amount of time and effort you have put into it.

What limits the successful reuse of legacy systems? How can we quantify the depreciation of a legacy asset?

A legacy system may not work all the time. It may have undocumented features or erratic behaviour, especially when exception conditions occur. It may have bugs or poor performance. But the same is often true of brand-new systems. This leads to the upgrade dilemma: do you want to exchange a familiar set of bugs for a new set of bugs?

A legacy system may have in-built constraints deriving from the way it was conceptualized or designed. The internal model may be adequate for a limited range of situations, but it may not be adequate for all situations. The design may make simplifying assumptions that limit future reuse.

For example, a legacy system may contain a batch procedure that is designed for single-threaded operation on a flat file. It would take a clever programmer indeed to wrap that procedure so that it would support multi-threaded operation.

A legacy system will usually be designed for operation on a specific technical platform. Considerable effort may be required to eliminate the dependency of the code on this platform, and to make it work on other platforms.

Furthermore, any poorly executed action on a legacy system, including wrapping, may worsen its quality and performance. Wrapping almost always introduces some performance overhead, and this is not always balanced by the technical superiority of the target platform: sometimes a poorly wrapped system can run slower on a high-performance machine than it did in its original technical environment.

Legacy thinking also applies to the use of COTS (commercial off-the-shelf) software as to in-house and bespoke applications. The specific ways that we use Lotus Notes in a given organization, or the specific implementation of SAP – these also constitute legacies, with many of the same issues. (There are also practical questions about whether and when to upgrade the package to the vendor's latest version, which also have to do with the legacy invested in the previous software version.)

Three perspectives on legacy systems.

There are three perspectives on legacy systems, which each has a different conceptual status. We need to articulate all three perspectives, if we want to have a complete theoretical and practical account.

PAST	Legacy as a sociotechnical artefact, the product of a past development process/project. Or perhaps the product of a sequence of maintenance actions on such an artefact. We must presume that such development or maintenance was carried out in terms of a set of intentions (business objectives, design priorities, etc.) then in force.
PRESENT	Legacy as a sociotechnical system-in-use. There is often a significant gap between a system-as-developed and a system-in-use. In the users' hands, the system moves away from the development intentions. The users often find ways to do things that were not anticipated by the developers, or even that the developers specifically sought to prevent.
FUTURE	Legacy as an asset with ongoing value, with the potential to survive and evolve, relative to emerging intentions. Rational managers might be expected to take this perspective, especially when evaluating legacy systems, and planning their transformation. There is a general management accounting principle involved here, known as Zero-Based Budgeting. This principle can be characterized informally by two contrary maxims: *Don't throw good money after bad* and *Don't throw away the baby with the bathwater*.

Table 5.2 Three perspectives on legacy systems.

The Italian food theory of legacy computer systems.

Within the software industry, there are two metaphors widely used to criticize the structure of an existing system: monolithic and spaghetti. Indeed, these metaphors are often used to describe the same system, without acknowledging any conflict between the metaphors. We'll come back to monolithic in the next section, but first let's suck the spaghetti metaphor and see if we can get any bolognaise.

The term spaghetti usually creates a mental image of a tangle.

Once upon a time, computer programmers could easily recognize spaghetti code by the presence of one word: GOTO. It was considered harmful; programming languages were developed in which GOTO was unnecessary or impossible; generations of programmers were trained to resist anything that resembled a GOTO. But the pattern mutates and reappears in a new form, designed to bypass our programmed resistances. Large complex computer systems are now being developed; each software component may be impeccably designed and coded, but these software components are wired together (using some form of scripting language) into something that we can only regard as a new manifestation of spaghetti.

(This example illustrates a more general idea, to which we shall return later. The use of good patterns, and the avoidance of negative patterns or anti-patterns, can easily become trite or obsessional. It's one of the features of evolution that an interesting pattern mutates, evolves, morphs. We must be alert to every new manifestation.)

It may be possible to teach individual software engineers to avoid creating spaghetti in software artefacts that are under their own control. What is more difficult is to teach them to prevent the emergence of spaghetti in situations where more than one software engineer is involved, making a series of changes over time. It takes two to tangle.

Legacy code is often compared to spaghetti, but lovers of Italian food will recognize that pizza provides a much better analogy. You try to cut out a wedge of pizza, but it remains connected to the rest of the pizza by innumerable strands of elastic cheese.

Or we might prefer to compare legacy code with lasagne. What were once separate layers of cheese, pasta and other ingredients have now been melted into a solid mass.

When we look at the legacy systems of a large company, we are usually presented with what appears to be a list of application systems. But this list can be misleading. The items in the list refer to the original system development projects – the layers of the lasagne. The systems have usually grown and changed, in functionality and architecture, often to the point where the original names no longer seem appropriate. New data stores, or interfaces to remote data stores, may have been added ad hoc.

Even if the applications were originally designed according to a well-thought-out architecture, with maximum cohesion and minimum coupling, evolution of the applications over time may have greatly reduced the cohesion within each application and increased the coupling between applications. So the segmentation of legacy code may not follow the apparent boundaries between the legacy applications.

 Under what circumstances do you think the interfaces may become clearer and better defined over time?

The geological theory of legacy computer systems.

When a system is described as monolithic, this implies homogeneity. It also implies that there are no fractures or internal interfaces.

 For whose purposes might this be an accurate or useful description of a typical computer system?

In geology, monolithic rock formations are usually attributed to a history of extreme temperature or pressure.

 What kind of pressures does a typical computer system undergo in its life? To what extent can the history of these pressures be read in its structure?

Buildings.

As Brand's book illustrates, structure, fabric and usage can all change quite significantly over the lifetime of a building. Some of these changes can be understood as slow accumulations of tinkering and fixing. Some of these changes represent sweeping redesigns, perhaps in order to rescue and redeploy a building that would otherwise be pulled down. Thus these changes may be seen as more or less evolutionary. Apart from Brand, there is remarkably little systematic study of change.

Organizational culture.

One of the most difficult things to change in a business organization is its culture. Indeed, some people seem to define culture in a way that makes this a truism – it's as if they are saying that culture is what remains when you've changed everything that can be changed. Culture is the excuse for the failure of any change programme, particularly from an engineering perspective.

Whatever culture actually is, it seem to be a consequence – or perhaps a complicated set of consequences – of things that have happened in the past, with a profound influence on the present and the future. In other words, legacy.

Like most legacies, culture is not static, but evolving. But can culture be deliberately changed? There have certainly been some brave attempts to change culture. Chairman Mao thought that the only way to change the culture of China was to initiate a Cultural Revolution. The enormous human cost of this programme raises important moral issues, but we can also ask about the practical effectiveness of the programme: to what extent were Mao's goals achieved, and have any cultural changes proved permanent? Our view of this episode may alter in a generation or two, of course, but I suspect that historians will struggle to find evidence of lasting and positive change.

 Do you think culture can be deliberately changed? Or do you think cultural change only occurs as a side effect of something else? How can this legacy be managed?

Technology.

Some of the pioneers of the World Wide Web are critical of many of the features of the web that have emerged, and express disappointment about some of the elements of his original vision that have not materialized. There are two points that are relevant here:

➢ The internet is already a technological legacy – we're stuck with an aggregation of past decisions and actions.

➢ The internet is a complex technological being, that has deviated (mutated, evolved?) from the original concept.

Another commonly cited technological legacy is the QWERTY keyboard. This keyboard layout was designed for mechanical typewriting machines, and these machines imposed some design constraints. These constraints are not relevant to computer keyboards, and the QWERTY layout is widely regarded as inefficient for these purposes. However, there are so many people who are accustomed to using QWERTY keyboards, that it's apparently easier to reuse this design than to convert everyone to a supposedly more efficient design.

Business patterns.

Finally in this section, let's look at business patterns as legacies. Business people and professionals get stuck with a particular mechanism, a particular notation, or a particular approach, and imagine that this is the only way of achieving a given outcome. In many places, this legacy manifests itself as a kind of inertia – not merely resisting innovation, but refusing to recognize the possibility of innovation.

Different layers transform themselves at different speeds.

In his book, **How Buildings Learn**, Stewart Brand identifies six different layers of a building, with different typical rates of change. These layers are described in Table 5.3.

Site	The location, boundaries and context of the plot of land. Can sometimes be extended, but cannot otherwise be altered, except in highly unusual cases. The same site may be used for many buildings in succession, often preserving the same shape.
Structure	The foundations and skeleton of the building. In engineering terms, this is what carries the physical weight of the building. Any alteration risks collapse of the building. The structure of a building typically lasts for decades.
Skin	The cladding of a building may change in accordance with changing fashions and tastes. In any case, the outer surface of a building may become weathered or grimy, and may require renovation or repair.
Services	Various services are piped into and around a building, including air, water, heat, electricity, security and communications. As well as toilets, there may also be kitchens and bathrooms. There may be moving parts, such as escalators and elevators. A commercial building may need to be rewired and refitted after as little as five years.
Space Plan	The layout and use of a building can be changed frequently. This may involve moving partitions and large storage units.
Stuff	The allocation and use of a particular space within a building may change on a daily basis. This includes small items of furniture and equipment.

Table 5.3 Layers of a building.
(source: Brand)

The relationship between these layers is depicted schematically in Figure 5.2.

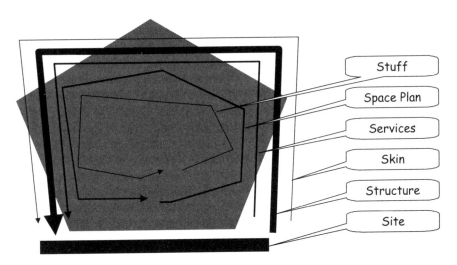

Stuff

Space Plan

Services

Skin

Structure

Site

Figure 5.2: Different layers transform themselves at different speeds.
(source: Brand)

This raises some practical issues about the articulation between the layers. In some buildings the layers are tightly coupled, and this makes any change more difficult and expensive. In other buildings, the layers are more loosely coupled. I think it's a consequence of Brand's argument that architects should (but usually don't) pay attention to the coupling between the layers, as well as to the layers themselves.

Similar theories could be constructed for business organizations, or could be inferred from various management writings, with similar consequences for business and system architecture and change management.

When I started practising structured systems methods in the early 1980s, it was common to claim that business data structures were more stable than business processes. Accordingly, software engineers were urged to design systems around a carefully articulated understanding of the business data structure.

However, although I heard these claims many times, I never saw a proper justification for them, neither based on theoretical argument nor on empirical evidence.

What certainly did happen in many cases was that software engineers analysed the data structures in great detail, and then froze them. They expected the business data structures to be unchanging, and so they built software artefacts with unchangeable software data structures – or at least structures that resisted change. The expectation that data structures wouldn't change was therefore self-fulfilling.

In any case, much of the technical difficulty of changing data structure was greatly eased during the 1980s by new data management technologies, such as relational databases. Ironically, the very software design methods intended to exploit these technologies, such as Information Engineering, were based on obsolete methodological principles (such as the inflexibility of data structures) that inhibited the designer from taking full advantage of these technologies. As often happens, the technological innovation had got out of step with the requirement.

Complex structures often tear themselves apart.

The surface of the earth is not a simple structure. It is composed of different geological materials and layers, and is subject to immense forces. There are large components, known as plates, which move in different directions, or at different speeds. These forces manifest themselves as earthquakes.

We sometimes need to think of a complex engineering artefact as an assembly of large components, each subject to forces pulling in different directions.

The slow-moving dominates the fast-moving. In the worst case, slow-moving and expensive structures need to be demolished or radically re-engineered, in order to enable the faster-moving changes. Imagine an office building where you had to take up the floorboards just to install an extra phone line. Imagine banking software that needed months of reprogramming in order to support a new kind of customer account, or a new kind of customer. That's hardly a great feat of imagination – you can find such artefacts all over the place.

Q What's the most extreme example of this you've experienced?

There is often a design conflict between short-term design goals and longer-term flexibility. For example, the designers may want to seal a unit, to keep out dust and human interference, but this may inhibit maintenance. In many industries, there is a separation between the original design and construction and the subsequent maintenance. This means that the designers have little incentive to produce flexible designs, and little or no feedback.

Flexible artefacts maintain an articulation between the layers.

In a flexible artefact, changes to the fast-moving components are anticipated and enabled. Most new offices are built with easily accessible wiring ducts, so that new equipment can be installed without major building alterations. In other words the services layer is separated (but connected to) the structural layer.

However, it is still rare for domestic housing to be built with equivalent flexibility. Electric wiring is buried in the walls. Sockets may be provided for telephones and television aerials, but these will become obsolete fairly quickly.

Although domestic kitchens are typically designed and built in a modular fashion, it's often very difficult to upgrade a kitchen without ripping out the whole thing and starting again.

In business systems, articulation means a separation of concerns. In technological systems, articulation means portability.

Alignment.

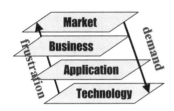

> Alignment is an ongoing process, not a one-time outcome.

> Deep alignment demands attention to the causes of misalignment, not just the symptoms.

> Alignment demands mutual adaptation of business plans, system plans and technology plans.

> Total alignment is unachievable – and probably undesirable.

Businesses need to align themselves to markets.

A business can be regarded as an adaptive system, whose environment is its marketplace. As we saw in Chapter 2, the survival and growth of a business is dependent on the intelligence and character of the business, which can be understood in terms of its flexible connection to its environment.

Does this mean that a business must follow the market? Or that it must predict the market, and follow its predictions? Neither of these – or perhaps both.

IT provision needs to be aligned with the business.

In Chapter 3, I put forward an ecological model of software supply, which showed how information and software services draw energy from the systems they are supporting. For this to be sustainable, these services must provide some value back to these systems.

For the purposes of this book, the systems we're interested in are business systems. This means that the value provided by IT services must be meaningful from a business perspective. Part of the problem of doing this is that the two domains are not as separate as the discussion implies.

IT systems and services are supposed to deliver business value. Whenever businessmen are asked to spend more money on IT, they are usually presented with a so-called business case, which offers various tangible and intangible benefits to the business. Some businessmen also demand a constant justification of ongoing IT expenditure, in terms of the value-for-money provided by IT.

Among other things, this entails some alignment of value systems. For something to be "worth doing" in IT terms, it must also be "worth doing" in business terms.

One common form of misalignment is the phenomenon of overengineering. This describes a situation where technical work goes beyond the business requirements, and cannot be mapped back onto business value. It appears to be worth doing from an IT perspective, but not from a business perspective.

Of course, claims of overengineering are always contentious. Such claims are usually found within a debate between one technocrat and another, each trying to demonstrate that he has a closer alignment with the business than his rival.

Alignment should be regarded as an ongoing process, not an idealized state.

Many people talk about alignment as if it were a state. "We are currently out of alignment, but if we do X then we'll get back into alignment." In other words, misalignment is a "problem", to which X is the "solution".

 What solutions have you seen proposed to the "problem" of business–IT misalignment? Have you seen any of them implemented? Was anything effective, and for how long?

Given the apparently rapid rates of change, both of business markets and of technology, we shouldn't expect alignment to be achieved by a single adjustment. Instead, alignment entails an ongoing series of alignments, probably involving both sides – what we're loosely calling co-evolution.

Alignment also entails anticipation. If you want to hit a moving target, you have to aim not at its present position, but at its expected future position. This is sometimes called feedforward. (But recall my earlier comments about feedback.)

Anticipation in turn entails a shared way of looking at the world, and a shared value system. The alignment process involves much more than simply aligning current artefacts and services with their business requirements.

How does IT accommodate business evolution?

We can identify many common patterns of business change. One challenge for IT is to build software systems that help to manage these transitions. In most cases, the software is unable to provide any help with the transitions, because it is struggling to keep itself up with the business.

Pattern 1: From one to many.

Many businesses start with a single product or brand, a single location or market. At some stage in their growth, these businesses may need to switch to multiple products, multiple brands, multiple locations and markets.

Data modellers imagine they can build systems to allow for multiple everything. And object modellers imagine they can abstract everything. But there is a fallacy here: although it is possible to multiply one dimension of the business, it is not possible to multiply all dimensions at the same time.

Pattern 2: From few to many.

Many small companies start with a small number of relatively high-value customers. At some stage in the growth of these companies, there is often a desire to expand the marketing, to access a much larger number of customers. This usually means a massive change to business processes, as customers can no longer expect the same level of personal attention.

At some stage, it may be decided to spin off high-value customers into a semi-autonomous unit. For example, a bank may provide special services for super-rich customers, and may set up an organization unit to provide them with personal attention, which may be similar to that provided to all customers in the early days of the company's history.

Pattern 3: From many to one.

We've looked at the transition from one to many. Now let's look at the reverse transition: from many to one.

Our first example is a drug company. Traditionally, pharmaceutical products are packaged and sold as lots of little pills, so much money a bottle. But for the patient or doctor, the pills are only a means to an end: the cure. Furthermore, there may be considerable variation in the number of pills a given patient needs to take, before a cure is achieved. It is possible to establish an entirely different deal with the drug company, where the payment is made for the cure, and the drug company provides enough pills to achieve the cure.

 What are the advantages of this arrangement for the drug company? What are the advantages for the health service or patient?

Another form of this pattern is the growth of one-stop shopping. Here the focus is on one supplier instead of many products.

And within the finance sector, there is a widespread shift from multiple accounts or policies, to a single customer focus.

Pattern 4: From many to few.

Another form of focusing is to reduce the variety in a given situation. This can be found at market level, where mergers and acquisitions serve to consolidate an industry. It can be found at product level, where the number of products and brands marketed by a company may be significantly reduced. It may be found in procurement, where a supply chain may be rationalized by greatly reducing the number of suppliers.

Pattern 5: From promiscuous to steady.

The Internet is noted for two extreme kinds of business relationship: promiscuous and steady. These can also be found in traditional business relationships.

Promiscuous	Steady
Opportunistic single transaction	Long-term relationship - based on growing trust
Narrow bandwidth	Broad bandwidth - may support many processes and products
High turnover or churn	Sharing intangible assets – including knowledge

Table 5.4 Two extreme kinds of business relationship.

There are two ways that this pattern can manifest itself. Some companies may themselves attempt to control the transition of relationships with its customers, from promiscuous to steady. In other situations, the pattern may be effected by brokers and intermediaries, creating a steady "hub" for a set of promiscuous suppliers. The idea behind this is that the customer prefers to deal with a large reliable intermediary, whether storefront or portal, rather than constantly building transitory relationships with one-off suppliers of information and services.

Of course, in some markets, the transition is the other way, from steady to promiscuous.

How does organizational culture accommodate business evolution?

This is another very broad question, which could easily take up an entire book. In this section I can only offer a few hints and examples.

In Chapter 4, we looked at the story of the businessman who rid himself of a division packed with poorly performing staff. In this example, the human and cultural factors may have been the sole reason for the demerger, but that's probably not a common situation. And although human and cultural factors may often influence a decision to merge or demerge, in many cases these factors are neglected completely.

Maintenance is the dominant paradigm for development and change.

In this section, we're going to see that "pure" development becomes increasingly rare. We're going to explore the growth of iterative and evolutionary development – in other words, maintenance by any other name. The maintenance paradigm addresses many important business and software concerns, including business/IT alignment, legacy renewal and reuse.

The fantasy of "pure" development.

All development is maintenance. The primary reason for building a new component is to deliver an improvement in some larger system or process.

However, many developers have a fantasy of "pure" development, which is sometimes called "greenfield" development. If you view a development project from a very narrow perspective, you can sometimes persuade yourself that everything you're doing is entirely new and innovative, building something, as it were, from scratch.

What is maintenance?

If you think of development as building some artefact, then it may be natural to think of maintenance as building (or establishing) a new version of an artefact. This means that maintenance is like development, but with some additional complications – such as reverse engineering, re-engineering and transition. Then a maintenance method is merely a somewhat complicated version of a standard development method. That's exactly how many formal software processes and methods regard maintenance.

From a software engineering perspective, "maintenance" refers to a piece of work that takes an existing software artefact and produces a new version, either to better satisfy the old requirements, or to satisfy some new requirements. This is not the same thing as producing new artefacts to satisfy new requirements, and demands rather different techniques – although perhaps the same notations.

From a business point of view, the purpose of a software project is to alter the characteristics of some business process. Practically all business processes these days already contain a considerable degree of software automation and electronically mediated communication. So from a business point of view, practically all software projects are carrying out a maintenance activity on a business system, regardless of how many new software artefacts they may generate. To describe such a project as a development project, or to use a method that is primarily designed for development, implies a restricted view of the project, foregrounding the new software elements and pushing the existing stuff (with which it must interoperate) to the background.

So is maintenance the same as development, or not? In this book, we don't see maintenance as a continuation or extension of development. On the contrary, we see development as merely a restricted view of maintenance. The same activity is described one way (as maintenance) from a business perspective, and another way (as development) from a narrow software perspective.

Business reengineering as maintenance.

'Modern' and 'postmodern' change.

"In the world of management and organizational change and development, the modernist tradition can be easily seen. It is the organization development scenario of demolish and/or rebuild around a central purpose, represented in town planning and architecture as demolish, clear, rebuild, start again on a green field site or new town development tradition. Post-modern organizational change might involve the quest to adapt existing organizations, recognize and build on existing features and strengths – restore rather than re-develop. It may recognize, too, that purposes are unclear, multiple, conflicting. It also brings into focus, but does not resolve, the relationship between a Learning Company that survives and prospers (against some criteria) and a company which is 'good' in some moral, ethical, social responsibility sense, in a world where 'good' is difficult or impossible to define." [M. Pedler, J. Burgoyne & T. Boydell, The Learning Company (London: McGraw-Hill, 1991)]

Town planning and urban development as maintenance.

Most town planning and urban development involves extending and building upon what already exists. However, there is a strong utopian tradition within writings on town planning, which focuses on the creation of new towns on so-called green fields, rather than the renewal of existing urban environments.

A evolutionary approach to town planning has been tried by Christopher Alexander and colleagues in California. They developed a set of principles for urban development, and then conducted a large-scale simulation to test the principles. A group of architecture students surveyed a real area of the city, discovered what kinds of buildings would be required in a redevelopment of the area, and used the principles to grow a series of coordinated designs, without any zoning or grand design. Although such an artificial experiment cannot be regarded as a definitive proof of the approach, the obvious merit of the models and drawings give some plausibility to its claims, at least as an alternative to traditional town planning.

Maintenance requires a different approach to management.

Why is maintenance a problem?

We often avoid calling maintenance by its true name, because "maintenance" is unpopular with staff and management alike. Maintenance is commonly regarded as the Cinderella of IT. It is unpopular with staff because:

➤ They are not confident of doing the job well.

➤ They expect it to be boring.

➤ They fear being blamed for other people's bad work (i.e. if a given task takes too long, or is not done well enough, it will be the "fault" of the person doing the maintenance rather than on the system or program being maintained).

➤ They suspect that new systems development would be better for their careers (i.e. if it is generally assumed that only second-raters get stuck with maintenance, nobody will volunteer).

➤ Maintenance is badly managed and inadequately resourced (for the reasons below).

It is unpopular with management because:

➤ Managerial objectives are often formulated in negative terms (e.g. avoid degradation to systems or interruption to services).

➤ It consumes resources without obvious results.

➤ It is difficult to motivate staff (for the reasons above).

Thus the best staff and the best managers tend to get the "plum" jobs in systems development, leaving the less glamorous, yet arguably more difficult, jobs to the others.

Many IT installations support their systems development team with tools and techniques, methodologies and standards. Yet the maintenance team often do not receive equivalent support, which confirms the low regard in which they are held. Maintenance may be assigned to those members of staff believed to be incapable of learning anything new. Or perhaps as punishment for building a bad system in the past, a programmer/analyst is condemned like Sisyphus to maintain it.

Because the structured methodologies are fairly new, they carry glamour. Then because they concentrate on systems development and ignore maintenance, this itself widens the "glamour gap", which may however be narrowed by enhancing those methodologies to cope with the extra complications of maintenance, and finding ways of applying the existing tools on existing systems.

Maintenance involves dealing with someone else's idea of order without the opportunity to impose your own. (As Bateson pointed out, what is tidy for one person is not tidy for another.) Shared values in terms of the orderly technical environment gets even less recognition and investment than shared business values. This may be at the root of many technological disputes and dogmata.

Old languages and old platforms are usually less glamorous than the new ones.

Maintenance often means working with old-fashioned data structures, COBOL rather than Java, IBM mainframes rather than Linux servers.

From a software engineering perspective, "maintenance" appears to be less glamorous than "development", even when they involve the same programming language and platform. Put this together with the fact that COBOL is less glamorous than Java, and IBM mainframes less glamorous than Linux servers, and it's not surprising that maintenance seems to have an image problem.

What's wrong with COBOL?

COBOL developers are not second-class citizens just because they're not doing it in Java or Visual Basic. COBOL remains a perfectly respectable way of developing software – including distributed components. It is the process that is important, not whether you're using a fashionable programming language.

The concerns of COBOL developers typically include legacy systems, legacy data stores, and (given that many of you have used structured methods) legacy models. Thanks to long attention to these concerns, COBOL developers can make a very useful contribution to the maintenance paradigm.

Development and maintenance methods converge, as the same (or similar) techniques and notations become available in both domains.

In the past, I took a methodological perspective on maintenance, seeing the virtues in bringing the prevailing practices of software maintenance up to the best practices of software development. In a paper I published in 1985, I outlined the piecemeal use of structured methods for the purposes of software maintenance.

In my 1994 book, I stated that many of the perceived distinctions between development and maintenance were in fact illusory, suggested that the traditional division between development and maintenance was going to disappear, and urged for common planning and methods across development and maintenance. (This was based in part on Christopher Alexander's 1987 book, which to my knowledge has not yet been taken up seriously by other software engineers. But then it did take about 15 years for each of his previous books to make the journey from architecture into software engineering, so there's still time.)

From Development Projects to a Maintenance Process.

Most development methods start from the notion of a development project. A project involves a project team, carrying out a defined collection of tasks, under the control of a project manager. A project delivers a product, which is first built, then tested, then installed. Within this notion of project, iteration merely means having several attempts at a given task, and parallelism merely means breaking the solution into subsystems or components, and doing the same development task on several components at the same time.

The new software process needs to be maintenance-focused rather than development focused. This means that I try to avoid talking about a development lifecycle, and prefer to talk about software and system evolution and alignment. Alignment as an ongoing process, not as a state of rest.

The world of maintenance (which of course many COBOL programmers inhabit) is often quite different to the world of development. Maintenance is a permanent evolutionary process, not a simple development process. The goal of maintenance is to realign things that are constantly getting out of alignment, thanks to changes in the business requirements, changes in user expectations, changes in the technological base, or the emergence of defects. The maintenance programmer is trying to do the best he can, despite the fact that many of the factors are out of his control. Maintenance activity is often squeezed into artificial projects, but this rarely aids management control.

Different metrics apply to maintenance as opposed to development. Even if we've agreed how to measure productivity of development, measuring the productivity of maintenance is a different kettle of function points.

Concurrent Engineering.

Modern manufacturing increasingly uses the notion of concurrent engineering, where instead of first designing a manufacturable product and then designing the manufacturing process, you do both at the same time. Successive versions of the product are "developed" in parallel – thus the designers have already started work on version n+2 before version n+1 has been put into production. (For one hardware manufacturer I worked with, a couple of years ago now, the entire lifespan of a laptop computer was 10 months – 3 months for design, 6 months for production and 1 month for disposing of the now obsolete stock. This was for major design versions, not just minor specification upgrades.)

This notion of concurrent engineering is increasingly relevant to software engineering, and is taken for granted in business. An insurance company nowadays must design a new kind of insurance policy in parallel with building the IT systems to support this policy, and the new components must plug into legacy systems that are constantly being altered, using interfaces that are frequently being redefined.

This means that you must do the strategic planning and the requirements analysis and the organizational design and the contractual negotiations and the software procurement and the prototyping and the testing all at the same time. Or rather, you must have all these activities going on in parallel, with regular alignment between them. The parallelism expresses the multiple conversations that must take place, instead of relying on a fantasy of communication in one direction.

If we divide the development process into separate interoperating activities, this has the additional benefit of allowing information and techniques specific to that activity to be encapsulated within the activity, rather than shared across the project. This reduces the otherwise exponential growth of project information, and helps manage the complexity of the software process.

Testing takes on a different role in the development/maintenance process.

Testing is not just finding out whether something works. In an open distributed world, such testing is unable to provide any guarantees of reliability or performance. Among other things, **feature interaction** is intractably difficult to test. Testing blurs into operational monitoring. We can no longer expect testing to be complete before a system goes into production.

Testing involves finding out about the (emergent) properties of a whole system. We can – indeed, we must – test the business for the desired quality (intelligence, flexibility, power or whatever).

Business management should be aware of business constraints and opportunities. This involves test cases, which we characterize as **business challenges**.

Planning.

This chapter is not about the design of individual artefacts, satisfying a set of requirements, built by individual projects. It is about programmes of designing many coordinated systems, satisfying the complete requirements of a large organization, forming a "whole". In this section, I shall draw heavily on the work of Christopher Alexander.

What do we mean by the word "whole"? We can recognize it even when we cannot describe it. It denotes coherence, lack of fragmentation. If a structure is whole, its parts are also in a sense whole, not fragmented but coherent. This may be because all parts are guided by the one single process, by a development programme which follows the same principles at all levels, from the preliminary sketch to the tiniest detail. Such a development programme will of course contain many projects, in series or in parallel, each developing one part. Any two parts are related, in sometimes very complex and indirect ways, but remain compatible, consistent. And yet the boundaries between parts can be clearly perceived, each part is visible and makes sense on its own, as well as within a wider context.

In most development programmes today, this vision of coherence is at best only partly achieved. We can analyse what goes wrong; more importantly, we can identify what improvements can be made in planning and executing these programmes, subject to the culture and environment of the organization.

Common sense and experience shows that such wholes cannot be implemented in a single step. Such projects are too large to be successful, producing a system too monolithic to be meaningful. The best we can achieve allows the whole to grow in many steps, over many years. Its final form cannot be predicted, except perhaps in ambiguous generalities, partly because the form is sensitive to details that cannot (and should not) be worked out in advance, but partly (and more importantly) because the organization itself learns during the development: the systems do not merely support the organization but transform it, or rather allow it to transform itself.

There are two common approaches to such multi-system design, with multi-project development. One can be called **hacking**, and the other can be called **grand plans**.

Some people ignore the complexities of systems, and merely hack with the pieces. Hacking doesn't work.

Hacking means that each system or individual component is built piecemeal, according to its own needs alone. Its features are determined by its direct costs and benefits. Each project is started and steered in isolation of other projects; communication between projects only takes place if of immediate benefit to the projects themselves. Piecemeal growth, by itself, will not create coherent wholes. This is exactly why people produce plans.

This is not to dismiss the value of the hacker's craft. Professional hackers can produce items of extreme elegance and beauty. The fragmentation doesn't come from the craft itself, but from the planning and management framework.

Few people have the luxury of controlling all aspects of the present, let alone fixing the future. Grand plans don't work either.

Grand plans means that each system is built to fit a prearranged position, within a preconfigured framework or blueprint. The aim of such planning is to create coherent wholes in advance, and thereby provide order and organization in the large. The trouble with this form of planning is that it often fails to achieve the sought order. In the worst case, such a plan can be a mixture of meaningless generalities and ill-considered rigidities.

It is worth noting here an important ambiguity in the word "plan". This word may be used to refer to a preconfiguration or blueprint, as in a building plan or an urban development plan. It may also refer to a scheme or schedule of activity, as in a military plan of action, or development programme. It may even refer to a combination of both.

In the 1970s and 1980s, strategic planning methods were widely recommended, and often attempted, to plan the entire system portfolio for a large enterprise. These methods were typically top-down approaches, in which an abstract "enterprise model" or "architecture" was used to scope and guide requirements for many projects.

In practice, these planned programmes often ran into difficulties. The emerging business requirements overwhelmed and overtook the architecture, and this was often quietly dropped or marginalized, becoming increasingly disconnected from the actual development work.

Instead, follow an organic process that allows the desired system properties to emerge.

The architect Christopher Alexander developed an **organic planning** approach originally for the purposes of town planning (as an alternative to the top-down approach adopted by both Ebenezer Howard and Le Corbusier). He uses a metaphorical language to describe the intended results: *whole, repair, fabric, centre, healing*. We shall adopt his metaphors, and then try to define what they mean for Information Systems.

The overriding principle is that every project must "make whole". It should repair and maintain existing wholes (this implies respect for the coherence of existing structure, although a project may abandon any particular mechanisms); it should create new wholes; it should establish a continuous fabric of wholes around itself. Thus a good project is not merely fabricating new fabric, but repairing and patching torn/worn places in the existing fabric. (Alexander calls this "healing".)

The wholes are of course sociotechnical ones. This means that there are several perspectives on wholeness, including the social and the technical. A range of stakeholders must perceive order and stability in the result.

Each project has a "centre". This may be either an entity type or a process. Around this centre is arrayed several other entity types or processes. The rule is that, as one such centre is produced, it must contribute to larger structures, and also bring together smaller structures – it must be both unifying and unified.

For example, consider a project that is centred around employee data. It will bring together, perhaps, aspects of personnel, payroll, work allocation, and other related applications. It therefore unifies many views of employee into a single data structure. And at the same time, employee may be recognized as a special case of payee, so that payments to employees may be unified into the larger structure of all outward payments.

For another example, consider a project centred around the issue purchase order process. It will bring together aspects of supplies, contracts, subcontracts, service contracts and perhaps even insurance policies. It therefore unifies several views of the same process. And at the same time, it contributes to a larger structure, containing deliveries and invoices and payments to suppliers.

In general, a data object contributes to a larger structure by being a subtype of a more general object, or by playing a role shared with other objects. And a process contributes to a larger structure by taking part either in the lifecycle of a given object, or in a control loop. Or both.

Peripheral objects will contribute by being part of the horizon of a central object, or by providing a supplementary information structure (e.g. an historical or geographical breakdown). Peripheral processes will contribute by establishing the preconditions for a central process. But these peripheral objects and processes become in turn the centres of their own, smaller areas.

Thus we can restate our goal as follows: to weave a fabric of centres, such that each centre supports one or more larger centre, and is supported by smaller centres. Furthermore, the fabric should be complete: there should be no "negative space".

In traditional design of computerized information systems, the spaces between systems are often merely the areas that nobody has bothered about. This is **negative space**. But the redress for this ill is not total automation, which leaves no space at all, but deliberately created space. Space in which the system users can be imaginative and innovative, freed of the burdens of repetitive and inflexible administration. This is **positive space**.

(Although these concepts of positive and negative space are metaphorical, they can be linked to notions of human-centred systems design developed in Scandinavia and elsewhere. The relevance of these notions has increased as IT projects moved from the automation of clerical transaction processing towards cooperative decision-support systems. Many people now believe that user-friendliness is profoundly affected by system scope and structure, and is not simply a matter of having the right front-end.)

Development principles.

In this approach, projects are selected, planned and managed according to a set of principles. Project proposals are put forward to be chosen on the basis of the expected contribution to wholeness. Each organization may define its own principles, but here is a reasonable set to start from:

There is a maximum project size. This may be defined in various ways, and will vary from one organization to another. An organic plan should provide firm guidelines ruling out excessively large projects, and restricting projects to what is feasible with existing project management skills and procedures. (It may be intended to enhance these skills and to redesign these procedures, but until the project management infrastructure is in place, large projects shouldn't be contemplated.)   Plans that are too big cannot contribute enough to the potential of the whole.

There is an ideal mixture of project sizes in progress at a given time. Within the maximum size already defined, there will be large, medium and small projects. A rough guideline should be established for the relative numbers of such projects, or for the proportion of resources devoted to projects of different sizes. (This will enable, among other things, a skills development path for project managers.) There should also be a mixture of high-risk and low-risk projects, and a mixture of urgent and non-urgent projects. Time-critical projects should be mixed with innovation-critical projects, and projects requiring much attention from senior management should be mixed with projects requiring relatively little attention.

The projects in progress at the same time should not all be concentrated on the same small corner of the overall fabric, but should be distributed between different functions, different groups of users. This allows not merely political balance but also systems balance and resource balance.

Each project must have an identifiable centre, and contribute to an identifiable larger whole, more significant than itself. Those managing the project must be able to show how their project will contribute to the overall fabric. The growing **awareness** of such larger wholes provides a helping hand towards our goal. Some of these wholes may be predicted, but some may emerge as you go along, and must be allowed to develop without preconceptions or forcing.

A larger whole has a discernible life cycle. First, one project hints at a more general structure, which it is outside its own scope and terms of reference to explore. Then other projects help to indicate the outlines of the larger whole, which gradually takes shape as each project enhances our understanding of it. A series of further projects then completes the whole.

A project will usually play simultaneous but different roles with respect to different larger wholes. Each project should therefore aim to do three things. First, it should help to complete at least one major whole that is already clearly defined. Second, it should help to pin down some other, less clearly defined whole(s), previously only hinted at. Third, it should hint at some entirely new whole(s), which will only clearly emerge with later projects. A project may use both development and maintenance tools and techniques.

Each project should be expressed clearly in advance. A communicable vision of the project can be provided through a well-defined portion of the conceptual structure, which the project is to analyse, or for which the project is to design a system.

Each project must create, and each system must have, coherent and well-shaped decision space next to it.

Each system must either be a simple and compact unity, or it must be made up of several simple and compact parts, one of these being major and the others minor, hanging onto it.

Interface bridges with other systems are built afterwards, incrementally. The bridges should serve the systems, and the systems serve the users. You don't design the systems to serve the bridges.

The conceptual structure will evolve as the organization develops new concepts. Each project may feed new insights back to the conceptual structure, making it richer and more powerful.

Requirements.

Getting a sporting chance.

The only requirement is excellence ...

Finally in this chapter, I want to expand the horizons of requirements engineering. I'm going to start with a domain that is not normally regarded as an engineering one. I believe that this domain illustrates some features that are already marginally relevant to requirements engineering, and could become more centrally relevant.

Imagine yourself as a sports coach, faced with four talented and highly motivated children. Each child presents a demand, which has to be translated into a ten-year training programme, building the physical and mental attributes necessary to compete in international sporting competitions. Not all the children will reach this level of excellence, but the training programme is (rightly or wrongly) going to be driven by this objective.

(I'm assuming that it takes around ten years to develop a world-class athlete. Many engineering projects have similar lead-times.)

The first child has great potential as a track athlete. She wants to be an Olympic sprinter. The task of the coach is to create a vision of a supremely fast, confident and competitive young woman, and to communicate this vision to the girl herself (and any other stakeholders, such as her parents). He then needs to decompose the vision into its components – speed, stamina, determination, recovery – and then to formulate a training plan that will help the girl herself to build and assemble these components. There may be some conflicts, trade-offs or sequence dependencies between these components, not to mention conflicting priorities between different stakeholders, and the coach will need to manage all of this. In some ways we can see this as a classic requirements engineering task: the requirement is pretty clear; much of the difficulty resides in the detail; the coach relies largely on past experience to find the best solution for the girl.

The second child has great potential as a footballer. He wants to represent his country in the World Cup. Now this presents a more complicated problem than the sprinter. The boy needs to develop into a useful member of an international team, but in order to do this he will need to be a useful player in a series of increasingly demanding junior teams. What counts as useful varies at different levels, and changes with different fashions over time. A boy with the wrong set of specialist footballing skills may be left out of the team, and thus fail to get the necessary match practice to develop to the next level. And there's no point in being the best Centre Forward in the world, if nobody wants to field Centre Forwards any more.

This means that the training plan needs to have a much higher degree of flexibility. The coach must understand changing team structures, and anticipate how these changing teams affect the requirements for individual players.

Thus the requirement is much less straightforward. The requirements analysis cannot be based purely on past experience, but must be influenced by some reasoning about the future. Coping with – or better, anticipating – requirements change has become an important theme within requirements engineering, and in this light we can still recognize the coach's task as a requirements engineering one.

The third child has great agility and enthusiasm for a wide range of individual and team sports. One option is to select a sport now, and to concentrate the training plan on the requirements for that sport. But better if possible to develop a training plan that is generic across the requirements for many sports. At some stage, it may be necessary to focus on a specific sport, but this choice can be left until later. This choice may depend on such factors as the popularity and television coverage of the sport, as well as the developing skills of the girl as compared to her peers.

Can we still regard this as an exercise in requirements engineering? Some rather generic skills requirements remain, plus a second-order requirement for opportunist responses to a wide range of sporting challenges. But these requirements are much more difficult to substantiate than for the first two children. They cannot be derived from observations of current sporting champions, except in a rather roundabout way, and may be based largely on hunch.

The fourth child isn't even committed to sport. He has something we can call an existential requirement: to be somebody. Becoming a sportsman is one way to fulfil this requirement – but only one way. A sports training programme may still give him something of value, even if he subsequently uses the components – stamina, determination, bonding and team spirit - in some other domain entirely. (But he will only get these components if he takes sports seriously to start with.)

What is the nature of the child's desire? Perhaps the child can only find out by exploring multiple options. This child's demand pulls the coach away from requirements engineering as most readers would recognize it, and towards something more akin to counselling. But of course the wise coach will acknowledge that this is not unique to the fourth child, but has been an integral part of the job in all four cases …

The only requirement is global domination …

Now imagine yourself as a requirements engineer, faced with four talented and highly motivated entrepreneurs …

One wants to build an efficient internet procurement process. One wants to construct a portal to which masses of other people will connect. One wants to build a website with a massive customer base, although she's open-minded as to the possible future uses of these assets. And the fourth simply wants to make money somehow.

A traditional requirements engineering exercise would elicit some verifiable requirements from some community of "users", and might build upon known solutions to similar requirements. But there aren't any users yet, and nothing to copy. To the extent that there are any other known solutions, there is a primary requirement to be significantly different (in some undefinable way) from any previous solution. But this is a negative requirement, not a positive one.

Do all these requests represent appropriate challenges for requirements engineering? (My answer is Yes.) Do requirements engineering techniques help you address these challenges? (My answer is: Yes to some extent.) And are there other complementary techniques that requirements engineers might usefully adopt? Undoubtedly.

Evolving requirements.

Much of the difficulty in traditional development projects comes from an artificial attempt to fix the requirements. As we've seen, in the real world, the requirements **evolve**. Look at the way the e-business market has unfolded over the past couple of years, with different players (with different or similar strategies) thriving at different stages. Overall, this evolution can be expected to continue, although there are undoubtedly some points of stability emerging. (Evolution can be detected in all areas of system requirements, not just e-business – but of course it's e-business where evolution is currently showing itself most strongly.)

The e-business marketplace can be regarded as a complex ecosystem, full of fierce competition and equally fierce innovation, both at the business level and at the software technology level. In designing system and component strategies for this marketplace, the ecological notion of fit seems much more relevant than the traditional engineering notion of fit.

In this world, gap analysis takes on an entirely different emphasis. Providers are looking for an ecological niche – gaps represent unsatisfied demands, or even as-yet unrecognized wants. Or they are looking for gaps in their competitors' or customer's defences – gaps represent ways that competitors or customers are vulnerable to attack.

In this world, traditional first-order requirements analysis is at best a starting point for a more complex analysis exercise. Whether at the business level or at the software level, we want our solutions to possess such second-order properties as flexibility (adaptability) and security (proof against the ingenious tricks of competitors and parasites). These are second-order requirements, because they specify an ongoing alignment between an engineered solution and the evolving first-order requirements.

Gap analysis.

So how do we do gap analysis? If there are gaps, where are they? There are two completely different kinds of gap we may want to consider:

Firstly, there may be gaps between the requirements and a proposed solution, where the solution is to be a defined assembly or configuration of several components. Gaps in the functional requirements may simply indicate that there are some specific holes in the solution into which additional components (yet to be identified) can be plugged. There may also be shortfalls in the predicted quality of service of the solution (often known as the non-functional requirements), and these often represent more intractable problems for the designer, indicating either that the overall solution is misconceived, or that there are serious incompatibilities in this particular combination of components. However, these gaps usually cannot be blamed on any component in particular; success or failure of a solution is a holistic property of the solution

Secondly there may be gaps between the components. A particular subassembly simply doesn't fit very well with together; the components making up this subassembly fails to collaborate effectively with one another. This kind of analysis can be done without having clear or explicit requirements at all, although you can't do it without having at the very least an implicit and imprecise notion of purpose. But collaboration failure is a joint failure of this particular set of components in this particular assembly; it should not automatically result either in the rejection of any one component, or the rejection of the whole lot.

In some cases, a single component turns out to be so poorly formed, that it fails to fit neatly with any other component. The gap analysis may indicate many problems with the use of this particular component, and the component may be deemed a **misfit**. But there will often be overwhelming reasons to go ahead with the use of this component anyway, and to find a way of tolerating the misfit. (This form of misfit is an aspect of the character of a component.)

Component- Level	Solution Level	Market Level
• Gap between this component and that component.	• Gap between this solution and today's requirements.	• Gap in the structure of demand
• Gap between this component and this solution-hole.	• Gap between this solution and any likely future requirements.	• Gap in the defences of competitors and customers
• Gap between this component and any likely solution-hole.	• Gap between this solution and the available components.	
• Gap between this component and this framework.	• Gap between this solution and this framework (set of frameworks).	

Table 5.5: Types of Gap Analysis

Recap.

In this chapter, we have explored some of the paradoxes of evolutionary change, and the practical limits to managing it effectively. The reason why a situation can be simultaneously regarded as revolutionary and evolutionary is that change and continuity are properties of descriptions – and the same situation may be validly described in contrasting ways, from different perspectives. It is sometimes possible to construct descriptions of systems such that they appear to be under management control, such that change can be centrally planned and managed. However, these descriptions fail to provide leverage on the kind of challenge presented by component-based business. The plans are typically narrow in scope and brittle in execution.

In this chapter, I have proposed a way of understanding global system change as a combination of discrete yet interacting local changes, over an extended time period. Our attention is drawn to the system that is being maintained by these changes, rather than restricted to the new artefact (or version) that is being developed. The ongoing result is a combination of things we can control, things we can partially control (or influence or negotiate) and things we cannot control. An organic approach to planning seems to offer much greater flexibility and richness in understanding and managing such changes than traditional approaches.

Afterword

After the Middle Ages comes the Baroque. Knowledge divided into compartments, systems divided into layers and folds, diplomacy becomes a formal game, elevation of intricacy and secrecy. Componentry. Something to look forward to?

Jerry Fodor once noted wisely that scholarship is the process by which butterflies are transmuted into caterpillars. This book has evolved through successive drafts, with new material folded in as it became available to me. I hope that this process has resulted in a more articulated and more accessible book, and not simply a more Baroque one.

Component-Based Business raises further questions. Component-Based Knowledge? Component-Based Action? I hope to be able to address these questions in the future. Readers are invited to contact me to discuss these or any other topics.

Richard Veryard

London, September 2000

richard@veryard.com

Recommended Reading

Christopher Alexander and associates, *A Pattern Language*. Oxford University Press, 1977. Christopher Alexander and different associates, *A New Theory of Urban Design*. Oxford University Press, 1987. I'm also eagerly awaiting the publication of his next book, *The Nature of Order*.

Gregory Bateson. Start with *Mind and Nature*. Bantam Books, 1979.

Hylton Boothroyd, *Articulate Intervention*. Taylor & Francis, 1978. Short and powerful monograph on systems and change. Long out of print, but some libraries have copies.

Stewart Brand, *How Buildings Learn: What Happens After They're Built*. Viking 1994. Read this to change the way you think about architecture.

Albert Borgmann, *Technology and the Character of Contemporary Life*. Chicago University Press, 1984. Read this to change the way you think about technology.

Douglas Flemons, *Completing Distinctions*. Shambala, Boston & London, 1991. A good study of articulation.

Paul S. Goodman and associates, *Change in Organizations*. Jossey-Bass, 1984. Especially recommended are the contributions by Chris Argyris, Kenwyn Smith and Karl Weick.

Larry Hirschhorn, *The Workplace Within*. MIT Press, 1988.

Kevin Kelly, *Out of Control: The New Biology of Machines*. UK edition, Fourth Estate, 1994. Kevin Kelly, *New Rules for the New Economy: 10 Ways the Network Economy is Changing Everything*. Viking Penguin, 1998.

Bruno Latour, *Science in Action*. Harvard University Press, 1987.

H. Maturana and Francisco Varela, *The Tree of Knowledge*. Shambala, 1992. Provides a readable discussion of the notion of closure in biology. A more theoretical presentation of their ideas can be found in H. Maturana & F. Varela, *Autopoiesis and Cognition: The realization of the living*. D. Reidel, 1980. See also Francisco Varela, *Principles of Biological Autonomy*. New York: Elsevier Science Publishers, 1979.

Gareth Morgan, *Images of Organization*. Sage, 1986.

Other References

Wiebe Bijker, *Of Bicycles, Bakelites and Bulbs: Towards a Theory of Sociotechnical Change*. MIT Press, 1995.

Desmond D'Souza & Alan Cameron Wills, *Objects Components and Frameworks with UML: The Catalysis Approach.* Addison Wesley, 1999. Formal techniques for modelling components and collaborations, with a strong emphasis on software.

F.E. Emery & E.L. Trist, "The Causal Texture of Organizational Environments" in *Human Relations*, Vol 18, 1965, pp 21-32.

Jerry Fodor, *The Modularity of Mind.* MIT Press, 1983.

Bruno Latour, *Aramis or the Love of Technology.* Translated by Catherine Porter. Harvard University Press, 1996.

P.R. Lawrence & J.W. Lorsch, "Differentiation and Integration in Complex Organizations" in *Administrative Science Quarterly*, Vol 12, 1967, pp 1-47.

Marvin Minsky, *The Society of Mind*, UK edition, Heinemann, 1987.

Geoff Mulgan, *Connexity: How to Live in a Connected World.* Chatto & Windus, 1997.

RM-ODP. *ISO 10746: The Reference Model for Open Distributed Processing.* Available at http://www.iso.ch:8000/RM-ODP/

Peter Rowe, *Design Thinking.* MIT Press, 1987. An excellent survey.

Adrian Slywotzky and associates, *Profit Patterns: 30 Ways to Anticipate and Profit from Strategic Forces Reshaping Your Business.* John Wiley, 1999.

Charles Smithson, "A Building Block Approach to Financial Engineering: An Introduction to Forwards, Futures, Swaps and Options" in *Midland Corporate Finance Journal*, Winter 1987. Available at http://www.schoolfp.cibc.com/articles/index.html

Piero Sraffa, *Production of Commodities by Means of Commodities*. Cambridge University Press, 1960.

See also the CBDi Forum website at http://www.cbdiforum.com

Glossary

This glossary contains the definitions and references of some of the key concepts used in the book. These are my own definitions; some of them are significantly different to those found elsewhere. I hope the reasons for these differences will be apparent from the discussion of the concepts in the book.

Term	Definition	Pages
Articulation	Articulation means both separation of parts and connection of parts – decoupling and recoupling. This is sometimes known as as loose coupling. (Articulation also implies clarity of structure. This results in a secondary meaning: clear communication.)	8, 12, 30, 34, 44, 67-76, 100, 134, 152, 157, 162, 166, 173, 198ff
Bandwidth	The quantity and complexity of interactions across an interface or business relationship. The capacity of an interface or relationship, in terms of its ability to handle quantity and complexity of interactions.	88, 138, 148, 150, 203
Baroque	A design style involving many layers and folds of complexity and detail. (In systems, this style often emerges without conscious intent from an evolutionary development process.)	10, 117, 219
Bearing Limit	The amount of cost or uncertainty that a given component can be expected to bear. (Uncertainty here may include risk, surprise, instability or variability.)	129
Binding	A decision to create or strengthen a relationship between two entities. The term "Late Binding" refers to policy of deferring binding decisions and commitments to the last possible moment.	137
Biodiversity	Healthy competition between components offering similar services. Choice of Opposite: Monoculture.	76ff, 94, 97, 119, 122, 175
Broker	A component that provides interfacing services.	5, 36, 112, 152
Character	The ability of an entity to relate productively and authentically to other entities.	12, 50, 52, 58-65, 67, 72, 76ff, 80, 90, 92, 100, 109, 112, 120, 128, 132ff, 152

Term	Definition	Pages
Cohesion	A measure of the unity or integrity of an entity or community – the degree to which it hangs together.	23, 108, 109, 194
Collaboration	A joint enterprise or activity involving two or more independent roles.	58ff, 89, 114, 133, 137, 145, 146, 147, 165, 217
Component	A dynamic packaging relationship between a set of services and a set of capabilities (possibly embedded in one or more devices).	passim
Component-Based Business	Construction of a business operation or process by connecting parts together from different sources.	2, 219
Component-Based Development (CBD)	See Component-Based Software Engineering (CBSE)	
Component-Based Software Engineering (CBSE)	The construction of large software systems from software components. Sometimes known as Component-Based Development (CBD).	4, 27ff
Componentry	A collection of components. The increasing articulation of systems into components.	4, 10ff, 18ff, 27-29, 44-47, 67, 91, 103, 167
Connectivity Principle	Use-value that derives from other people's usage of the same component. Economists sometimes refer to this as Network Externalities.	95
Consistency Principle	The ability to reliably manage the delivery of services (and their associated benefits) from a given configuration of devices. This in turn relies on an ability to predict and control the behaviour of components-in-use, including the emergent properties of large distributed systems.	97
Coupling	A measure of the linkages between entities: the extent and rapidity with which changes within one entity impact on another entity, or the requisite degree of coordination between entities. Tight Coupling is contrasted with Loose Coupling.	50, 67, 71, 73, 108, 109, 173, 176, 184, 194, 198
Creativity	A generative principle. Sometimes associated with the generation of ideas, but better associated with the generation of completed works.	20, 64, 76
Critical Mass	The point where a process (like a chemical or nuclear reaction) becomes self-sustaining, generating more energy than it absorbs. In other words, a defined threshold at which there is a qualitative change.	94ff, 121-123

Term	Definition	Pages
Design Heuristic	A principle, procedure or other device that contributes to reduction in the search for a satisfactory solution. As far as I know, this term was introduced by Allan Newell, J.C. Shaw and Herbert Simon, in work that dates back to the 1950s.	20, 56, 83, 99
Device	An artefact or instrument or tool, which may be physical or conceptual. Includes hardware and software.	1, 14, 20, 27ff, 48, 85, 94, 97, 102, 104, 113ff, 138, 142, 155
Device Paradigm	Viewing any new technology exclusively as a kind of device or gadget, and evaluating the technical features and powers of this device, without having any other perspective. (Source: Borgmann)	27ff, 142
Domain	A generic business process or context, or a generic area of knowledge.	34, 38, 56, 69, 89, 152, 163, 170ff, 180, 214, 216
Drill-Down	Progressive decapsulation – getting more and more detail and complexity on demand.	143
Ecosystem	A field of interaction in which entities compete for survival.	30, 87, 91-103, 114, 123, 132, 175, 217
Emergence	(The appearance of) properties of a whole system that are not located in its parts. With engineered systems, these properties don't manifest themselves until the whole system is assembled and commissioned. With evolved systems, these properties often disappear when the system is taken apart.	56, 170, 172, 174, 194, 208
Encapsulation	The opacity of an interface. Encapsulation is often taken to mean that some person is not supposed to be able to see inside. (This depends which person we're talking about, in which role. There are different degrees of opacity, from different perspectives.) It is also taken to mean the converse: that a person responsible for the insides of a component shouldn't know anything about how the component is going to be used, lest this knowledge corrupt the technical purity and perfection of the component. Opposite: Decapsulation.	14, 36, 80-83, 89, 100, 143, 158, 180ff
Energy Conservation Principle	Getting the maximum value from the minimum exertion. This is the basis for the economics of scale or scope, and for reuse.	96ff

Term	Definition	Pages
Evolution	Something interesting emerges (develops, unfolds) from a large number of small changes and interactions.	15, 28, 31, 66, 72, 75ff, 92, 97, 113, 149, 151, 169-181, 186, 194, 201, 203, 208, 216
Feature Interaction	A form of (usually destructive) emergence, in which the feature or properties of separate components interact in an unpredicted (perhaps unpredictable) way.	87, 109, 110, 111, 173, 186, 209
Fetishism	The tendency to describe something as a property of an isolated entity, instead of describing it through relationships with other entities. In particular, the tendency to describe technical artefacts as if they were independent of any socio-economic context.	
Fit	Alignment between a system and its environment (or a system possessing a reasonable degree of alignment – as in "survival of the fit"). Alignment between an artefact and a set of requirements – as in "a good fit". Connectivity of two or more components.	48, 82, 86ff, 101, 104ff, 112, 127, 133ff, 138, 148-150, 169, 175, 178, 181, 186, 191, 210, 217
Flexibility Principle	The ability to easily substitute devices and reconfigure systems, in order to satisfy changing requirements.	97
Grand Plans	An overall structure is defined at the start, and all artefacts are designed to fit this structure. All projects are managed and coordinated under a single integrated programme.	210
Hacking	Artefacts are built and maintained adhoc, piecemeal, according to their own needs alone, their features determined solely by direct costs and benefits. Each project is started and steered in isolation of other projects; communication between projects only takes place if of immediate benefit to the projects themselves.	210
Heuristic	See Design Heuristic.	
Impedance Mismatch	See Interaction Distance.	136
Intelligence	How a complex system behaves in relation to knowledge, complexity and change. Practical cognitive ability.	12, 23, 26, 37, 46, 48, 50-77, 82, 105, 106, 127, 133, 152, 166, 169, 179, 185, 200, 209

Term	Definition	Pages
Interaction Distance	A measure of the difficulty of communication or bridging between two entities. Sometimes called Impedance Mismatch.	148
Interface	Something that connects and separates components.	30, 34 Chapter 4 passim
Late Binding	See Binding.	137
Legacy System	A system with memory that resists necessary change.	7, 15, 28, 33, 42, 65ff, 72, 113, 119, 124, 136, 164, 191-196, 204, 207, 209
Memory	Tight coupling with the past.	65, 88, 164ff
Monoculture	Where one component or service has a dominant market share, leaving consumers of the service with little effective choice. Opposite: Biodiversity.	8, 10, 76ff
Much Binding	A restrictive tangle of commitment and coupling.	137
Organic Planning	An approach to planning that allows integrated structures to emerge, rather than expecting them to be identified from the start.	211
Pattern	A judgement of some kind – typically, but not necessarily a design judgement - partially abstracted from its context.	3, 20, 24, 27, 34, 56, 64, 87, 137, 141, 145, 161ff, 191, 193ff, 202ff
Platform	A collection of (generic) services supporting the implementation of many different service specifications.	9, 34, 76, 96, 107, 110, 123, 159, 192, 207
Pleasure Principle	A good balance between attention (excitement) and inattention (statis).	95, 128
Plug-and-Play	The connection of two or more components into a temporary or permanent system that can be operated immediately, with no further hassle.	2, 5, 126, 134
Policy Management	Rule-based management of an enterprise as a dynamic network of collaborating services.	37
Proxy	One entity or class stands for (represents itself as, takes the identity of) another entity or class, for some purpose within some context.	68, 71, 89
Reification	An attempt to view the world (or some aspects of the world) as composed of things. The philosophical basis of the so-called Object Oriented approach.	

Term	Definition	Pages
Repetition	The unplanned or unconscious re-enactment of some pattern. *Wiederholungszwang*.	64
Requisite Variety	Just enough complexity of response to the complexity of demand.	76, 117
Resistance	A manifestation of system stability, frustrating to those desiring to make systems change.	10, 16, 65, 127, 149, 165
Schismogenesis	A progressive loss of homogeneity or cohesion, a fragmentation. Note also Bateson's definition: "A process of differentiation in the norms of individual behaviour resulting from cumulative interaction between individuals".	164
Sociotechnical	A description of something that identifies both socially mediated relationships and technically mediated relationships.	55, 65, 66, 140, 148, 190, 193, 211
Specification	A description to which some artefact (or class of artefacts) is to conform.	19, 90, 102, 106, 127, 129, 208
Stakeholder	A person or community regarded as having a legitimate interest in some system or change programme.	50, 51, 144, 148
System	A bounded description of something as a set of interconnected parts.	passim
Tolerance	Good enough fit. Give and take in a relationship or collaboration.	16, 48, 83, 105, 120, 148
Trust	A property of a system or relationship based on expectations of reasonable and fair behaviour.	1, 11, 12, 50, 60, 119, 125, 133, 136, 158, 166, 203
Uptight	Near to the limits of what this entity can bear, and therefore unable to tolerate much more.	50, 133
Vertical Integration	Single point of control of a business process or value chain, from one end to the other.	3, 71, 124
Virtual Diversification	Using Component-Based Business to achieve some of the strategic benefits of diversification.	6, 40
Vitality	Survival. An ongoing transformation of energy into value.	87